FIERCE
Illumination

Grief as a
Spiritual Teacher

MARTIN CHESLER

Foreword by Pat McCabe (Woman Stands Shining)

Waterside Press

Published by: Waterside Press
2055 Oxford Avenue
Cardiff by the Sea, CA 92007

Editor: JoAnne O'Brian-Levin

Book interior, cover design, and production:
Ann Lowe, graphicdesignforbooks.com

Website design by: ladesignhouse.com

ISBN 978-1-9391160-9-3

BISAC: OCC011020, BODY, MIND & SPIRIT/Healing/Prayer & Spiritual

Printed in the United States of America by CreateSpace.

WWW.FIERCEILLUMINATION.COM

For Ofir, Rachel, Tal and Daniel

Sa'ah Naaghai Bik'eh Hozhoon:
May you walk your Beauty Paths in harmony with all that is.
Ubuntu: I am because you are.
Sawu Bona: I see you.

Mitákuye Oyás'in: To all my relations,

I am eternally grateful.

TABLE *of* CONTENTS

FOREWORD

FIERCE ILLUMINATION is the diary of a Phoenix. It is a recounting of the proverbial, victorious, and purportedly joyful rise from the ashes; it is also the story of a life and the burning that came before. In its scrupulous attention to emotional detail, it will provide the deepest solace to those who have experienced the loss of a child.

But *Fierce Illumination* is also something more. It is Exhibit A of a process that is being exacted from all parts of the globe at this time. Never before in humanity's current incarnation have feelings of grief, devastation, and loss been so profoundly collective and widespread. Whole generations now have never known a time when they were not presented with over-whelming statistics as to the fragility of life on the planet; many scientists attest to what they name a "mass extinction event" as precious life forms disappear forever from the waters, the air, the land. At the same time, live video feeds bring the reality of war, conflict, and violence into our living rooms; we watch as helpless victims reach out to us, seeking validation of the value of their very lives.

Fierce Illumination provides a medicine for the many experiences of loss that are so prevalent at this hour. Yes, as strange as it may seem, this is the perfect time for a detailed account of how devastation operates, its symptoms and rhythms; its logic, its illogic; how it can dismantle family and community, and the bone-deep reckoning it demands—often unbidden.

It is because my work involves, at times, serving as a voice and guide for these times, working with others to unravel our concepts of "Masculine" and "Feminine," and particularly how the dynamics between these relate to our species' current dilemmas, that I find Martin's willingness to divulge his thoughts, feelings, and process around the devastating loss of his son here, so very precious. The author's awareness of his position in the hierarchical, power-driven human society that dominates the planet is a key part of why this account has so much to offer to us at this time. He understands that, by all accounts of the modern world, he, a white, successful businessman, holds a place at "the top of the food chain." His upbringing in South Africa imposes this understanding upon him in ways that are both validating and uneasy.

Here, in this accounting of a life, he describes the confusion he encountered when the maps he had faithfully followed and the bargains he had made with the Universe all fell apart. He had trained his will to be a force unstoppable; he had played by all the rules, and did it all correctly. Still, his mastery of this textbook version of manhood could not shield him from the chaos of having a heart vulnerable to a true love and the deeper realities of the fabric of this Life, realities that modern culture does not acknowledge, much less prepare a man for. Martin's book is a deeply personal look at not only that dilemma, but also the possibilities that might arise from the crumbling of the isolated, hierarchical, masculine-dominated system that shaped him—including the possibility of the seemingly displaced male discovering, instead, a new kind of liberation.

Indigenous elders from all over the world have expressed that, in order to "right ourselves," the Sacred Feminine and, in fact, women themselves, need to be restored to their rightful place of participation, and leadership, in every aspect of our functioning as a species. In popular culture as well, a women's movement is brewing unlike any other, as is evidenced by the 2017 global Women's March, in which hundreds of thousands of women took to the streets in every major city, and in tiny bergs on the ice, in the forests, and deserts, too. This movement is unsettling for many, yet in that unrest can be found an opening for light. The day after The March, I spoke at a church to an audience of mainly women. As is my habit, I spoke on behalf of Men's Nation, naming their inherent Holiness as the

Sacred Masculine. Several men broke down in tears on the spot. This told me just how deep run the emotions of the men of the world. In the face of half of our species railing and rising, they must be wondering: Are we inherently flawed just by the fact of our maleness? Can we still rightfully claim a place on this Mother Earth?

In my work, I express the need for a rebalancing of the Masculine and the Feminine. I see this as part and parcel of a much larger movement. The paradigm under which we have chosen to live, with its roots in the Social Darwinist concept of "survival of the fittest," is radically hierarchical and, as such, it creates the circumstance and the desire to isolate and compete, often at the expense of Life itself. This is in direct opposition to the methodologies of the construct in which we live. As scientific evidence increasingly attests, this construct we call "Earth" responds to cooperation and collaboration. These are the kinds of actions that will foster not merely surviving, but thriving. And not just the thriving of our own kind, but the thriving of the vast, interrelated community we have called "Life."

And so, we are being called to shapeshift, to move away from the pyramidal "Power-Over" paradigm that supports all fruits and profits flowing to the top, and to embrace a more inclusive paradigm exemplified by the circle. In this "Power With" paradigm, "Everybody Wins, and All the Children are Fed." What this asks from men is that they give up their position in the hierarchy and move into, co-created with women, new structures entirely.

As the author takes on in this writing, a key question of our time is: What does it take to give up privilege and power? I would suggest that, first, it takes a reframing of the concept of "power." I propose that true power creates and furthers Life in all its fullness; it does not impede or destroy it. In other words, contrary to popular mythology, there's no sense in winning the throne of a dead kingdom.

In this writing, Martin describes, in a tender, human narrative, his process of dismantling, reorganizing, reframing, and reorienting to a new version of power, as a human, yes, but more particularly—and certainly more rarely—as a male of our kind. He gives us here a view that most have never witnessed before. This offering, in its particular voice, in its inquiry, in its emotional depth, in its vulnerability, is therefore more than just a truly moving story of triumph over indescribable loss, it is a also a map of understanding and perhaps an invitation to the process of deep transformation that is calling to our kind, and, specifically, to Men's Nation.

> −Pat McCabe, known as *Women Stands Shining*, is a
> Dine' (Navajo) mother, grandmother, activist, artist,
> writer, ceremonial leader and international speaker

PROLOGUE

ON THE LONG FLIGHT BACK TO AMERICA I had tried to sleep, but it would not come. So, I'd read for a while, then I'd fidgeted, and then I'd lifted the flap and just stared out the window at the composite wings cutting through the air. Soon, I'd found myself lost in reflection. I flashed back to a lazy, quiet day not so long ago. I was hanging out with the children of a dear friend when the seven-year-old happened to see a picture on my phone.

"Is that your son?" he asked.

"Yes," I replied.

"Is he dead?" I nodded assent, stifling my shock. *How on Earth did he know?*

"Then why are you still alive?"

It was the most innocent of questions, uttered by a little child, but it pierced right to my core. Even at his tender age, he knew that the order was all wrong. *Why was I still alive?* That was the question that had haunted me from the beginning.

It had been years since I'd embarked on my journey, maybe an impossible one, to unearth the hidden Nature of Reality, the discovery of which I had hoped would then lead me to my son. It was all for that—to find him and bring him back. I'd covered what felt like was a huge amount of territory, but where was I? What, if anything, had it all added up to?

As I returned from the land of my birth, something was telling me that I might have finally stumbled upon the key. But how and in what way everything was all connected, I still did not understand. I knew then what I had to do. I needed to piece together the story, to write it down so I wouldn't forget. This book is that story. I wrote it to make peace with it, though it hurts even now. I wrote in order to exorcise it, though it will always be part of me. I wrote it to honor what had been lost but also to honor what had been gained.

I wrote to discover why I was still alive.

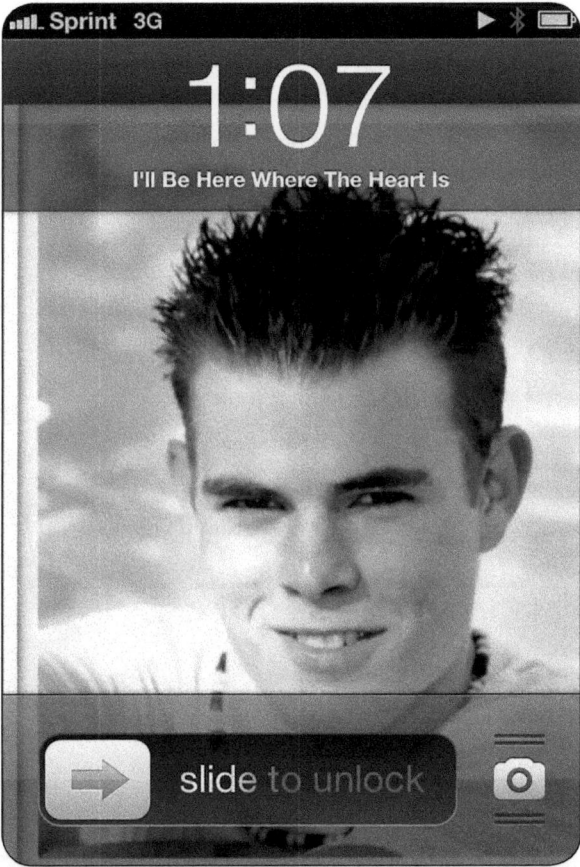

*Your children are not your children.
They are the sons and daughters of
Life's longing for itself. They came
through you but not from you and
though they are with you yet they
belong not to you.*

— Kahlil Gibran

1. Stupid Happy

THIS WAS SUPPOSED TO BE A NIGHT like every other: serene and tranquil, the perfect complement to a calm, lazy day in May. Hours before, the hot spring sun had given way to a waning crescent moon in a seamless transition without changing the mood. Now, the desert lay hushed and still beneath a clear sky punctuated with stars. Even at 3:30 a.m. the temperature remained warm, a soothing balm. Cocooned in their homes, the residents of the valley slept soundly, assured of awakening to yet another perfect, slow-paced day.

We were no different.

A blinding flash of light shot through our bedroom, jolting us upright out of a deep sleep. My wife, Rachel, and I looked around, disoriented, trying to get our bearings. Then we heard what sounded like a mumbling voice. As my eyes began to focus, I could make out a figure standing by the light switch. It was our eldest son, Tal. I gave him a confused look, which was closely followed with one of irritation. He had turned our lights on in the middle of the night! Why on earth would he do something so annoying?

At first, I thought his voice only sounded mumbled because I was not yet fully awake, but it quickly became apparent that I wasn't mishearing— he *was* in fact mumbling. He was trying to get some words out but was unable to do so.

I was genuinely irritated now and became aggressive with him. I raised my voice and blurted out, "Tal, just say it."

My words hung in the empty air for just a bit too long. Seconds only, but long enough for Rachel and me to look at each other and then back at Tal. Why wasn't he speaking? Later, I'd berate myself for acting as if the fault were in him. I just didn't know that what he needed to say no son should ever have to tell his parents.

As we waited for a reply, my thoughts inexplicably jumped back in time.

Spring is the season for sitting outside in the evenings, a popular choice for area residents and visitors alike. But, I had selected a time earlier in the day and had spent a large part the previous afternoon alone outside in deep reflection, something that I did not do very often. This rare event had taken place on the patio of our new home. For some unknown reason, I'd had the urge to pause, step outside, and take in the scenery, which got me to thinking about the land where I lived and about my life there.

The Coachella Valley desert is nestled at the very bottom of Southern California between the San Bernardino Mountains and the Salton Sea. Nine cities dot the valley, including well-known Palm Springs and Rancho Mirage, where I made my home. There, the weather in May is perfect.

In the winter, the mountains in the distance are very often snow-capped adding that much more contrast to an already diverse landscape. In May, though, when I stood on my back patio, the peaks were bare of snow as the melt had already rushed down forming little swollen streams and rivulets that replenished the groundwater reserves in the belly of the desert floor. All around, the cacti stood guard, like silent overseers just about to begin their flowering cycle, hinting at the impending summer when the temperature would zoom into the hundreds.

Throughout most of the year, cacti stand stark and resolute, convey-ing an almost angry demeanor. Devoid of leaves, they proudly display their "I am going to stick you good" spines. But when they bloom, all that changes and it is truly show stopping. Their typically large, white

DESERT CACTUS IN BLOOM

flowers give the cactus a soft, sensuous look that is inviting—even sexy. Hypnotized by their sudden transition into a softer, more feminine guise, I find it tempting to get closer, to handle or even caress them. I don't. The spines are still angry.

On that comfortable May afternoon, bathed in the magical light that came just before sunset, it was hard to anticipate the scorching fever of summer that lay just around the corner. Enduring that oppressive heat was the price we residents paid for the other three, glorious seasons, when Nature revealed herself in all her raw beauty and when many refugees from Northern climes—we locals called them snowbirds—sought relief from the harshness of winter, trading snow for sun.

Apparently, Nature is just not enough for us humans, for each fall all the lawns and golf courses are reseeded and within weeks the landscape is transformed into a lush sea of green—unnatural, but gorgeous. The residents also plant annual flowers in a kaleidoscope of colors that instantly transforms the area.

That day on the patio, as all this ran through my mind, I found myself conjecturing that the desert where Moses wandered for forty years probably didn't look anything like ours.

Life in the valley was relatively quiet and slow and, although I was a man of action, that suited me, perhaps because it calmed me down. The local economy was dominated by two very different industries: the aforementioned tourism and agriculture. The agriculture here was and is quite diverse. Crops include grapes, fruits, vegetables, citrus, some cotton, alfalfa, and, of course, dates. The Coachella Valley grows almost 100% of the country's dates.

My businesses were predominantly in the agricultural field; I grew vegetables and it was a good living. I had always been passionate about my work, especially when I was walking the fields. It was a business, to be sure. Yet money was never the primary motivator; it was the joy I found in growing things. I loved interacting with the plants and watching their progress. It was beyond rewarding to place tiny transplants in the ground

Manicured lawn in Palm Desert, Ca.

in early spring and then experience their coming into maturity, culminating in the harvest of their fruit. In fact, growing was so much fun that it would have been easy to lose myself in it to the detriment of the business side. However, I seemed able to shift my focus back and forth, and maybe that was why I'd been relatively successful.

Growing things was by no means an easy business because it was quite risky—both in its very nature and because of Nature—so it had always demanded great attention. But I'd been fortunate. I was a serial entrepreneur who, over time, had developed a number of successful businesses that then basically ran themselves. Part of my contemplation that afternoon was my gratitude that, at last, I could spend more time with my family.

I had just turned fifty-one and, although I still did some business, most of my days were spent either playing golf or whiling away evenings with Rachel. It felt like we were getting reacquainted after a life of hard work. I found myself appreciating Rachel more and I genuinely enjoyed spending time with her. I felt our relationship was actually strengthening with time and that I was getting much closer to her. I sensed this might be unusual for a couple who had been married for more than thirty years, yet it was very real.

Having my life consist mostly of golf and family was more than enough. In fact, that was a very good time of life for me personally precisely because I was evolving into more of a family man and less of a businessman. I also took great satisfaction in the fact that everyone in the family was doing very well. The boys were all busy with their lives and projects, and Rachel and I had recently completed a major task, the construction of our "dream" home.

Not a single aspect of building our home was done without my knowledge or instruction. I had never built a home before but, like every endeavor I had ever undertaken, I gave it my all and, therefore, had no doubt that it would succeed. This was not arrogance; I simply knew it to be so. I say this with such confidence because, for as long as I can remember, I possessed a kind of uncanny knowing, a clarity and conviction about certain things. It told me that, once I set my sights on something, achievement was virtually guaranteed. All that was required was for me to be in full control. The source of this prescience was beyond my understanding; nonetheless, I trusted it without question and acted without doubt. And, I always made sure that everything went according to my plan, regardless of the effort it demanded.

In addition to the big project, I was also very much enjoying being the father of three boys, now young men. They had grown into fine human beings, yet each was very different in his nature and disposition. Tal had recently graduated from college with a degree in Ag-Business and he was taking life a step at a time. Easy-going and calm in temperament, Tal marched to the beat of his own drum. He didn't need to chase happiness; he was there already.

Ofir, our middle son, was pursuing a graduate program in psychology at a nearby university and excelling in his studies just as he always had. In fact, he had completed his four-year undergraduate program in three and was well on the road to achieving his dream of gaining a PhD. In my mind, Ofir and I were cut from identical cloth. Like me, he was very serious, intense and goal-orientated, only he was more refined, softer.

Our youngest, Daniel, was still in high school. Daniel seemed to be somewhat of a hybrid of Tal and Ofir—outgoing, yet introspective in his demeanor. Because of the demands of work, I had missed out on a lot with the older boys, so I was determined not to have that happen with Daniel. Mostly more time with him involved taking him places in the car. I thoroughly enjoyed every moment I spent with him because it gave us the kinds of experiences I never got to have with Tal and Ofir. We seemed to really enjoy each other's company and I felt we were becoming very close. Yet, whenever he was about to meet up with his friends, the whole dynamic would change. The closer we got to his drop-off point, the further away he drifted, to the point where I realized he must be feeling downright embarrassed. I actually thought I was kind of a cool dude; but apparently Daniel did not, at least not in front of his friends. In fact, there were times when I had to drop him hundreds of yards away from his actual destination! But I delighted in all of it. Most of all, I enjoyed going to his basketball games and never missed one. He was an outstanding player, and it was simply a joy to watch him and his teammates succeed on the court.

I was proud of our boys and proud to be Rachel's husband. Rachel was a homemaker, no—better yet and put much more accurately—she was a family maker. She had nurtured our boys in a way only a mother knows how, consistently, passionately, and above all selflessly. She kept our family intact. I sensed that at a very deep level she knew who we each were as human beings and she knew what each of us needed. In particular, I felt her understanding of what made me "tick" was truly remarkable; she was extraordinarily patient with me.

On that early evening, for afternoon had slipped into evening, sitting on our patio alone, I felt particularly grateful to her for the selfless devotion she had given to the boys and to me.

Along with my gratitude, I was feeling very confident that I knew how life worked: control was the key to navigating life successfully. So long as I was at the helm with the steering wheel held firmly in my hands, the ship would always go in the right direction, regardless of the prevailing currents or winds. This philosophy was firmly embedded in my psyche. It had proven itself over and over again, so I knew it had to be right.

Because I was so confident in my worldview, I wanted desperately to pass this knowledge on to my boys. I fully expected them to follow in my footsteps, not necessarily in the details but definitely in the way I functioned—take control; get the job done. I especially wanted to pass this knowledge to Ofir. Because he and I were so similar, I was certain that my understanding of life would be a great resource to him and that he could absolutely take it to the next level. At the same time, I was also a little afraid for him. I could see that, like me, he tended to set the bar really high for himself. I loved that about him, but a part of me also feared

Chesler family in new home – January 2007
L-R: Daniel, Me, Rachel, Ofir and Tal

that one day he'd set it so high that he might not be able to handle the consequences.

As I reflected on this, a memory flickered across my mind. I had been doing some work on the computer one evening last year when something suddenly popped up on the screen, startling me. It was an instant message from Ofir. I remember wondering why he did not simply call me on the phone, but the question faded as we began an online conversation that soon became serious in nature. He was trying to decide whether to pursue graduate studies in medicine or in psychology, and he was second-guessing his intelligence and abilities.

I knew his concerns were totally unfounded but also perfectly normal. After all, he was in the throes of making a huge decision about his life's direction; and although he did not ask me directly, I sensed that he was fishing for my advice. We communicated back and forth for a while, and then finally I told him that I could not tell him what to do, that the decision had to come from him. But not wanting to leave him empty handed, I tried to give him my best fatherly counsel.

Hoping to help him temper that tendency to push himself too hard, I told him that to be successful in life it was not necessary to be overly strong or gifted in any one aspect; it was much more desirable to have a broad spectrum of life's tools. A well-rounded toolkit should include intellect, common sense, knowledge, and things like emotional intelligence, energy, and desire. I used a metaphor to try and drive this home. I told him it was like baking a cake. A tasty cake needs only the correct amount of each ingredient; too much of any one element does not make the cake better. Then it was the oven that ultimately baked the cake. I finished by explaining that, in the metaphor that I was using, the baking oven represented *passion*, which I knew he had, as I did, and then some. As we disconnected, I found myself hoping I'd made a difference.

Thinking about that conversation reminded me how the notion of success had always been a bit of a conundrum for me. Despite my financial accomplishments, our family had always lived below our means. It was a matter of values; material rewards were just not that important to us. In fact, I actually found excess disturbing. Our new house was the exception. It was spectacular by any measure, certainly more than any family could ever need. For that reason, I had also been determined to view it as yet another business venture, to see it as a challenging construction project, rather than a place we could genuinely call home. Thinking of it that way kept my qualms about materialism at bay, though they still lingered just beneath the surface. And, yet, I couldn't deny that the house was also a symbol, the ultimate evidence that we had made it.

Rachel and I had come to America twenty-five years earlier bringing with us nothing but our backpacks, our youth and energy, and a passionate desire to make a life for ourselves and eventually for our family. For, despite my disdain for consumption, my worldview was distinctly materialistic—what else was there? To me, America was the epitome of capitalism, the world capital of rational thinking, and so, whether I consciously knew it or not, I'd come here to test myself, to validate my worldview.

Sitting outside our beautiful new home in that perfect setting, I was certain that we had come to the right place. We had been well rewarded for our efforts, not only financially but in other ways as well. We were living testimony that the American Dream was alive and well. I have a deep love and respect for this country, especially its ability to reward diligence, responsibility, passion and good, old-fashioned hard labor. Nothing is perfect and certainly our country is no exception, but I have always felt a deep allegiance to her for the simple reason that I am here not by default, but by choice. As Lee Greenwood sings, "'Cause there ain't no doubt I love this land. God bless the USA."

Yes, life was very good indeed. In fact, life had been exceptionally kind to my family and me. I rarely thought about it that way, but those were the facts. I was confident that our lives, both as individuals and as a family, were as good and satisfying as anyone could ask for. Feeling a deep sense of contentment, I cast one last, parting glance out on the magical vista, and went inside.

That evening, we had invited some friends from the neighborhood to share a meal. Since they were older and did not like to be out late, they arrived early, around five o'clock. Rachel had prepared a fabulous trout dinner, which we all enjoyed. The food was as delicious as the evening air, the view from our dining room, and the warmth of our friendship. Afterwards, we spent a wonderful evening chatting about various things. Rachel and I always enjoyed their company; the conversation always flowed and the subjects were varied, never boring. They, too, had just finished building their dream home, but this had been their second go-around, so they had given us the benefit of their wisdom. Of course, we bragged about our kids a lot, as proud parents tend to do. They, in turn, partook of the joy of bragging about their grandkids. Also, as good friends do, we touched on some of the difficulties our families had faced. Sadly, they had lost a child under tragic circumstances seven years earlier. I had recently lost my brother to cancer and my dad as well, twenty years earlier, so I felt I understood their loss.

Around nine o'clock, the evening began to wind down. Our friends left, and Rachel rushed to call Ofir as she was accustomed to do most evenings. But just as she was about to dial out, the phone rang. It was Daniel's art teacher wanting to let Rachel know how well Daniel was doing in class. To this day, it is still unclear why his teacher called at such an odd hour or even why she called at all. Although Rachel was anxious to speak with Ofir, she did not want to be rude, so they ended up chatting for quite a long time. Rachel never got to make that call.

After Rachael had hung up, we went to bed. We kissed each other goodnight like we had each night for the past thirty-one years, secure in the ongoing story that had become our life. Life as we knew it was simply beautiful. There was an order to it all, and a beauty to that order. This was the universe we knew; and as we drifted off to sleep, we left the universe to continue on, trusting in it, as we had done every other night, to take care of its portion of the grand story while we slept.

I did not understand this at the time, but order is fundamentally important to the human psyche. For the human mind to function properly, the parameters of life must remain within a certain range. I say this now, but this was not obvious to me then; it was simply so.

Neither was I cognizant of the contract I had made with the Universe. I just assumed that, as long as I did my part, the universe was honor-bound to take care of the rest. That's why I always made such a great effort to control my small slice—because then the Universe would have to honor our agreement. It always had, and I was sure that was because I always kept my side of the bargain. I had no idea that this sacred pact was unilateral, and that it was about to be broken in the most excruciating and savage way possible.

The Universe was not only about to devastate our family and shatter our dreams, but it was also about to obliterate everything I thought I knew about how life worked. And it was to do this all without warning, without harbinger. We were given no clue, not even the remotest hint that this was to be our last real and true goodnight kiss, ever. An irreversible catastrophe had already been set in motion. Our world as we knew it had already begun to disintegrate, but we were still innocents. Sleep comforted us for a few more hours.

You left and I cried tears of blood.
My sorrow grows. It is not just that
You left. But when You left my eyes
went with You. Now, how will I cry?

—Rumi

2. Are We Dreaming?

FULLY AWAKE I STARED INTENTLY at Tal, waiting for him to talk. Finally, finally, he was able to get it out in a somewhat coherent manner. "Ofir's been in a car accident," he said.

"Is he okay?"

"No."

I pressed. "How badly is he hurt?"

His answer was brief and confusing. "It does not look good."

I immediately began to barrage him with questions. "What do you mean? Is he going to be all right?"

Tal kept on trying to sugarcoat his responses. To this day, I'm certain he was trying to shield his mom from the reality of the facts. He managed to tell us that the sister of Ofir's close childhood friend, Michael, had called Tal to tell him that Michael and Ofir had been in a car accident and that Michael had been killed instantly. It is hard to admit this even now, but hearing that Michael had been killed simply did not register with me the way it should have. At that moment, I was so totally focused on Ofir that I was incapable of comprehending anything else.

Tal then told us that Ofir was in the hospital.

At last, we knew what to do. Rachel and I threw off the covers, staggered toward our respective closets and began putting on some clothes to go to the hospital.

Tal followed me into my closet and it was then that he told me what he really knew. Ofir had been driving with his friend Michael in the passenger seat, when he lost control of his vehicle and crashed. Michael had

15

L-R: Ofir, Brandon (Ofir and Michael's
best friend), and Michael

been killed instantly. Tal had spoken with a doctor, and the doctor had told him that Ofir was in a coma in very serious condition. The doctor had then told Tal that there was not much hope for any kind of recovery.

When I heard this, I froze. Then I looked at Tal and said, "This is all my fault. I should never have bought him that car."

I will never forget Tal's response. Even though the exact words he spoke are not clear in my mind, the message will remain with me forever. He tried to reassure me that it was in no way my fault. He did this in a way that was exceedingly kind, compassionate, and gentle. It was as if we had instantly reversed roles. He became the dad and I was the son.

I had never realized what a sensitive being Tal was until that moment. He had been away at college for the past five years; he had left us a boy and returned a man. Since then, I have many times experienced his many incredible qualities: his capacity to be totally selfless, for example. He has opened my heart and taught me so much, and I will forever admire and respect him for his incredibly caring spirit. Every time I think back on his standing by the light switch, unable to utter a word, my heart aches for him. For the longest time I felt so guilty for my impatience and the way I had verbally attacked him.

Together, we then went to rouse Daniel, telling him as little as possible so as not to alarm him. We all piled into the car and began the two-hour car trip to Scripps Hospital in La Jolla. The drive was nothing short of torture. We were tired, worried and traumatized, so the trip seemed to go on for hours during which very little was said. What was there to say, anyway? Each one of us was simply trying to process the unthinkable. How I was able to keep the car on the road, I will never know. The fog in my head was so intense that I could barely see through it. The car's headlights definitely provided no solution to the problem, but I kept flicking the brights on and off anyway.

All the while, I was telling myself that things like this happened in the world, but they could never happen to us. This is and must be impossible. We would get to the hospital soon and sort it all out. Everything would be okay; it had to be. Did rivers ever flow upstream? Did the sun rise in the west? No, no, there was an order to things. These things cannot happen, and so neither could anything happen to our beloved son. It was all a huge misunderstanding, soon to be resolved. If I could just get there, I could take control and make it be all right. I knew I could; I always had.

After what seemed like an eternity, we pulled into the hospital parking lot at about 5:30 a.m. We dumped the car and raced into the main entrance. It was still very dark outside, so the brightly lit interior was a shock. The hospital also seemed eerily deserted. For a moment we just stopped, completely disoriented and bewildered.

I had no idea where to go, yet I charged ahead with my little band not far behind. I remember racing from corridor to corridor with Rachel, Tal, and Daniel trailing after me, running up to different nurses and asking if they knew where Ofir was, as if everyone in the hospital knew Ofir by name and what his circumstances were. No one could tell us anything. In truth, we were so mentally overloaded that we were lost beings, both figuratively and literally. If the situation had not been so tragic, the scene could only have been described as comical.

My emotions were running wild and my exasperation level rising. Why were the corridors so empty? Why did it feel like a maze? Where were we supposed to go for information? It was all so like a strange dream.

We raced down yet another corridor and came upon yet another nurse. This time, though, when I asked if she knew where we could find Ofir Chesler, she responded, "Do you mean the John Doe?"

WHAT??? I was horrified, and I remember my very angry response verbatim: "My son's name is Ofir, not John Doe."

Later, I learned that they had been unable to identify Ofir because he either did not have I.D. on him or they could not find it. Looking back, I now see that eruption of anger for what it really was—my first act of denial, the first indication that I might not be able to accept the reality of Ofir's status, that I might fight it every step of the way, no matter the cost or consequences. But how could I accept it? Everything was simply happening too fast.

Finally, we found him. He was in the ER, lying in bed on his back, hooked up to many different kinds of machines, tubes, and wires, none of which I recognized or understood. The nurse who ushered us in told us that he was still in a coma and that the doctor would come and speak to us soon.

The whole situation was becoming more surreal. On the one hand, I was told that Ofir had been in a terrible high-speed car accident and that the injuries he had sustained were so serious that they put him in a coma. But when I looked at him, he just seemed to be sleeping. His body was pristine, and he looked as handsome as he always did. No injury, not a single scratch visible, on him. Later, Rachel saw a small bandage on the back of his head, but at that moment, what I was hearing and what I was seeing contradicted each other to such an extreme that I was unable to process the situation.

I walked out into the corridor to try to collect myself and make some sense of it. When I returned, a little more composed, I looked at him again. A sudden feeling overwhelmed me. Despite the protests raging in my head, my gut told me that he had already left us and that I was looking at a shell. I will never understand how or why I knew that, but the feeling was extremely strong. In fact, the entire time we were in the hospital I refused to touch Ofir because I knew in my heart that he was no longer with us.

I felt sick to my stomach. I tried to stay strong for Rachel and the boys, but I am sure I failed dismally. Finally, a doctor came into the room. With practiced objectivity, he gave us the verdict. He told us that all the tests pointed to zero chance of any kind of recovery. Blood flow to the brain had ceased. The damage was irreversible. He said he felt there was no point keeping Ofir alive artificially via the machines, but then he suggested that we wait another day and "see."

See??? Even to my scrambled brain, it was abundantly clear that the doc was simply offering us some time to absorb the reality of the situation.

By now, dawn had turned into morning. It was maybe eight or even nine. Completely at a loss, Rachel and I began keeping vigil, taking turns checking in on Ofir. When we weren't doing that, we wandered the corridors aimlessly, like rudderless ships. Trying to be helpful, the staff suggested we call a Rabbi. I had no desire for a Rabbi; I saw no point in it. What could a Rabbi do? Would the Rabbi pray to God and then everything would be okay? All my adult life I had been a practical and grounded man, not a spiritual one. I did not just pray for problems to go away; I always took the reins and resolved them. Besides, I knew in every fiber of my body that it was too late, too late for prayer or anything else. And yet, and yet, I knew I had to somehow fix this for my family. I had to; I always did. I just didn't know how quite yet, but I knew I would find a way. Rachel wanted the Rabbi to come, so I relented. The Rabbi spent the afternoon with Ofir and prayed. Even though we did not go to synagogue much, I knew this Rabbi really liked Ofir. He had helped him prepare for his Bar Mitzvah at age thirteen, tutoring him in the portion of the Torah that he had recited in the synagogue. Even though I did not have much time for organized religion and the hypocrisy that tended to accompany it, I had gained a lot of respect for this Rabbi as a human being. He was kind, understanding and, most of all, humble. He did not invoke God nor did he preach to us. Instead, he displayed a very humanistic and emotional presence. He cried with us and repeated over and over, "I simply cannot believe it." The Rabbi was being authentic, and that was all we could ask for, all *I* could ask for. And then it struck me: I wondered if even the Rabbi was questioning God at that moment. I could certainly feel that Rachel was not only questioning God but was downright angry with God.

We camped out in the hospital all that day and most of that night, claiming ownership through adverse possession of a little piece of real estate in one corner of a large waiting room.

Clear memory of what transpired at the hospital is difficult to come by. My recollections don't play back like a continuous movie, but more like scattered still shots. I remember, for example, that Michael's mom came to visit Ofir, but I don't know how I knew because I do not remember that we met there.

I do not believe she wanted to see us, and I certainly did not have the strength to meet with her. Nevertheless, I have a vivid memory of her. I was struck by how business-like she seemed, how devoid of emotion her face was. It was a defense, I was sure, because I felt her pain shoot through me. It was then that the full force of Michael's death hit me. Suddenly, my brain was screaming. Again, I was overcome by a feeling of helplessness. I was so sad for Michael's mom and family; but I did not know how to begin to be present for her, so I was not.

My heart broke a thousand times watching Rachel. I could not imagine the pain she was in. She had carried Ofir within her body for nine months and subsequently nurtured him with such love and grace. Whenever this thought presented, my psyche, always so ready to act, became paralyzed. I knew I had to make this right but simply did not know how. I felt as powerless as a newborn. To be a functioning and rational adult and then suddenly to have my mind overtaken, usurped by pure emotion because of the loss of Ofir, was the most excruciating feeling, beyond anything I had ever experienced.

They continued to do scans of Ofir, looking for any kind of blood flow to the brain. There was none. We were again told that the doctors were recommending we disconnect him from the life support systems. If we did, they said, his heart would simply stop pumping blood to the rest of his body and he would die very quickly. This was their attempt to reassure us. It didn't.

In a desperate attempt to forestall this, I talked with multiple doctors at the hospital and even reached out to specialists in Los Angeles. I was groping for a solution, a lifeline, a sliver of hope; but all I got was discouragement followed by apology, over and over. The letdowns accumulated like broken pieces of straw.

In the back of my mind, I kept wondering: *were we doing this right?* I didn't know then and never will, really. All I know is that we did the very best we could, but Rachel and I were beyond distraught and more alone than we had ever felt in all our lives. Were we even capable of thinking straight? It was a great and tragic irony that we had to attend to these most dire and delicate matters—both emotional and practical—when we were least equipped to do so. At the same time, we were trying to protect Tal and Daniel as much as possible. We wanted to shield them from having to hear the doctor's words or having to go through any of the decision-making process. We considered it to be simply too much for them.

Adding to our hardship was the fact that both of our families lived overseas, so they weren't there to support us in the way we needed. We might have leaned on our friends, but we never contacted them. I don't know if we even considered it; that's how out of our minds we were. Maybe, deep down, we were afraid to be so vulnerable in front of them. So, we were riding solo. The only people who actually came to see Ofir were his friends—still kids, really. They kept company with us, and we were grateful for their presence.

Behind the scenes, though, we were getting some much-needed help. It came from my bookkeeper/secretary/*everything*, Lily. She is a beautiful spirit and to me she is like a daughter. Lily took charge of many things we just didn't even think about. She informed those who needed to know, made other necessary arrangements, and visited with us at the hospital. It was truly remarkable how much she did, especially without being asked, and I will be forever grateful.

The next day, after a prolonged discussion, Rachel and I decided to go ahead and do the unthinkable, the incomprehensible. I relayed to the doctor on duty that we had made a decision, but that we also had a request. We just could not rely on any one doctor's opinion; so, before any action could be taken, we wanted three doctors to sit in front of Rachel and me and for each to give us their professional opinion, one-by-one.

I remember pacing those bleak, colorless corridors, trying to fill up the time until three doctors could assemble. After a while, they called us into a small room. Three white coats were sitting side-by-side at a table. For some reason, when I replay the scene in my mind I never see faces, only those three white coats. For all I knew, they could have been janitors.

It was unanimous. One by one, they told us that there was no hope of our son ever waking up. All the while, the camera that was my memory was stuttering, skipping over things it did not want to record, going AWOL. It did not document any response from Rachel or me. To the best of my recollection, we merely sat slumped in our chairs, exhausted, devastated and feeling very, very abandoned. The film reel that is my memory freezes then and momentarily goes black. Then it flickers and jumps to another point a few minutes hence to an indelible scene.

Just when I thought the meeting was over, just when I'd managed to find a way to keep my heart beating, one of the white coats threw a last and final blow. "Do you want to donate his organs?" he asked. The question landed squarely and took down whatever was left of us. *This is just too much.* I wanted to scream in anguish, but I didn't, I couldn't. Instead, a burst of anger surged through me and I blurted out, "No! No one touches him. Enough is enough." I have since come to regret that decision. I wish we had decided differently, but we just couldn't at the time.

The white coats then filed out of the room, leaving us behind in the sterile, fluorescent hell that was now our reality. We remained seated, immobile and lifeless. The life force had been sucked out of us. But I was not a zombie. I couldn't be because there was too much going on inside. I just couldn't turn any of it into any action. So, I sat there helplessly listening as my mind writhed in agony: *We gave life to our boy and now they have asked us for permission to terminate that life. As if it was not devastating enough to be told that our child is going to die, we his parents, the people who gave him life are now being asked to take his life. How is this even possible?*

Somewhere along the line, I had become aware of a curious fact: we have a word for children who lose their parents and we have words to describe people who have lost their spouses, but there exists no word in the English language for a parent who has lost a child. For some reason, in that precise moment, my mind retrieved that obscure fact from somewhere in its recesses and proceeded to torment me with it. If there was no word for that, then how could there ever be a word for a parent who ends his or her own child's life? Perhaps there are no words for these things because they are so beyond comprehension, so beyond the natural order, so beyond the laws of the universe.

How could I be expected to make a decision like this? I am his father. Nothing, nothing has prepared me for this.

Years later, I realized why I could not look into the faces of those doctors. It was because I was certain that they were filled with contempt. I was positive that this tribunal of men was silently accusing me of the worst of crimes—of failing to protect my son—and that if I had dared to look into their eyes, I would have seen that. "Man to man, we see you as a disgrace," their eyes would have said. "You are no longer one of us. Your once exemplary track record has been expunged, and you are hereby condemned to punishment. Leave now, go." Without a single word being spoken aloud, I knew beyond doubt that I had been banished, exiled from the community of men. It was a sentence that only men could confer upon other men, and I accepted it.

How long it was before we finally left that room, I don't recall. I only know I walked out a sick and broken man.

Rachel and I chose not to be present when they disconnected Ofir from all the machines. We returned to our little piece of waiting-area real estate, where we huddled with Tal and Daniel and Ofir's friends, and waited. After what seemed like hours a nurse came in and told us that Ofir's heart had stopped.

Our son was dead.
Our son was dead.

May 14, 2007. They turned off all the machines, his heart stopped, and we went home.

Thankfully, a family friend drove us. I don't remember if anyone said a word on the long ride home because my mind was reeling, racing with questions, doubts, and judgments. They besieged me, relentlessly. Among them was the realization that we were now just four; the Chesler family had consisted of five. I no longer recognized my family.

Outside the car windows, the countryside slid by, but I didn't draw any comfort from the serene beauty of the landscape. The conflagration in my head was raging too high. *This cannot be, cannot be. No, I'll wake up and everything will be back the way it was, the way it should be, the way it has to be. But what if, in some dreadful alternative universe, this has all really happened? What then? Then the white coats are right: it is my fault. I have failed my son. I have failed as a father. No matter how I look at it, I am responsible, if not for the car accident, then definitely for the events in the hospital. I could not protect my son. I have failed as a father and I have failed as a husband as well, allowing my wife's son to be taken from her on my watch. The doctors said it with their eyes, "You are a failure as a man and human being."*

My brain was short-circuiting and drowning all at the same time, and I had the sensation of fading in and out of consciousness. I tried to grab for something solid, something to stabilize me so I could get my bearings, but I couldn't find anything. In fact, I did not recognize my surroundings. I didn't even recognize myself. And worst of all, the control I had worked so hard to maintain all my life was gone, stripped away by a terrible storm. Not only was I no longer standing at the helm holding the steering wheel firmly in my hands, but the boat had capsized, taking all of us with it.

It was then I realized that I was falling.

Falling in and of itself is not a terrible thing. I had experienced something like it several times in the past with the deaths of my grandmother, father, and brother. But this time, everything was different. I was in a free-fall dropping farther and farther down into a pit that was so deep and so black that it felt both spaceless and timeless. Never before had I felt so utterly lost.

I just kept falling.

SON

You left
They tell me not
They live not in my heart
Drowning in tears of sadness

My shadow my reality
Moving with the sun
Noise my ears' companion
Feelings rage in the furnace

Our future stolen, so alone
Mind body and soul
Empty smiles, meaningless words
Devastation my oxygen

Purpose not
Compass gone
Exist by instinct
Why?

—M.C.

3. Descent

THERE WERE FOUR DAYS between when we arrived back home and the funeral. I wish I could recount what happened accurately, but my memories of that time are disjointed at best. Perhaps it was because the boundaries between what was true and real and what was fantasy or nightmare had become so blurry I might as well have been declared legally insane. Perhaps it was because I had also lost all sense of time, I am not sure what came before or after. All I know is that my memories make everything seem disconnected and all my actions look jerky, indecisive and clumsy in direct contradiction to how I had conducted my life previously.

Yet, even in this state of utter disorganization, I had absolute clarity about certain things. I understood, for example, that from the moment we left the hospital everything in my life would now become a subset of two distinct epochs: life Before Ofir and life After Ofir.

Some events during that time left no trace. I have no doubt that they occurred; I know they *must* have, but I have no recollection of them. Other incidents are forever etched in my memory.

One of those vivid memories occurred the first night we were home. I did something then that I will never fully understand. Rachel and I first made sure the boys were asleep, and then we went to bed. We lay there wracked with fatigue but unable to sleep. The crying never ceased. I don't believe that either one of us could imagine that we would never see or touch Ofir or hear his voice ever again. How could he simply be gone? For hours, we alternated between wailing, weeping, or just whimpering, depending on the level of energy. Then an overwhelming impulse came

27

OFIR UNDERGRAD GRADUATION WITH HONORS

over me to have sex, and we did. Rachel did not actively participate and it certainly was not lovemaking. Afterwards, I felt awful about it. I could not understand why the drive was so strong, as it was so incongruent with where our hearts and minds were. It was as if our bodies had disconnected from us and were having a life of their own.

I felt shame about this and buried it deep. In fact, I never mentioned this to anyone until recently. The person I spoke to was not shocked, but reassuring. She told me that she had heard firsthand of a similar occurrence under the same circumstances. So maybe, in that moment, instincts took over. Maybe we felt so dead inside, that the subconscious instinct was to seek life again, to remind ourselves that we in fact were not dead as well. What better way to do that than to induce the act of sex, which is life making? Maybe, as repugnant as it may seem, it was natural, the natural expression of a deep subconscious drive to respond to death by making another child.

In the Jewish tradition, burial is supposed to take place twenty-four hours after death, but we had to wait for family to arrive from overseas. In the interim, we tried to distract ourselves as best we could. The boys had friends over, Rachel had a few visitors, and I kept myself busy by taking charge of whatever tasks needed to be done. I went to the funeral home to make all the arrangements, leaving Rachel at home with the kids. I was not going to have her go through the ordeal of choosing a casket and a gravesite or tend to all the legal, administrative and financial work that needed to be done. I would handle it all. This was a change, for up until now, Rachel had taken care of all arrangements for Ofir, from taking him to nursery school to seeing him off for his first day at college. Now I was arranging his burial site, his final stop. Thank God, I did not fully comprehend the implications. There was to be no more taking Ofir anywhere, no more firsts, no more anything. This was it, his final milestone, and a huge part of our future was to be buried with him.

The Rabbi who had come to the hospital volunteered to go to the funeral home with me, and this time I was very happy to have him. He was all the support I had, and I loved him for offering. We met in the foyer and were ushered into a room where a variety of miniature caskets were on display in a manner not dissimilar to how floor tiling is exhibited at Home Depot. I clearly recall thinking "how clever." The kind of casket did not matter much to me. I chose one quickly, and the Rabbi and I talked a little as I waited for the paperwork to be processed.

At one point, he turned to me and said, "I cannot believe how strong you are and how well you are functioning." That statement made me freeze. I did not know what he meant by "strong," but I did get the "functioning" part. I really was functioning well—on the outside. Maybe that was what made me appear strong. The only explanation I had for being able to "function well" was that I knew certain things had to get done. I was instinctively drawing upon my business background. I was used to organizing and performing in all kinds of situations and under all kinds of conditions. The strong part may also have been due to massive doses of adrenaline that had to be pushing me on, because the truth was, I felt dead inside. If I was functioning, it was like a robot. But then I wondered, do robots observe tiny caskets on display and think "how clever"?

At some point while I was still at the funeral home, Michael's mom and sister arrived, needing to do what I had just done. Like me, they were also handling things alone. The mom was divorced and her ex was not with her. As I completed my business, I could overhear them struggling with decision-making. My heart ached for them and I really wanted to help, to make up for my inaction at the hospital. I was ready to do anything for them, and more. They turned down my offer to help with office matters, but we did go outside together to look at burial sites.

Although we were restrained by having to bury our sons in two different sections of the cemetery—Jewish and Christian—we were able to find sites fairly close together. Ofir's grave was to be beneath a tree and Michael's across the path, surrounded by trees. These gravesites were to be their new home, but I tried to avoid dwelling on that thought, for it just shattered me. These childhood friends who had grown up in the same neighborhood, attended the same high school, rode the same bus every day, and who had both attended college in the San Diego area would now be together forever in the Palm Springs cemetery. Both were such good kids with so much to offer, so much. *Why? Why? Why?* The question hammered me.

Michael's mom and I decided that we would have the services for both of our sons together, followed by Ofir's burial ceremony and then Michael's. To plan the services, Michael's mom, sister and their priest came to our house. I have no recollection of the specifics of the meeting. I just have a mental picture of us sitting in our living room, where we must have been talking through the details. Rachel, meanwhile, spent most of her time in our bedroom either alone or with her sister. Again, I never bothered her with any of the planning. I was trying as hard as possible to insulate her from any additional pain.

The next morning, the day of the funerals, we were taken to the cemetery and dropped off at the entrance to the hall where the services were to be held. By now, our families had arrived from overseas. It was comforting for us to have their help, support, and presence. My brother took care of the boys while I made it a point of paying close attention to Rachel, worried that she might not make it through the day.

I was told, days later, that there were hundreds of people in attendance at the funerals, but I have no sense of that; my sensory apparatus was not working, disabled by the loud screaming in my head and the dark, black, sinister fog that had become my aura. I only saw vague images, and voices were only background noise. I did register, though, the fact that Michael's family had chosen an open casket. We did not.

We four sat in the front row and I did my best not to look at the caskets, for the thought that my son was lying inside one was unbearable. I can remember forcing myself to look away, trying to focus on anything but that. For some reason I remember looking to my right and staring at a golfing friend for what seemed like hours. He was a much older man who always seemed very wise. I believe I was asking him telepathically to please tell me why this was happening. I was waiting for his answer, maybe even silently pleading for it, but an answer never came. In my mind's eye, I still see him as I imagined then, sitting in the distance, staring back at me, his face cold and stoic. In his eyes, I see the same look I'd imagined seeing in those of the white coats.

During the preceding few days, we had heard many people, both our family and his friends, talk about Ofir. Through those conversations, I learned so much about him. Some things felt familiar, reinforcing the Ofir I knew, but others were somewhat mystifying. My sister-in-law, who practiced healing, had worked on him and said that she had never before felt such a strong and heavy spirit and that it had actually scared her at first. She believed that Ofir was an Indigo or Crystal Child. In a similar vein, one of his friends told us that Ofir had once confided to him that he had become aware of spirit beings at a very young age but that he never mentioned this to us, his parents, because he thought we would not believe him. He was right; I would not have.

We also heard several of his friends recount how Ofir had encouraged them to reach for the stars, to live up to their full potential. He didn't just do this with words, they said; he also set the example. Over and over again, I heard the same thing being said, "If it were not for Ofir . . ."

These things pierced me to the heart. Who was this young man we had lost? Did I ever really know him? Thinking about this opened the chasm. Once again, I found myself falling, falling through dark, fathomless space. Then with a start, I was jolted back to consensus reality, back to the funeral, and I realized that Ofir's best friend was in the middle of offering his eulogy. I strained to absorb every word of his speech, as if his words were life-giving oxygen, as if they might save me from asphyxiating on my own black, bloody vomit, as if they had the power to somehow bring him back.

This is what he said. "I grew up with Ofir. He was my best friend, but he was more like a brother to me. So many of the things that I am today are because of Ofir. So full of life and inspiration, he was one of the few

people who knew what they wanted in life and actually had the motivation and willpower to make it happen.

"I talked to Ofir for hours every day, whether in person, over the
phone, or on the Internet—ANYWHERE—and it would NEVER get
old or boring. We would often build upon each other's knowledge in such
conversations, and in doing so he often left me with a burst of inspiration
to learn and research more about whatever it was we were talking about.

"Probably the most striking characteristic about Ofir was his drive
to succeed. We often would have long conversations that consisted completely of how, in the future, we saw each other being the most successful
people at the top of our fields and that any lower fate was unacceptable.

"Ofir not only finished his undergraduate career in a short amount
of time that few people could ever claim, he did so with great excellence,
graduating with honors among the brightest in his class. I remember
being at his graduation with his mother, whom he would always call
ema'shalee, and I remember the sparkle in his eyes as he took pictures
with his colleagues. He knew that his mother was at that very moment
the proudest mother on Earth, and it showed in her continuous loving
care and ever-present confidence in him that was apparent whenever I
saw them together.

"Most definitely Ofir's greatest role model was his father. On many
occasions he would tell me with much honor and pride stories of how
his father started out from scratch to become the successful businessman
that he is today. I know that his motivation to not only succeed but to
be the best was because of his father's strong presence as a role model
throughout his life. Ofir would always call him 'Hero,' and that nickname
was created because he truly viewed his father as his Hero, whom he
hoped someday to become.

"You both did a wonderful job of raising Ofir to be the successful, yet
loving and caring, person that he was, and he was truly proud to be your son."

At the mention of the word "hero," my heart startled. It was true; he'd
say it to me a lot, as in, "Hi, Hero, how's it going?" We were always playful

with each other, and I figured he was just mocking me. Anyway, I was uncomfortable with the term, so I ignored it and shrugged it off. Rachel, however, being aware of all family dynamics, told me that this was Ofir's way of telling me that he looked up to me. I remembered her telling me again and again that I ought to feel proud and that I should acknowledge Ofir for doing it. If I didn't, she said, I would come to regret it.

She was right. Regret gushed from my heart, searing down my arteries and through my veins, and I felt an even deeper wave of sadness flushing through me, which I would have thought impossible.

Many other eulogies were delivered, and then it was time for mine. Somehow, I made it to the podium for I remember standing behind it with Tal by my side, supporting me, as he always seemed to be doing now. I was wearing my reading glasses, but I could not see the words I'd written on the paper in front of me because tears were flowing down the lenses. I tried to stop crying, but I could not. I tried wiping my glasses, but that only made things worse. I felt so helpless and frustrated. I turned to Tal in desperation and said, like a little child, "I can't see. What should I do?" In that moment, my brokenness was evident to all. I could not think or function on my own, and I did not care. I just wanted to be plucked up, carried away, and dropped at the very top of the county dump, so I could roll down the side into oblivion.

After the service, we were taken to the gravesite for Ofir's burial service. As they began lowering the coffin into the ground, Rachel lost all control and wanted to follow. I screamed for my brother to help me and together we restrained her, never letting go, until she finally stopped struggling and went limp. She did, however, summon the strength to cast a hand-written note into the grave just before they began to fill it with earth. What does a mother write to her son as he is being lowered into his final resting place? I have never asked her, for that is between the two of them and should remain that way; but, to this day, it makes me physically ill to think about it.

With Ofir's service over, it was time for Michael's to begin, but Rachel could not move. I pleaded with her to please make an effort to come to Michael's service, reminding her that we owed him and his family this final respect. Also, I wanted her away from Ofir's grave. When I tried to gently guide her away, she slumped against me, as limp as a rag doll. But then, in an amazing display of strength, she assented and we walked across the path to join Michael's family.

For three consecutive nights after the funeral, we held prayers at our home, as was the custom. Many people came. Afterwards, I can remember sitting out on our patio with a group of our friends as they began discussing current events and engaging in general chitchat. I witnessed it, but I could not enter into it. Only later would I realize that this was the first hint of what awaited us in the coming days, weeks, months, and years. All the people who surrounded us now would return to their own lives; without meaning to, they would desert us, like a tide going out, never to return. For them, life would be "business as usual," while our world had changed irrevocably.

But I did not understand that then. All I knew at the time was that I was in a dark, suffocating pit and that from that vantage point the words being spoken bore no meaning. At best, I heard only echoes. Meanwhile, my mind wandered in circles, like a drunken ghost. *Had I stopped falling?* I wondered. *If I had, was it for good? Or just for now?*

ME?

You left
I am no longer complete
I gaze upon a world I once knew
I meander through a strange landscape

I am now a foreigner
In an infinitely distant world
I fail to participate
I have become an observer

Talk has become mindless chatter
Odors from another time
I know not what I am looking at
Meaning left with you

I go on purposeless and disorientated
I saunter here then there
Who am I?
Where are you?

—M.C.

4. The Beast

WITHIN A FEW DAYS of the funeral, our family members left for home. Almost from the moment the door closed on the last departure, our home transformed. Signs of life all but vanished. After all the hoopla of that first week, it was now eerily quiet. An unnatural silence echoed through the halls, and it was deafening.

Our beautiful dream house was bereft, hollow, empty—and yet it wasn't; it was permeated by death. Grief, sadness, pain, despair, and many other emotions yet to be identified filled it to the bursting point, suffocating us. The heart and soul of our family had been ravaged and we were gasping for breath. Or so it seemed, anyway. We needed the presence of others—were desperate for it—but the phone took a hiatus; the doorbell rarely rang. At first, a few friends came by, which was helpful; but soon their visits became less and less frequent.

Bit by bit, we began to realize that we'd been given a front-row seat to a very sad cultural phenomenon. We were witnessing firsthand how gracelessly our society relates to death and grief. Our culture fears death, so most of us want to sweep it under the rug, run away from it. The fact we had lost a child only served to exacerbate this cultural characteristic. Our experience was so outside the natural order that it scared people. The depth of our grief terrified them and made them run away from us even faster and farther.

Later, friends tried to apologize, telling us that they stayed away because they wanted to give us our "space," but I felt people were afraid to show up or even call. I could even understand why they felt that way.

What does one say? The situation becomes too awkward. In wanting to say something wise, people unintentionally say the most hurtful things.

"He is in a better place."

"God had a plan for him."

"Time will heal and you will move on."

And then there was my all-time personal favorite: "I had a cat that died suddenly, so I know exactly how you feel."

These efforts were all well intentioned, but it was garbage as far as I was concerned, and it made me secretly angry. But that anger was only the tip of the iceberg; I had absolutely no idea how angry I really was.

For several weeks we endured this isolation. Then, in desperation, Rachel and I decided to attend a support group dedicated to parents who had lost children. It took us over an hour to get there; and then when we walked in, we found everyone standing around chatting. Some were even laughing! I could not process what I was observing. I could not understand how any of them could be smiling, let alone laughing. *Were we in the wrong place? What the hell was going on?*

Soon, someone walked up to us and introduced himself as the head of the chapter. He informed us that the timing for our first meeting was good because there was to be a special event that evening: a worldwide releasing of balloons by bereaved parents. Rachel and I conformed to the plan. We grabbed balloons, attached a message and then, along with everyone else, released them to the heavens. I vividly remember breaking down at the sight of all those colored orbs ascending into the twilight sky. I bawled like a baby, as did Rachel.

Up until that point in the evening, we had been able to keep our emotions under control; but for some reason releasing the balloons devastated us. And then my anger flared. What was the purpose of the balloons? Was it to send them up to heaven, where our kids supposedly were? I did not know and I did not care. I was not interested in symbolic messages. *I just wanted Ofir back.* How was a goddamn balloon going to bring him back?

The group then went back inside and sat down in chairs arranged in a circle. Over to the side was a basket of teddy bears you could pick up and hold onto during the session or even take home to keep. I chose a white teddy, which still sits opposite my bed. Then the meeting began. We went around the room introducing ourselves with parents having the opportunity to talk about their children and the circumstances surrounding the child's death.

That evening, I learned something about how strong a grip grief can have and for how long it can hold a parent hostage. Some talked about how they had touched nothing in their child's room since the day he or she had died, not even ten years later. These rooms were frozen in time, like shrines to loss. One parent told the group that only the previous night had she finally been able to unpack some boxes that had belonged to her child. This, too, was many years later. Hearing this made me think about how Rachel had managed to pack up and remove Ofir's personal items from his condo, but so far none of us had had the courage to log onto his computer. I knew why. Once, Ofir had told us about some of his dreams. For example, he was working on some ideas about how to reform education. Deep down, we must have all believed that he had written about those dreams on his computer and that maybe, if we didn't touch it, those dreams would stay alive.

Rachel and I attended maybe three of these meetings but then decided that they provided no comfort to us, at least at that time. It was so sad to hear other parents talk about the death of their kids that we found it downright depressing. Especially disturbing were the stories involving suicide and murder. Perhaps it was just too soon. In any event, we quit going. But if these meetings helped in any way, it was that I came to understand how much parents who have lost kids all have in common. No matter how old the child is or how old the parent is, when a child dies, the feelings are the same. One young woman had miscarried. Her child had never been born, yet her pain and sadness was every bit as real as ours.

Conversely, a woman in her late eighties also showed up every week. Her son was in his sixties when he died, a good long life by many measures; but her pain and sadness, too, was every bit as wrenching as ours. Then there was a young mother with a baby in a carriage. She had given birth to twins, but one had died. The baby in the carriage was terminally ill; and as if that were not enough, the baby was also blind. The attitude of this young mother was so courageous in the face of such hardship that I remember her well even after all these years. She has served as a source of strength for me on many different occasions.

Our support group venture having been a failure in terms of relieving our pain, Rachel and I retreated back into our house. Then, as the days progressed, something inexplicable happened; the four of us began to drift farther and farther away from each other, like icebergs on the open sea. We could have banded together and maybe we should have, but instead we chose isolation. Perhaps we were so raw that contact seemed intolerable. Perhaps we were so consumed by grief that we needed every ounce of energy for sheer survival. If that was it, we didn't know it. We only knew we couldn't talk about Ofir or express our feelings to one another. But, how could we? We had no idea what we were feeling.

I remember being vaguely aware of the contrast between how icy things seemed on the surface, yet how underneath emotions burned like an inferno. These feelings were so intense and foreign that I began to wonder if we were not all going insane. For one, our paranoia levels were raging off the charts. Rachel and I were both terrified, especially at nighttime. If Tal went out, we could not leave our phones alone for a second. I actually slept with mine just in case we were to get the call, again.

Meanwhile, I felt a draining fatigue unlike anything I had ever experienced. Yet, as exhausted as I was, I could not rest or sleep. The truth is I did not want to. I feared that if I stopped moving, I would have to acknowledge a reality I did not want to be in. So, I behaved like a robot gone rogue, active day and night. There was no way to shut me down.

I was a warrior by nature and also by training and had lived my life as one. Believe me, I was as tough as the next guy. I had left home at seventeen and survived by my own hand ever since. I had lived in multiple countries, served in the military, started and grown several successful businesses from scratch. I had lived life according to me, answering to no one.

The picture I am attempting to convey is not of an arrogant man, just a highly independent, confident, and passionate one. I was most proud of the fact that I had provided for and protected my family with the same passion, energy, and strength. I had suffered losses and failures along the way, but they had all been rather easily overcome. I was independent, perhaps to a fault, and always in full control. On May 14, 2007, all that changed. The passing of my son had brought me to my knees.

From that moment, I began to experience a degree of pain and sadness that I could never have imagined. Absolutely nothing in my previous fifty-one years on the planet had prepared me for this. The truth is, had I lived for a million years, I would still not have been prepared. Instructions for how to cope with this particular event are not included in the operating manual of the universe. I now know this for a fact. In the years since, I have read and reread the manual a thousand times looking for what I thought I had missed, and they are just not there. Whoever put together the master plan for the universe forgot to include the loss of a child in the software.

I had experienced grief before, but this was different, so different that it scared me. Before, when someone close to me died, I was able to process it in a relatively short period and return to full functionality very quickly.

Not this time.

This time, I just couldn't seem to function right. On more than one occasion, I backed out of a parking space and didn't stop until I hit whatever was behind me. It didn't take long before my vehicle looked like it had reigned supreme in the National Demolition Derby Tournament of Champions. I would go out to do an errand and wind up in the wrong kind of store altogether, without even noticing. Then I'd proceed to traipse through the aisles, endlessly searching for something that was not remotely related to what that particular store sold—fruit at a pharmacy or aspirin at a hardware store. That's how bad it was. I'd keep searching and searching, and it wouldn't even occur to me to leave until a clerk pointed out my mistake. "Sir, we are not a pharmacy," he or she would say with just a hint of alarm in his or her eyes. Sometimes when I was driving, I'd reach out for what I thought was my drink, put my mouth over what I thought was the straw and not understand why nothing was coming out. Only after a few moments of puzzlement would I think to look down. Then I'd see that I had the antenna of my phone in my mouth! Maybe this wasn't so crazy the first time, but by the third time I knew something was really wrong. Again I questioned, *was I losing my mind?*

I have subsequently learned some things about the nature of the mind. For a mind to be healthy, there needs to exist a balance between the rational and emotional components. When these are in dynamic balance, we function well. But push a mind too far—stress it, traumatize it, force it to suffer something unconscionable—and it will eject some of the rational portion; keep pushing and it will eject all of it. With rationality out the window, emotions take over. That's what was happening to me. My mind, overtaken by pure emotion, was ill equipped to deal with the day-to-day stuff that we so take for granted, let alone make rational decisions. The consequences could be dire; but, up until then, mine had only been embarrassing. I was mortified, but I soon got used to it.

There was one thing, though, that I couldn't get used to: the loss of control. Once the steadfast commander of our little band, I had lost control of the ship and our lives were in complete disarray. The shame I felt was nearly physical. It hurt the most to look at Rachel. She had lost her son, and I was sick to my stomach that I hadn't been able to shield her from that.

How could Ofir be gone? Somehow, my fractured mind was not convinced that he was. I knew that children died, but not mine. That was impossible. My denial was so strong that I began to invent stories and scenarios. One such scenario involved the saleswoman at the car dealership where I'd gone to purchase two new cars, one for Tal to replace his old one and another for Daniel, who was learning to drive. There was a story behind that: Rachel insisted that if the boys were going to drive, they needed the safest car ever made and it was my job to find out what that car was. She was relentless, questioning me on every detail of every car that I researched. I finally found one that she agreed to, and I immediately drove down to the dealership to purchase two of them.

During the negotiations, the saleswoman and I actually became friends, and she would listen to me with patience and compassion. She was pregnant at the time, and I remember looking at her tummy and thinking maybe Ofir was going to be reincarnated as her child. I even decided that I was going to come back after she gave birth to check the baby over to see if there were any clues that it was, indeed, Ofir. I even planned to go about it like Tibetan monks when searching for their next Dalai Lama, by testing the child to see if it remembers its previous life. The feeling was that strong.

And then, one day, the falling sensation returned.

It started again as abruptly as it had stopped; and I kept falling, faster and faster and deeper down—hell, for all I knew I was falling upward—until I reached what felt like terminal velocity. In that moment, I began to sense a presence. Even though it was pitch black where I was, this presence was even darker. It had a sinister and ominous feel to it. As I fell ever further, that presence began to materialize into form, and it did not take long for me to come face to face with an animal the likes of which I had never before encountered. And yet, somehow, it was also strangely familiar.

I thought back to the death of my grandmother when I was thirteen, the death of my dad—I was thirty-one then—and then to the death of my brother, who died the previous year, when I was fifty. Each time, grief had lurked in wait; but, true to form, I'd quickly taken control. I'd looked at grief like a wild animal I had to wrestle into submission, and I never had any doubt that I was capable of overcoming it. But it was different this time. This thing had fangs, not normal teeth; it was huge and looked unimaginably powerful. Also, the environment was different. I had previously faced off against those animals on my terms in broad daylight. Now I was falling through a scary, dark, black pit.

Bizarrely, even though terrified, I began to see a twisted logic in this. The more extreme the loss, the more ferocious the animal it summoned. Of course, the beast released upon me was preternaturally savage, monstrous, and grotesque beyond belief; it was the perfect expression of just how unnatural and incomprehensible our loss was.

Then, suddenly, before I could process any further, before any declaration of war or even an introduction, it attacked, swiftly and decisively. It lunged at me, somehow knowing exactly where to strike. With a searing pain, I felt its fangs sink into my neck. I attempted to fight it off, but it was futile. Even as I continued to fall, it did not let go, its teeth firmly embedded in me.

I tried to take stock of the situation. Here I was, falling helplessly with that animal hanging from my neck. At the time, it seemed clear that this animal knew only one thing: kill, kill, kill. It had it in its power to deal a deathblow at any time it chose; and, if it did, I did not believe for one second that I could possibly survive. It seemed obvious that this animal was not leaving voluntarily any time soon. And, if I fought it, I would surely lose.

I felt myself wanting to give up; in fact, I would have welcomed death. But then I thought of Rachel and the boys. I knew I had to survive for them. If I could not slay it, then I would have to learn to live with this animal; I had no recourse. But how did one go through life attached to a mutant animal endowed with what could only be described as superpowers? I needed some guidance, but I wasn't ready to communicate about this with any other human, professional or otherwise. So, I turned to a source that was, for me, quite unlikely: books. I vowed to discover everything there was to know about this beast. Through devout study, I would learn how to defeat it.

It made the most sense to learn from those who had experience with this same kind of grief, so I ordered multiple books by or about parents who had lost kids. I was barely able to handle my own grief, let alone that of others, but it had to be done. Within days the books arrived, and I began to read voraciously.

By the fourth week, I had entered into a daily routine. I would be at the coffee shop at 5:50 a.m., waiting for them to open at 6:00. There I would read, cry intermittently, and then stare at I-don't-know-what until it was finally noon. At that point, I would attempt to eat some sort of lunch, and then I would spend the rest of the afternoon at a different coffee shop. I would go home late in the afternoon and spend the evening there, also reading.

This routine gave me a sense of order; it kept me busy and somewhat distracted. I had always liked being a creature of routine, for it gave me a kind of comfort. Some mornings I awoke even earlier and would arrive at the coffee shop a full hour or more before it opened. I would then either read on a bench outside or put my earphones on and circle the block continuously until I could go inside. Those were never easy walks. I would cry from the moment I began until the moment I entered the coffee shop.

Once inside the cafe, I felt like an alien species. There were people chatting all around me, but I swear I never heard words; I heard only an annoying drone. It was so overwhelming to my senses that at times I would run outside to recoup and reset. I distinctly remember wondering, *What was it that people could possibly be talking about, sometimes for hours? What was there to say?* I spoke to no one and no one spoke to me. At the time, I did not even know how to put a sentence together. It was like I had no past and only a blurry present from which to draw. And if there was a future at all, it was meaningless. In short, there was not much in my life to talk about unless the subject was the loss of my son.

Meantime, the Beast accompanied me everywhere; no matter where I went or what I did, this thing would follow. It had become my Siamese twin; we were joined together by throat and mouth. Yet, somehow, I actually began to adapt to it, like Rosemary to her baby. In fact, when I was out and about I wanted people to acknowledge my new twin, but it was quite elusive. Being from another realm, it had powers unfamiliar to this world; it could go invisible at will. It would never share me with anyone else. In fact, it did not seem to like anyone except me, and it made sure that I never forgot that. Yet, it never did my bidding. Whatever I wanted, it would do the exact opposite or whatever would be the most humiliating or embarrassing to me.

In short, the Beast ruled supreme. It made every decision in our Siamese twinship, and thus it taught me a great lesson about what total control *really* looked like. I became a slave to its every need and whim, and it would never allow me any downtime.

Soon I realized that the Beast was usurping all my power, almost to the extent that free will was no longer a part of my life. As I was soon to learn, its bag of tricks was never empty. Somehow, it was able to cause my body to twitch terribly, the worst happening at night when I was lying in bed. The twitching was not continuous, but came in intervals. Then, my torso would jump, not unlike when one is startled. Yet, it could get so intense at times that I did not know if it would ever stop. Soon after, I began to have issues with noise, the absolute worst being sudden noises. Any unexpected sound, no matter how faint or innocuous, stopped me dead in my tracks. I also could not handle anything loud. I would get very angry if someone turned the TV or radio up. It freaked me out.

But none of this deterred me from my mission. After racing through maybe six books written by or about parents who had lost children, I came to a basic understanding that my family and I were *not* going crazy. The extreme feelings we were experiencing and our bizarre behavioral patterns were perfectly normal under the circumstances.

Then after wading through a few more books, I came to a quite stunning realization: some of these parents had survived the loss and gone on to live productive lives, albeit very different ones. So, apparently some of these parents had tamed this animal. That realization gave me a tiny glimmer of hope, but it was not long lived. I just could not see any way to make progress. It seemed so hopeless that I decided there was only one possible explanation: not all of these Beasts were alike, and the animals sent to those parents were not as ferocious as mine. My animal was the most savage of all; so savage that it might never be reined in.

By the second month I was done reading books on grief and had progressed to more esoteric subjects: the soul, past lives, mediums, and everything in between. I read about these things because I wanted so badly for someone to tell me that Ofir was not simply gone. I needed to know that a part of him carried on, maybe in another life or form.

Over the next three-month period I read sixteen books of that genre, and all the while the animal held on tightly. It would not let go nor lighten up on its grip. Just as the Beast couldn't let go of me, I couldn't let go of the hope of finding Ofir. I contacted people from all over the world looking for answers or comfort or God knows what. Rachel and I even contacted a medium. He offered us a phone reading months in the future. We took it. Prior to Ofir's leaving, I would never have considered anything like this. As far as I was concerned it was voodoo BS. But now I was willing to try anything.

Around this time, the idea of writing to Ofir came to me. Maybe if I wrote to him, I might somehow maintain the connection. But it was more than that, too. I could say things to him that hadn't occurred to me to say while he was alive. Now there was so much in my heart. I seemed to see Ofir more clearly now, as if a curtain had been lifted. I set up a remembrance site on the web and entered my first posting. It turned out to be a tribute.

Ofir:

This will now be my venue for writing to you. Not a second, minute or hour goes by that I do not think about you. You are my Hero and shining light (how appropriate for an advanced soul like yours). How does a man of my limited abilities honor such a great being like you? My only answer is I will try with all my heart and soul until my dying breath. I am in awe of you. God bless you.

Love and respect you always. I am so, so sorry.
Dad

During the first few months with the Beast, it had seemed very much up in the air as to whether it was going to kill me or not. Death could be a quick way out for me, but it didn't seem to be what either of us wanted. Then, in a flash of insight, I became aware of a hidden dynamic: the Beast was feeding off of me—it was a bona fide parasite. I took some pleasure in realizing that. No, the Beast didn't want to kill me because that would have meant suicide for it. It just wanted to feed on me for as long as it could, as long as I could endure it.

The Beast seemed more than happy with the status quo of just hanging onto me, its teeth embedded deep in my throat. And the bizarre truth was, so long as I was breathing, I did not want it to leave, either.

Why?

As that thought was stewing in my minimally functioning brain, the strangest revelation came to me. I saw that this relentless animal was serving a dual purpose. First, it was carrying out the orders of that white-coated tribunal back at the hospital; it was punishing me and ensuring my exile. I, for one, was fine with that. I was convinced that my son's passing was my fault and did not want to hear otherwise. Then I saw that the Beast was not merely my tormentor; it was also my only lifeline to Ofir. In the pit of my soul, I believed that if I lost the Beast, then Ofir too would be lost to me with a finality I couldn't endure.

Now, at last, I saw the genius and cunning of the Beast. It had put a spell on me; it had made me believe that it was *I* who needed the relationship, not it. This strategy was hugely successful. The sick truth was that I did not want to lose this animal because I was imprisoned in a desperate love-hate relationship with it. I despised it for supplanting my son in my life, but I also loved it for its connection to Ofir.

So, I clung to my grief and I clung to the Beast, just as it clung to me. I guarded it with my life. Just as it would not allow anyone near me, I would not let anyone near it, for fear they might try to take it away and with it the last trace of Ofir.

Perhaps by then I was starting to glimpse a more accurate view of reality; but those fleeting insights didn't matter, so absolute was the Beast's power over me. I did not know if I could survive the Beast, if I could hold up under its constant dictatorship, but I knew I had to try.

CHILD

They leave us
So suddenly
We are lost
Who are we now?

We pretend
We follow time
Our hearts are not present
They are but shards

Our compass fails us
Yet we journey on
We seem fine
But sadness is our existence

Why do they do that?
Don't they know?
They take the best of us with them
Only empty shells remain

We are fatigued by why
The questions fade
What is left?
Purpose is forgotten

—M.C.

5. The Debt

THE MONTHS IMMEDIATELY FOLLOWING the funeral were possibly the loneliest I have ever encountered. For the most part, each family member dealt with his or her grief independently in the best way each knew how. Locked away in our solitary sorrow, we couldn't help each other; we were all shadows of death and there was no way death could console death. We needed life. It was not there.

All the while, time inched on.

Rachel and I never went out with friends because we had become a plague of sorts. Whether that was self-induced or by their choice, we weren't sure. Sometimes, though, Rachel and I made feeble attempts to connect with each other and with the living. We would go out in the evenings to sit outside a place called The River, a small outdoor mall, so that we could see what life looked like, to remind ourselves. One evening, we decided to go get a bite to eat at a local restaurant. There, we saw a waiter whom we both decided looked "exactly" like Ofir. We called him over to our table and talked to him at length, not allowing him to leave. The poor kid, he had no clue how to extricate himself from our overwhelming attack. Finally, he somehow managed to escape us, but we could not take our eyes off him for the entire evening.

Overall, though, Rachel and I seemed to handle our grief within the framework of our personalities. She tended to be a very private individual who kept things to herself, so she dealt with her grief alone. Mostly, she stayed at home, rarely leaving. I, on the other hand, despite the insular character of my excursions to the cafes, craved contact. So, I tried to reach out, at least at first. In all the reading I had done about the loss of a child, one theme that seemed to surface over and over: the desire of the bereaved parent to be heard and acknowledged, especially by family members. I, too, had a deep need to be heard and acknowledged, especially by my family overseas. I tried talking and writing and eventually sending them books on grief in the hopes that these things would help them understand what we were dealing with and also give them some guidance as to how to communicate with us. I got nowhere. Things got progressively worse until finally there was a full breakdown in communications.

At the time, I had been signing my emails to them, "Ofir's dad." It was my way of declaring to the Universe that even though it had taken away my son, I was still his father. Then, one day, a family member wrote back, "How you ended the letter upset me. You are Ofir's dad but also Tal and Daniel's dad. I know your thoughts—and perhaps your very being—are filled with memories, disappointments, achievements and everything this unique boy was; but you need to encourage, love, and accept Tal and Danny as much as you do Ofir."

I was horrified. My signing my emails that way had never been about loving one son more than another; it was only a father's desperate attempt to hold onto his identity as the father of three, not two.

After that incident, I began distancing myself from my family overseas. It happened just like all the grief books said: grieving parents often break communications with family members because they feel they are being insensitive, hurtful, impatient, selfish, or misunderstanding. My emotions were so fragile and raw that I could not risk any kind of additional hurt, and I certainly did not want to lash out at anybody. I did not have the energy for a watch-my-every-step kind of dance. In turn, they did not know what to say or how to relate to me. I did not want to put them in an untenable situation of having to try and get it "right," so I just pulled back.

From then on, I handled my grief in what I guess might be considered a very "male" way. I channeled it into action. I went out looking for

ways to numb the pain, but most of all I isolated myself. I holed up reading, searching for some way to understand what had happened to us, to
Ofir. But all the while, the deep, unprocessed sadness and the companion
feelings of extreme guilt and responsibility for not being able to protect
my son, festered. They grew like a virulent virus, plotting their takeover.

One weekend morning, I did not go out to read, which was rare. I
tried to concentrate, but my mind was leapfrogging in a thousand different directions. I was uneasy, sensing that if I did not take a timeout of
some kind, I would implode. So, although it was summertime and the
temperatures were well into the hundreds, I decided to go outside anyway
and pull weeds, hoping to give my mind a rest.

I walked over to the garden barefoot, wearing only swimming trunks.
Oblivious to the oppressive heat and to everything else for that matter, I
knelt down and, like a repetitive mechanical device, began pulling weed
after weed after weed. It was grueling, but I welcomed the physical hardship and the discomfort of the heat, hoping they would help distract me
from the mental agony.

It worked. For a time, I was in a world of my own, a world without
pain. Then, after about maybe a half-hour, I happened to glance down at
my legs; they were covered in red ants all the way up to my thighs. It was
the strangest thing, but only after actually seeing them did my brain/nervous
system kick in and transport me back into consensus reality. Only then
did I begin to experience the severe stinging. It was also only at this point
that I finally felt the heat of the sun beating down on my body, turning it
the color of a ripe, red tomato. My senses, now awake, signaled alarm and
I immediately ran towards the pool, not far away, and dove in. I stayed in
the pool until the stinging began to subside; but once I got out and dried
off, I felt a terrible itch. The itching bothered me more than the stinging,
and it seemed to intensify rapidly. I raced for the house, scratching all the
while. I can't even imagine what that must have looked like!

When I reached our bedroom, I came to a stop and literally fell to
my knees. Between my overloaded mind and the intense itching, it was

all too much. I felt helpless to relieve the itching, but mostly I felt helpless to understand what had happened to Ofir. I began to sob, wail really, like never before or since, a wail so pitiable that it reverberated through the halls. *I want my son back. I want my son back. I want my son back.*

I don't know if the sobbing was due to repressed emotions, though I can't imagine how, as I had been crying profusely daily, or if it was a final plea to the Universe to return my son. Whichever it was, it shook the ramparts. Our house was very big and the bedroom was very far away from the family room, where Rachel was lying down; but apparently she heard me because she ran into the bedroom, where she found me on my knees. She was caught off guard by the intensity of my sobbing and kept asking me repeatedly what had happened. But how could I answer that question? How could I possibly tell her that it was ants that had brought me, a grown man, to my knees wailing like a madman? *How could I tell her that I was weeping because we could not process together the fact that Ofir had left us?*

I was so pitiable that Rachel also fell to her knees and held me and did not let go. I don't know why, but, except for just one other time, that was the last time I recall us holding each other. I don't understand it, but apparently we were simply incapable of taking on each other's grief in addition to our own.

And so, another dynamic was set in motion.

Meanwhile, Tal was attempting to cope by spending most of his time with friends. Actually, he was spending more and more time with Ofir's friends, ultimately adopting them as his own. Tal, being as sensitive and compassionate as he is, was deeply affected by Ofir's passing; but, like his mother, he did not share his feelings openly. The signs were there, though, if you looked. When Ofir's college held a memorial, after the service, Tal signed the guestbook, "See you soon." When Rachel saw that, it shook her deeply; so, he changed it to read something like "See you when I see you." I was touched and again I looked at Tal in a new way. Prior to that, I had no idea that Tal ever thought about life after death.

We wanted Daniel to go back to school as soon as possible. In part, it was to get him back on track, but mostly it was so that he could be among his friends and engaged in life. Behind it, too, was the larger truth that Rachel and I did not have it in us to give Daniel the attention he sorely needed.

Thankfully, of all of us, Daniel had by far the strongest support group. He had recently found a girlfriend. She was sweet and gentle, and the closeness and physical contact she gave him helped provide some consolation. Daniel also had three best friends, each so different. There was the serious one, exceptionally bright and talented, with a bright future ahead of him. Then there was the musician, a longhaired, easy-going kid. The third was a girl, who was the life of the group, always smiling, happy, and positive. The three of them came to our house almost daily, so I witnessed firsthand how thoughtful, kind, and compassionate they were towards Daniel as he grieved the loss of his brother. It warmed my heart to watch his friends take such good care of him. All in all, Daniel seemed to be making good progress. He was re-engaging with life, which was encouraging to see. He re-joined the basketball team and was one of the star players. Rachel and I never missed a game; it was one of the few things I could look forward to.

We were about four months into Life After Ofir, and September 26, 2007 seemed like just another in a series of grief-tinged days. It was late on a Wednesday afternoon and we were all home, busying ourselves with various things. Suddenly, Daniel rushed out of his room and stood before Rachel and me, visibly shaken.

Time and space both froze as we heard him tell us something that could not possibly be true: there had been a terrible car accident close to school and his three best friends were all possibly involved. He was not certain, but apparently information to that effect was circulating among the students on cell phones and social media sites.

I heard what he said, but the story had to be overblown. Yes, of course, it was. Having convinced myself of that, I chopped through the glacier that had gripped the room and tried to calm Daniel down with a dose

Daniel, 2014

of rational thinking. I suggested we wait until we heard something more definitive from a reliable source.

Daniel nodded assent and went back to his room while Rachel and I resumed going about our day. An hour passed, then a little more time, and our vigilance began to ebb away. Then I thought I heard something out of the ordinary. Was Daniel crying? I rushed to his room and found him hysterical, banging his fists against the wall. "It has been confirmed," he managed to say in between sobs. His best friends in the world had been in a single-car accident and all three had been killed instantly.

I stood by as Daniel banged on the wall, repeating over and over and over, "What the f . . . ? Why is this happening?" I knew this question was not directed at the Universe; it was directed at me. And it hit home, like a bullet right between the eyes. Daniel was pleading for me to help him make some kind of sense of all of this. He needed an answer; he wanted it from me and immediately. The anguish in his voice told me that if he did not get it, he might lose the last bit of sanity that he was so desperately clinging to. His despair tore at my barely functioning heart. I wanted so desperately to have an answer to give him, but the room was filling with that thick, dark fog and the only response I could utter was the truth: "I don't know, I don't know, I don't know." I just kept repeating this pathetically inadequate mantra as I cried with him.

I will never get the sight and sound of that moment out of my head. In that instant, I knew that just four short months after losing Ofir, we were now in danger of losing Daniel, too, only in a very different way. After all this, how would he look at life? At seventeen, I had thought I was invincible, that I would live forever; but Daniel did not have that luxury any longer. No, Daniel knew too much about death.

I took full responsibility for this, too, and it re-confirmed what a failure I had become to my kids, to my family. My role had been straightforward— provide and protect. I had done the first part right, but I had been unable to safeguard my family, and the shame of that was consuming me, piece by piece. I knew that God could not be this cruel, that the Universe could not be this horribly wrong for no reason, so the fault had to be mine. I had to be to blame. I had to have broken the contract. *But what had I done wrong?*

I was more lost then than I had ever been. My head felt like an inflated balloon that had just been punctured from all sides in a zillion places and the air was trying to escape from each hole, sending the balloon careening off in one direction then another. And yet, on the outside, I was still somehow able to function; I was even aware of the pain of others. The day after Daniel's friends' accident, I volunteered to accompany the school principal as he went to pay his respects to the families of the three teens. As we made our way from one home to another, offering condolences, my heart broke to see the families in so much pain and shock. I remember thinking to myself that the worst had not even begun for them.

We attended services for the two boys locally, and then Daniel and I flew up to Portland, Oregon, to attend a service for the girl. Her mother had requested that Daniel give a eulogy and he agreed. Remembering how I had struggled to deliver my eulogy at Ofir's services, I was a bit worried for Daniel. I suggested he might want to reconsider, but he insisted on doing it. Still, I was concerned that he would not be able to find the words, so before we left I asked if he wanted me to help him prepare. He declined. Then, on the plane I asked again if he had written his eulogy to which he calmly said, no. I was uneasy, to say the least and suggested we work on it right there and then. Once more, he refused.

The next day we arrived at the chapel for the services. The hall was packed, standing room only. Daniel was sitting with his friends up front while I sat alone toward the middle. I was feeling very emotional and could not stop crying as I listened to the eulogies. When Daniel was called up, I prayed that he would be able to get through it okay. He stood behind the podium with his long hair and shabby clothing, looking for all the world like he had just come off the streets, but what followed can only be described as Herculean and genius. He was confident and strong in his delivery, and what came out of his mouth was loving and beautiful, validating the strong and profound friendship that had existed between his friend and him. I was in total awe of him.

I do not remember any of the actual words he said. I only remember the depth of love, strength, and class my son displayed. I understood at that moment that I had much to learn from him, too, just as I did from Tal. That was a real life lesson, for I had grown up in an environment where "kids should be seen and not heard." I realized in that moment that I had come to believe that kids had nothing to offer, neither in conversation nor in life. But first Tal and now Daniel were proving that understanding to be not just wrong, but insane. This realization was like a grenade going off in my misinformed mind.

By the time Daniel finished, I could not stand any more emotion, so I ran outside and let it all out. I wept uncontrollably. I wept for the family in the chapel, for the other two boys' families, and for my family, too.

Then, on the plane ride back to California, Daniel made a confession. He told me that he was supposed to have been in that car with his friends. But just before he was to enter the vehicle, his girlfriend called telling him not to go, to wait for her, that she was on her way. I sat there, stunned into silence, feeling absolutely terrified by the fragility of life.

Our grief seemed to intensify over the months that followed, heightened by our awareness of the baggage that Daniel was now carrying. Ever since Ofir's death, Rachel and I had both been asking the same question over and over. *Why, why, why?* We repeated it like a mantra, and the only answer we were ever able to agree upon, the only one that seemed logical, was that we were being punished. Why were we being punished? We had found an answer to that, too. Our life had been good, too good, and now it was time to repay the debt.

If our genius theory was, in fact, correct, then our life must have been beyond good. It had to have been spectacular for apparently the loss of our son was not enough to repay our debt; we needed to pony up the rest. What angered me to the core was the fact that this debt was handed not to me, but to all those innocents. Now three families' lives were turned upside down, and all the other students' lives were forever changed. *And what about Daniel?*

For the next few weeks, he rarely came out of his room. We suggested counseling, but he refused. Night after night either Rachel or I would sit outside his closed bedroom door and wait until we were certain he had fallen asleep. We refused to sleep until we knew that he had.

Maybe, before this, I might have thought I'd stopped falling. Maybe I thought I'd finally hit bottom and that I was beginning to gain a tiny modicum of equilibrium. But after this, all that changed. Now the abyss opened directly underneath me, and I was falling even faster and deeper into that bottomless pit where there was no light and no companionship except for the Beast.

✦

The superior man thinks always
of virtue;
the common man thinks of comfort.

—Confucius

6. The Search Begins

THE DEATH OF DANIEL'S FRIENDS was like an echo reverberating and magnifying the original loss. Nothing made sense any more. I was consumed by grief and, even worse for one so in love with control, by a pervasive sense of my own inadequacy. In desperation, I turned to the only person I thought might really understand, Ofir. Immediately after the kids' accident, I wrote him a letter. I didn't think about the words; they just came out. This is what I wrote:

Sept 28, 2007

> *Ofir:*
>
> *Think about you every second of every day. You are my Hero and shining light. You humble me. We were so alike — only you were 1,000 times better.*
>
> *Love you always,*
> *Dad*

It may sound like something any father might say about his son, but I knew in my soul that it was true. Ofir was better, kinder, and more aware than me or almost anyone. I hadn't really seen it when he was still alive, but I saw it now. Ever since he had left us, our roles had reversed. Now, Ofir was my hero and my light; and wherever he led, I vowed to follow.

And then there was Daniel. I was achingly proud of him, even as I feared he would slip from our grasp. I had to tell Ofir. He needed to hear it from me.

October 5, 2007

    Ofir:

Daniel lost three of his best friends in a car accident last week. At one of the funerals the family requested that Daniel speak. Ofir, you would have been so proud of him. There must have been 500 people present. Daniel spoke with such confidence and eloquence. He was truly amazing. As parents we can only hope that our kids are better than we are. Daniel was and is, as you are. Maybe you know all this, I truly wish so, more than anything in this world.

    This past week I have been talking to different people about you, and I keep learning how special you were in this world but also what a unique soul you were. You definitely are a very advanced soul, and I have no doubt in this matter.

    Love you and think of you all day and night,
    Dad

I wrote to him again the next day. Maybe in my mind if I kept writing to him, then he was not gone.

October 8, 2007

    Ofir:

We all miss you so much. We are thinking about you all the time. You are and always will be with us and in our thoughts. This will go on till the day we die. Not only will you never be forgotten but your memory will continue to inspire your family and friends forever. So young, but what a legacy! You are such an inspiration to our family. You are what most people strive to be throughout a lifetime. You earned the respect and love from all who knew you.

    Love and miss you,
    Dad

After the loss of Daniel's friends, the level of emotions at home amped up to such a degree that the very air was saturated with pain. As for me, the deaths of all these young people had so tested my ability to cope that I felt my head was ready to explode. Everything I thought I understood about how life functioned, about being a father and a husband, had been upturned. I felt I was witnessing my sanity slipping right down the drain.

I was feeling so much emotion that I needed some release, but did not know where to turn. Then, one evening, a friend invited me out to dinner. This rarely happened. So, I readily accepted, welcoming anything that seemed normal. He was a single man and, when eating out, typically sat at the bar, so that's what we did. Actually, bars were very foreign to me. Neither Rachel nor I consumed alcohol, so I had never even sat at a bar before. However, I soon learned why the bar scene is attractive to so many people. Almost immediately, we were joined by a group of guys we knew, and the evening evolved into a night of laughter and joking. Mostly, I stood on the sidelines, not participating and not drinking. The conversation was light and mostly shallow, frankly bordering on downright stupid, but something about it lifted my spirits just a little. That night, it became clear that this could be a way to escape from the pain. And by now, escape was very attractive.

Whenever I did something, I gave it my all, so in short order I became a fixture at the nightly bar scene, but I wasn't there to drink. I was there for the lights, the people, and the babble. It was just about being there, being a part of the silliness of our group of guys. Even though I rarely interacted with anyone, I had a front row seat where I could at least observe normal life, something I had come to believe would never happen for me ever again.

This went on for months, and in all those months, I only had one truly meaningful experience, which mystifies me to this day. One evening I was standing behind the guys, as I was accustomed to doing, not thinking or saying much, when a woman sitting a few chairs down signaled me to come over. I thought it strange, but out of politeness, I walked over. After we introduced ourselves, she asked me if she could ask me a personal question. When I agreed, she looked me straight in the eye and asked me if I had lost a child. Having never seen this woman before, my first reaction was to blurt out, "Who told you?" She indicated that her friend, who was sitting next to her, had reached that conclusion from observing me all evening. She then introduced her friend who was from Canada and worked as a psychic of sorts. After talking to them for a little while I returned to my place. The skeptic in me wondered was it really a psychic thing or was it just so damn obvious? I know one can quickly identify physical anomalies in others, but how does one identify a broken heart from across a counter?

Despite my cynicism, that evening, I wrote another letter.

> *Ofir:*
>
> *I think about you every day. There are days I just cannot believe we will never see you again. I cannot get over what a waste of a truly good human being occurred when we lost you. You deserved so much more. I miss you every day. You were my Hero. I wish I could have done more for you.*
>
> *Love and honor you always,*
> *Dad*

The truth is, I actually hated being at those bars, but it was infinitely better than being home, sad and alone. By now it had become clear that Rachel and I could not give each other what we needed. For my part, I knew I was guilty, guilty, guilty, and I felt deeply ashamed. I simply could not come home to her every day and look her in the eyes. I know this may sound insane, but nevertheless it was 100% true.

And, so, it was probably inevitable that I would meet a woman one of those evenings. After we met, we started chatting and texting daily. Pretty soon I was hooked—not just by her but by the whole thing; I began to crave encounters with women. Why? To this day, I'm not entirely sure;

but in an effort to rationalize, I've come up with many excuses. First, since I was so emotional, I found it more comforting—and probably safer—to talk to women versus men. The pressure relief valve just had to be bled from time to time, otherwise the vessel would have undoubtedly exploded; and with women, I was able to be more vulnerable and express my true feelings without fear of judgment or embarrassment. Second, it was exciting; the flurry of texting and talking that ensued provided a much-needed distraction. Finally, the physical contact became my numbing "drug of choice." The numbing began the instant the thought of contact entered my mind and lasted well beyond the end of the "fix." For a little while, I could forget. The relief these negative behaviors provided was so effective that no regard was paid to consequences or morality. In short, it became an obsession, and I was a full-blown junky.

It continued this way for several months. Then it was January 24, 2008: my first birthday after the accidents. I wrote again to Ofir:

> *Ofir,*
>
> *It is my birthday today and will not celebrate. I cannot understand how I have been given fifty-three years and you only twenty-two. You were so much better than me.*
>
> *I look around and see all the kids your age wasting their lives away, lost and non-productive. I do not understand why you were not allowed to realize your dreams—you had so many. You understood that nothing is given and nothing is easy. You worked so hard and gave up so much to live out your dreams. It was all taken from you. You deserved so much more. You earned it. I wish I could have done something. With so many young kids wasting their lives away, your death is even a greater waste. I am so sorry. You were better than me and deserved so much more than I have received. Love, honor and respect you always.*
>
> *Love,*
> *Dad*

This letter provides another insight into how poorly my mind was functioning: I had actually turned fifty-two, not fifty-three.

After months of being out at night, the intensity and variety of those escapes had grown like a cancer to the point that something had to give. My life was spinning out of control. On April 30, 2008, this was confirmed. I moved out.

Rachel had agreed that it was best for me to leave because of how disconnected from her I had become. I was out all day, every day, reading, and then at nighttime I was out with the boys, looking for women. In short, I was already gone in every other way, yet a bond still existed with Rachel. The night before I was to move out, we lay on our bed, held each other, and cried profusely. Then, in the morning, as if it were the most natural thing in the world, I got up, took some clothes, and left. I walked out of a thirty-one-year marriage with the only woman I had ever loved.

If anyone had told me that I would one day walk out of my home and my marriage, I would have thought the idea insane and preposterous; Rachel and I had been together for more than thirty years. Until May 11, 2007, we had been very happy living and loving life together; and yet here I was, a mere year later, walking out. Even more incomprehensible is the fact that I that moved out on Rachel's birthday, something Rachel enlightened me about years later. Up until then, I had no clue.

I still struggle to understand why, exactly, I did this unthinkable thing; the dynamics are so complicated that they defy my understanding. All I know is that the pain was so deep that it seemed to penetrate all the way down to my DNA and I felt like a cornered animal. So, despite everything I stood to lose by giving up on our marriage, I felt I had no choice. I had to escape to survive. It still amazes me how the loss of a child can so often result in such cruel and devastating collateral damage. For us, it was scorched earth, an outcome I played no small part in creating.

When I walked out, I had no idea what I had set in motion. The grief and sadness associated with the loss of my marriage to the woman who had stuck it out with me through thick and thin since we were teenagers was to compound my self-loathing exponentially. Many times, my guilt overwhelmed me to the point where I could not function, and I would lie in bed for days, unable to rise. Often, on my numerous sleepless nights, I would text Rachel, "Sorry" or "I am so sorry," or some variation thereof, a mournful message to which she would never reply. Rachel was angry with me and rightfully so. My guilt was so intolerable at times that I considered going back, but every time I thought about it, I would go into total overload and retreat.

In time, I would draw some comfort from an online relationship with a mother who had lost her daughter. She was going through something similar. One day, she wrote to me about the difficulties she was having in trying to be compassionate toward her husband. Her words resonated in my heart, "I think I have distanced myself from him because my own nightmare of loss is staring me right back in my face. My husband and I have an emotional and physical connection to the same pain and loss that is so deep. His pain mirrors my pain and sometimes I can't even handle my own pain . . . and maybe that is why I am distancing. I still love him dearly."

Most of the time, though, I felt pushed to the very edge.

And then I noticed something else. Even though my sadness never let up, I could sometimes feel it transmuting into a fierce, white-hot anger, an anger so intense and potentially explosive that it scared me. I had to do something to channel it. Prior to the accident I had worked out a good five times a week, but for months now I'd engaged in very little physical exercise, so I decided to give the gym a shot. It turned out to be a good idea. Not only did intense physical exercise help keep my anger in check, it also proved to be a way to escape from my other feelings. Soon, intense physical exercise became another addiction.

Simultaneous with re-joining the gym, I also began hiking in the surrounding mountains. I approached those hikes looking for another escape, but that's not really what they turned out to be. The hikes felt good in a way that was unfamiliar; they quieted me. Immediately after the hike, I would sink right back into my screaming head; but, looking back, it is now clear that those hikes were a form of meditation and served as my introduction to the realm of spirit. I was a practical man who put no faith in religion or spirituality, but those hikes opened me to Nature, and Nature spoke my language. This might seem like a really insignificant thing; but it wasn't, not at all, even though I myself was unaware of it then. Somehow, in those mountains I crossed an invisible boundary; I left the material/rational plane and entered the sphere of spirit and heart. Though I might reside on that plane for only a few moments each time I hiked, the effect reverberated. What seemed then like a minor tremor was setting in motion a whole cascade of events.

I didn't understand any of that then, so I just kept seeking a physical outlet for my inner turmoil. Soon, I returned to the golf course. Golf seemed to do very little for my emotional state of mind, but I continued playing because it kept me busy for a few hours. To my surprise, within a few months my game returned; I was playing at almost the same level as before Ofir left, but with some major differences. In the same way that I would twitch in life, so I had developed a twitch in my golf swing. It was a real burden, but I learned to live with it. Also, my deep anger would flare up from time to time, and it was not uncommon for me to have to replace the shafts on some of my clubs. Over the years I had come to love and respect the game of golf in all its facets, so these outbursts disturbed me deeply. But my anger won out every time.

Then golf gave me an opportunity to really run away, and I took it.

A month earlier, just as a way to get my mind off the grief, I had decided to enter a tournament that our golf club held annually. I was paired against a seasoned player who had beaten me in previous tournaments. On this occasion, however, I was able to somehow win. After the match it was he who suggested I give the Maccabi Games a shot. I was quite taken back by his suggestion, but when he went on to tell me that the qualifiers were to be held in West Palm Beach, it sounded appealing. I decided that getting away for a while might do me good, even if I didn't qualify.

Hiking San Jacinto mountains

The day after arriving in Florida, I played a practice round with two other players. When a woman approached us asking if she could join us to make up a foursome, I was the first to agree. Given my state of mind, that "practice round" became much more about the woman than the golf.

The following day, the qualifiers began. I played well enough the first two days, but I had no expectations. Then, to my surprise, on the last day I played quite well. I wound up in third place, which was good enough to qualify! Since my head was never in my game, no one was more shocked than I. The truth was that I had flown clear across country primarily to run away from the oppressive, stifling grief. I had given very little thought to the idea that I might actually qualify for the Games, which would, in turn, obligate me to fly to Israel next year to play golf. I told myself that, since the games weren't taking place until the following summer, I had lots of time to back out, and that's how it ended. What might have once been a proud moment proved instead to be flat and flavorless, just like everything else. With the distraction over, I flew home feeling no better than the day I had left.

It was now the end of July. More than a year had passed since Ofir's death. I had become so debilitated from being eaten alive by guilt that I finally gave in and decided to seek therapy. I had resisted therapy until then for multiple reasons. First and foremost, it had always been very difficult for me to ask for help. Second, I did not want some therapist confirming that Ofir was not coming back; I simply did not want to hear it. Furthermore, how could anyone who had not lost a child identify with me? The excuses went on and on. But I knew I was in trouble, so I did it anyway; I found a therapist.

I was not an easy patient, to say the least. Recently, I asked the therapist to write a brief synopsis of her impression of me during those first months. Here it is, unedited:

Hi Martin:

A comment that one of the staff said to me before the first time we met was "He won't last long; he is so angry. I don't know what you can even do with him."

Your anger was actually scary. You appeared like you could have killed someone with the rage you had. It was very extreme. I truthfully wasn't afraid, but the intensity that you had was difficult to process much with you.

After looking at some of my notes these are some of the things that I noted:

Avoidance; you were acting out sexually. There is no clarity from you on a way to move forward in the grief process.

Some of the things that you said were: "My life is upside down." "Can't focus." "Can't sleep." "He (Ofir) had it all, the drive, the smarts." "I am the kids' dad." Extreme guilt. "No one in the family is talking about Ofir."

I think what I remember the most was the extreme responsibility you took for the accident. There was no rationalizing with you. You were desperate for help on how to cope or function, but [had]no way to process anything constructively. Since your family was so devastated, there was no way to come together to grieve it together or come together to even talk. Your guilt was extreme. As if the father role has all the responsibility for anything or everything that happens, and you perceived that you had control over it. It was like a hurricane that had to blow itself out before there was any way to use processing of the emotions.

As a therapist, I just had to listen and follow your train of thought and move with you on a trail of misery and self-destruction and drop bread crumbs that maybe you could follow at some point in time as a rational way to process the unimaginable emotions you were going through. I felt I had to stay centered and allow your process to happen, send you compassion and love without you knowing it, since the pain was so great and you didn't want that.

That is all I can think of at the moment. I hope this helps some.

Early on in therapy, I almost walked out when the therapist made an assertion that challenged the very ground I walked on. She said that we humans really do not control anything. Since I had lived my whole life believing that I *was* in full control, my anger flared up. I contested her statement and I was on my feet, about to exit, when she said, "And you could not control what happened to Ofir."

I stopped in my tracks. This statement felt incredibly brutal to me, yet it was also profound. The last thing a grieving father wants to hear is that he could not have protected his child, that he was powerless to do so. I cannot speak for other fathers, but for me this issue superseded all others by far. It was the major source of my guilt and shame. Now this therapist was saying that the belief I had held onto so dearly all my life— the belief that I was in full control—was but an illusion. She was telling me that I had never had control over . . . anything.

A volcanic anger rose up inside me. I felt incredibly betrayed, lied to. By whom, I wasn't sure. What about the bargain I had made with the Universe, the one that said if I did my part, the Universe would do its part and all would be well? I had kept my part of the deal; I'd followed all the rules, given it my all. Now I was being told that humans do not—cannot— control anything. Well, if I did not control things, then who or what did? *Who the hell was writing this story?*

I was so shattered that I don't know how I made it through the rest of that session or any of the others. I only know that I somehow kept going back, even though I could not process the information I was receiving, for my brain was barely working or so I thought. I did not understand this at the time, but even though my conscious mind was not functioning well at all, my subconscious was. In fact, it had taken over. It was directing the show. But I didn't know that then; I just thought I was broken. I didn't understand I needed to shatter in order to let the light in.

A few months later my therapist asked me what seemed to be a very strange question, "Who are 'they'?"

I looked at her, confused. "What are you talking about?"

"Throughout all our previous sessions," she said, "there has been one statement that you have made repeatedly: 'They took Ofir.'"

I was dumbstruck. I had not been even remotely aware of this. Since I was as baffled as she was, we moved on, and I do not recall our ever addressing this again. But I never forgot it, and over the years I struggled to understand the meaning behind my own words. In time, I think I began to get a glimmer.

In the early days of therapy, I was functioning in a purely emotional state. I had very little rationality at my disposal; it had been demolished by that "why" question. I could almost understand why Rachel and I might need to be punished, but why Daniel? There was just no rational explanation to be found, so my mind just snapped loose; it broke loose like a mustang slipping its halter. My busted, wild mind simply could not process the idea that my son had died on my watch. He just could *not* be dead. And if he was not dead, but just "gone," then the only "logical" explanation was that someone had to have taken him. Someone had stolen him. And because I could not as yet identify who had done this, I just addressed them as "they."

"They took him."

This hypothesis might have been the product of a broken mind, but it gave me hope when I needed it most. If Ofir was not really dead; but only gone, then I would be able to find him. I could reclaim my manhood, my dignity, and my self-respect; I'd be able to look Rachel in the eyes again.

Yes, that's what I would do. I would go get him and bring him back and make it all right again for his mother and brothers. Now my life had a purpose again. I had a reason to be alive.

Even with my fractured mind, I had to have known at some level that this would not be easy; that the search would take me beyond my known universe, that it would challenge all my assumptions, all my deepest beliefs, even my identity. Knowing, deep down, how stubborn I was, I must have also figured I was in for a hell of a ride.

REASON OR NOT

Where did the light go?
Why are flowers colorless?
Why is music noise?
Why did taste drown in the food?

Why has hope left?
Why is the path mocking me?
Why did winter replace the seasons?
Why does each footprint weep?

Where did you go?
Why did you leave?
Did they not know
We had a future?

Sadness my reflection
Anger my anchor
Why he me preceded
What happened to order?

I don't understand
I don't feel
I am a grounded eagle
Universe, you are the grand composer.

—M.C.

7. Where is Ofir?

M Y LIFE NOW HAD ONE AND ONLY ONE PURPOSE: *find Ofir and bring him back.*

He had gone from here, from this plane of reality, but I knew he was not gone completely. He was somewhere, of that I was certain. Was that somewhere another world, another dimension or another form? That is what I needed to find out. How to proceed? I took stock. It seemed clear to me that, in order to find Ofir, I would first need to understand the Nature of Reality. I would need to survey, map, and understand the very mind of the Universe and find out exactly how it functioned. I realize this goal might sound ridiculous to those of sane mind, but I never gave it a second thought. As far as I was concerned, this was just another job to get done. I knew I had a laser-like ability to focus on an objective, and I had always accomplished whatever I set my mind to. Why should this be any different?

Now that I had a specific objective, I made a plan. I decided I would undertake my search the only way I knew how: by treating it as a project and immersing myself fully. I was fortunate in that I had the financial means to take whatever time would be needed. I remember wondering what other parents did after they had lost a child. Did some go out searching as I intended to do? Did they continue on, "dead and numb" to the world? Did they simply give up? I decided to take this journey on behalf of all those who had lost children.

Before proceeding, I set one rule of engagement: I would follow wherever the trail led. I made the commitment that nothing would be out of bounds, no matter how alien or foreign it initially seemed. I would listen to, look at, and experience anything and everything I encountered without pre-judging. This was a huge step for me because I *always* pre-judged. I always instantly chose the option that aligned with my philosophy and that was that. Up to this point, life had always been drawn in black and white with no grey areas, and I liked it that way. But now, there was a crack in that foundation.

What was my next step? In the months prior, I had purchased book after book about grief and then about more esoteric subjects and consumed them like a starving man. These latter books professed that there was a life after death in the form of reincarnation. This felt mostly right to me, but the fact that it felt right or that I somewhat believed in the idea could never be enough for me. I needed much more data. Though those books had provided much in the way of illumination, guidance, and solace, I now needed to delve deeper and broaden my search. But how?

Right at the outset, I arrived at a major fork in the road. It seemed to me that there were two clear options, each very different from the other. I could embark on the path of religion or the one of science. A decision had to be made: left or right, the blue pill or the red pill. How was I to decide?

I knew very little about my own religious tradition, Judaism, let alone any other; but then again, I knew even less about the sciences. Still, I gravitated toward science. My understanding of life had always been one of existentialism with a strong tendency towards the philosophies of determinism, positivism, and materialism. It had worked, so it had to be right. Plus, I reasoned, the sciences had created everything that made our material existence work so well. Science was at the core of the most prestigious and brilliant institutions in the world, and science and technology had both played a huge part in my success in life. Science and particularly physics seemed to be constantly coming up with new and intriguing answers about the Nature of Reality; whereas, in my mind, religion had gained no new ground in the last 2,000 years. We still had no solid evidence that God existed. Yes, I wanted hard proof, not faith, and only science could give it to me. In sum, it seemed most logical to follow the path of science, particularly physics.

That settled, I focused on the next step. Books, I knew, would be my pathway into the science of physics, but not just any books. The search would require that I read and study academic books, something I had engaged in only sparingly before. A self-educated man, I had always chosen the experiential route over the academic one; and, so, it was a huge step for me to engage with the very institutions I had avoided, even shunned. But I'd vowed to go wherever the path led, so there was no backing out. I set out to learn what the great scientific thinkers thought about the Nature of Reality to see if they could shed some light on where Ofir might be.

And so, the search began.

I conducted my search with a degree of dedication and efficiency that would have made any military commander proud. I bought dozens and dozens of scientific books and poured over them each day at the coffee shop looking for clues as to the Nature of Reality. While reading, my mind could be amazingly clear, focused, and resolute. It took a huge effort, but I was generally able to maintain some level of calm. Still, as intent as I was on my objective, the pain and sadness were ever present, bubbling just beneath the surface and threatening to break through at any instant. Although during my hours of reading, I could generally keep a lid on my emotions, not always; sometimes my sorrow and rage just gushed out before I was able to stop them.

On one occasion, for example, while reading, something triggered a deep response. I burst into tears, put away my book, got in my car and headed for home, still crying. On the way home, a cop stopped me. When he reached the driver's side window, he asked for my license and registration. As I handed them to him, he looked at me quizzically and asked if everything was all right. I can't imagine how I might have looked, having been sobbing profusely for the previous ten minutes.

The policeman told me I had not come to a complete stop at a small, quiet intersection. I was agitated that he had stopped me for such a trivial reason but said nothing. When he returned to my window, he looked at me again. He obviously thought that maybe I was on drugs or who knows what, so he began to look around inside my truck. He peered into the back and then asked me what I had on the seat. That question was like a needle piercing the swollen balloon of my pent-up emotion. The balloon detonated in one huge outburst, and I verbally attacked him. Before I knew it, another cop appeared at the passenger window. What ensued was not pretty; I let them both have it—all of it. I was certain they were going to arrest me, and that did not bother me one bit.

Miraculously, however, they let me go. It took me a while, but I finally calmed down. Then I felt terrible for I realized that they were only doing their job. This incident showed me how very, very angry I was and how out-of-control I could be. Again, the vehemence of my anger scared me. I was especially worried that I might direct my anger towards others, as I just had. I knew I had to channel that anger in a productive way, so I vowed to use it as fuel and to re-double my efforts.

I was relentless in my study and quickly found myself fascinated by a mystifying branch of physics called quantum mechanics. The principle known as Occam's Razor tells us that the simplest explanation is usually the best. I generally agreed with that; but where my quest was concerned, my intuition told me otherwise. It told me that, since we humans had not yet been able to identify the Nature of Reality, the answer had to lie in something beyond our current thinking. So maybe, in this case, the simplest answer *wasn't* the best. Thus, when I stumbled across the relatively new sub-field of quantum theory, it immediately intrigued me because it pointed to some very surprising phenomena. For example, when viewed at the subatomic level, matter apparently behaves in a way that is very counterintuitive. When I read that, something clicked, so I dove deep into the latest findings.

I learned that quantum physics had not only shown but had actually proven some pretty remarkable things including that matter is both a wave and a particle and that a particle could be in two places at the same time and that particles under certain conditions could communicate with each other faster than the speed of light, regardless of distance. It was also showing us that material existence was not absolute, but only existed as possibilities and potentialities!

These findings were so unexpected that I was absolutely convinced that studying them would lead me toward a better understanding of the Ultimate Nature of Reality. If such weird things or events were possible, then surely other possibilities existed as well including the possibility that Ofir was somewhere and that I could find him. If, in fact, a particle could be in two places at the same time, then it was not such a huge leap to think that, even if Ofir had been taken from this reality, he might still exist in other dimensions or places or times or . . .? If the particle/wave duality was a fact, then maybe it applied to human beings. Maybe Ofir had once been like a particle, existing in the physical realm, but now he had returned to waveform.

Also, according to Einstein's conservation of energy theory, energy cannot die, but only change form. If the soul is a form of energy, then Ofir's soul could not have died; it could only have changed form. Did all this mean that he was still here but camouflaged in some way? Could that be?

All this quantum strangeness gave me hope, which strengthened my resolve. I vowed to forge on, to find out more. I read voraciously on the history and interpretations of quantum theory going all the way back to the beginning of the twentieth century, to the father of quantum theory, Max Planck. I found, that although many of the details of quantum theory had been proven over and over again, they had yet to be explained. In fact, *every quantum theorist including Einstein struggled to accept what quantum mechanics was telling them.* A multitude of quotes by famous physicists describe their reactions to the "disturbing" behavior of particles. Erwin Schrödinger, a Nobel Prize laureate and key contributor in the early years of quantum mechanics, said, "I don't like it and I am sorry I had anything to do with it." Richard Feynman, also a Nobel Prize laureate, is quoted as saying, "What I am going to tell you about is what we teach our physics students in the third or fourth year of graduate school . . . It is my task to convince you not to turn away because you don't understand it. You see my physics students don't understand it . . . That is because I don't understand it. Nobody does."

These brilliant physicists were able to describe *what* was going on in the most detailed way, empirically, through mathematics and replicable experiments. Yet, what they could not do—and what physicists still cannot do—is tell us *why* or *how*.

All this discovery was both stimulating and very humbling, and it pulled me further into an even deeper fascination with quantum physics. I was reading about the "measurement problem" in physics when I came upon something quite startling. Simply put, the "observer effect" suggests that the mere act of observation can affect how particles behave. This was astonishing to me. All my life I had believed that the physical/material world was distinct and separate from the non-material. But, if mere observation could affect the behavior of particles, that had to mean that the physical world was somehow connected with the non-material. For me, this was an earth-shattering revelation! Finally, I had stumbled upon something that might help me build a bridge from the material to the immaterial, from the physical to the transcendent. This was the key I was looking for, the key to open the door to another realm.

Deep in my bones I sensed this had some very meaningful implications for my search for Ofir and the Ultimate Truth, so I waded in deeper. I ordered even more books and read hungrily, seeking to discover what the best minds were saying about this.

The road led to the subject of consciousness.

I discovered that a few brilliant scientific minds were conjecturing that consciousness played a key role in manifestation on the material plane. Of course, this got my attention and raised important questions that began to rock my world. Did that mean that the material world actually originated in the non-material? Was the material world affected or even *controlled* by the non-material? And, there was an even more fundamental question: Was there really something beyond the material? If there was, why had I not previously read about that anywhere in physics?

The very narrow path where I had begun my journey was slowly, but miraculously, opening up a new tributary. The path labeled "consciousness" had appeared, and I took it.

Exploring the idea of consciousness was like encountering a whole new world. The more I delved, the more thoroughly convinced I became that I was on the right track. I knew that the subject of consciousness would play a key role in my uncovering the Ultimate Truth, and that my understanding of that Truth would lead me to Ofir. But once again, I was humbled. What did I know about consciousness? It seemed almost unbelievable, but up until that time this conscious being (me) knew absolutely nothing about consciousness! My mind was *so* full of ideas, thoughts, facts and memories, and yet it was not conscious of its own consciousness. I was never even conscious enough to think of asking the question, "*What is consciousness?*"

I decided to rise to the challenge and set myself a task. I would attempt to articulate my own view of what consciousness was and also address the more important question, "*Where did consciousness originate?*" I sat down and got to work, but after several hours, I had written only one lonely sentence. I remained seated staring at it for what seemed like hours until the realization sunk in that I had already written everything I knew. However, over the next week or two, I was able to construct something that expressed my understanding up to that point in time.

WHAT IS CONSCIOUSNESS? –Martin Chesler

Inspired by Ofir Chesler

IN ORDER TO PURSUE THE "TRUTH" ABOUT CONSCIOUSNESS *I must ask many questions. I doubt that I will arrive at or even stumble on a definitive answer, but I must continue on this quest to establish at least clarity, if not actual answers.*

I recognize that I am not suitably equipped with the knowledge, brainpower or experience to embark on such an impossible journey, but I continue to do so anyway inspired by Ofir and people like Schrödinger, Plank, Einstein, Bohr, Pauli, Born, Dirac, Heisenberg, Rutherford, Wheeler, Feynman and others.

These men were geniuses and more, but history has also witnessed many an occasion where ordinary people have accomplished extraordinary things. This journey is a selfish one. It is not for any altruistic purpose other than to understand where my son is. I would rather die looking than just exist because that, in essence, is all that is left for me.

There can only be two possible outcomes once the answer is known.

1. Consciousness dies with the body.

2. Consciousness is not part of the physical and does not die with the body.

If number 1 is true then another question is generated: Is that the end game or does something else survive, like the soul or some other form of energy and how does that relate to the death of consciousness?

If number 2 is true, then the possibilities are endless.

I do believe that the explanation has to come from quantum mechanics or beyond. The "old one" has revealed all his secrets in regard to Newtonian classical physics. In regard to quantum mechanics, Niels Bohr felt that the "old one" did not intend for us to know all his secrets. Einstein argued that the "old one" had revealed the secrets, and they are for us to find. So far, we have not uncovered any further secrets since Bohr's or Einstein's time. Yet, I would not bet against Einstein. Even his greatest blunder (by his own admission) turned out to be no blunder at all. It does "scare" me to think, though, that we will find a hidden variable and quantum mechanics will be as deterministic as classical physics. I still have great hope that the "old one" is what we all would like him to be regardless of his secrets.

Here goes:

"I" can be broken into four parts.
Three are higher functioning parts
- the brain
- the conscious
- the unconscious

One is a lower functioning part
- the body

The brain is a well-studied organ and we do know it dies with the body. Also, to a relatively high degree, we know how it functions. I, therefore, must come to the conclusion that the brain has the same physicality as the rest of the body and is one of the lower-functioning parts of "I." However, I group the brain with the higher functioning parts because the brain is the connection or bridge between the conscious/ unconscious and the rest of the body and because it is a high-functioning entity. The brain executes the conscious' s and the unconscious's wants and needs.

The conscious is the "I am aware" in the I. As noted above, the brain carries out all of its desires. Is consciousness a physical, energetic or spiritually related entity? Are we born with it? Does it evolve? Does it grow in ability and scope with time? Can it be influenced? If so, by what? When we die, does our consciousness die, too, with our bodies? If not, where does it go?

Everything we have repeated enough times and are familiar with is sent and stored in the unconscious. An example of this is walking, driving, eating, etc. When the unconscious does not function as planned, who observes and realizes this, our consciousness or our brain? Who monitors the unconscious, the brain, the conscious or all these?

Reading the above today, it is clear that my inquiry was very shallow and naive. Clearly, I knew nothing, but this did not stop me. Nothing could. I ordered more books and kept at it. And meantime, I kept writing to Ofir. I think it was my way of saying, "Please wait; I am coming to find you."

November 16, 2008

Ofir:

I think of you every day. I sincerely believe I have incorporated a large part of you and of what you represented and stood for deep within me. It is so much better being me now. I cannot begin to imagine how beautiful and rewarding it must have been for you living with the gifts and GREAT spirit that you had. Just the little bit of you that I have managed to find and make my own has enriched my very being.

Little by little I am getting to feel you and get a real sense of YOUR essence. You are truly special and a shining light. I only hope I can carry this energy that you have so graciously bestowed upon me for the rest of my life. Will never understand how I am still here and you are not, NEVER. Love and MISS YOU all day to the point of mental numbness.

Love,
Dad

December 18, 2008

Ofir:

Today is Our birthday. I write Our because I do not celebrate mine any more. I have adopted yours. I have been thinking about you all day today; there is nothing special in that. I just spoiled myself a little in allowing myself to think of what could have been, but of course I KNOW what would have been. You always excelled in achieving your goals and dreams.

What a waste of talent and a good human being. I will never understand why. Maybe there is no why, there just IS. Still looking for you and will never give up. Miss you every second of every day.

Love you always,
Dad.

Then, after further reading on the subject of consciousness I came to a stunning realization: the vast majority of scientists believe that consciousness is but an epiphenomenon of the brain. In other words, they believe that consciousness is a purely physical phenomenon, i.e., that all mental events are caused by physical events in the brain and that consciousness has no power to affect those processes. Most physicists believe this quite dogmatically!

Tied in as I was to physics and the philosophy of materialism, it never crossed my mind that that could be so. To me, consciousness was not born out of the physical; I was absolutely certain it was the exact opposite. Looking back, why I was so certain is a matter of great curiosity. Up to that point I had been a devout materialist, so why did I not willingly resign myself to materialism in the same dogmatic way that these respected physicists had?

After less than a year of intense research, I reached the shocking conclusion that science and some of the most brilliant people in the world really did not have much more to say on the subject of consciousness, particularly regarding its source. There were hundreds of hypotheses, volumes of details and a myriad of studies on the subject of consciousness; but when it came to addressing the question of source, it all added up to little more than what I had written months earlier. In fact, what science terms the "hard" problem of consciousness (i.e., how something immaterial—consciousness—emerges from something material—the brain) is no closer to being resolved today than it was at any other time in human history.

And so, I remained steadfast in my belief that consciousness held the key to a door, which, when opened, would reveal the Ultimate Truth and lead me to Ofir. This left me with a dilemma: if science could not tell me the source of consciousness, then who or what could? I knew this simple question would set me on a new path. I respectfully said my goodbyes to science and began to look for another direction.

Teach me how to trust
my heart,
my mind,
my intuition,
my inner knowing,
the senses
of my body,
the blessings of my spirit,
teach me to trust these
things
so that I may enter my
sacred space and love
beyond my fear And thus
walk in balance with
the passing of each
glorious sun...

−Lakota Prayer−

KNOWING – PERCEPTION

I know
You see intuition
I am experiences
You see wisdom

My heart listens
You see presence
My mind perceives
You see intelligence

I journey
You see worldly
I remember
You see esoteric

I am on the path
You see dedication
I seek home
You see longing

Do not see me
Join me
Awareness is the way
Return home with me

—M.C.

8. The Place Beyond

IN MY SEARCH FOR OFIR to this point, the focus of my inquiry had been books. Gradually I had expanded the type of books I was reading, moving on from pure physics to books about consciousness. While some of these books tested my tolerance; others seemed to strike a chord. Thus encouraged, I felt the urge to investigate more broadly. While surfing the web, I happened upon a conference that soon was going to take place in Los Angeles, the "Conscious Life Expo." Something about it felt right. These days, I was basing more and more of my decisions on feelings, not rational thinking, though even that was a bit rational. For this journey to have had any chance of success, I knew it was crucial to engage the tools of the non-physical realm, such as intuition, creativity, and wisdom. When one is exploring a foreign land, it is always best to speak the language of the local culture. So, I rationally decided to pay attention to the non-rational.

Reviewing the online brochure, I became even more excited by the subject matter and the variety of presenters. In fact, the authors of some of the books I had already read were scheduled to speak. This seemed to be exactly what I was looking for! I eagerly went to the registration form, but then hesitated. Would I have to interact with people? Reading books and researching were solitary endeavors; they were also very forgiving, allowing me to be what I had become, a sad and angry, malfunctioning being. People, on the other hand, were generally not so tolerant.

Whatever uncertainties I might have had, the need to find Ofir trumped everything; I filled out the registration form. In fact, I was feeling so stoked that I signed up for all the pre- and post-conference workshops and everything in between. A few weeks later, I was on my way to L.A.

The conference was truly virgin territory for me. I had never before attended a conference of any kind, so I had no idea how it was done. There were so many different talks and presenters and I wanted to hear them all, every last one of them. With crushing disappointment, however, I soon realized that would be impossible. The lecture times often conflicted, so I had to prioritize. I studied the program carefully and planned a grueling schedule. On each of the five days, I began at 8:00 a.m. and kept going straight until 10:00 p.m. or later. I had to draw up that schedule on a five-page spreadsheet in multiple colors and multiple columns just to make sense of it all. Otherwise, I could never have kept track of times, rooms, and presenters. I even had to tape extra paper at the bottom of each sheet because of the number of lectures I planned to attend each day. I don't even remember if I had allotted any time for meals. Food? Not necessary, irrelevant. I only wanted to listen to the experts; maybe they would lead me to Ofir! I was as excited as a "dad-to-be," and maybe that was exactly what I thought I was. Maybe I thought I would actually find a way to get my son back. By the end of the final day of the conference, I was—to put it mildly—exhausted.

There had been no major breakthroughs in my search for Ofir, but I wasn't discouraged. I had many new leads about information, people, and events to research further. Even more than that, something had occurred that I couldn't quite put my finger on. Only much, much later would I realize that, without being fully aware of what I was doing, I had designed a very intense, all-consuming experience with no escape route. This meant that, for the first time since Ofir's leaving, I was experiencing a prolonged period during which my emotions were not screaming at me. But even beyond that, I was all but forced to stay in the "soup" of the conference for five full days. Perhaps this was just long enough for this rough oyster to begin turning all the grit of its life into its first coarse

pearl. Something about being in that saturated environment—a crucible, really—and listening intently from morning till night to people
speaking in a vocabulary that was completely unfamiliar to me seemed
to have catalyzed a kind of alchemical alteration of my consciousness.
Though I didn't necessarily understand it, I could feel it.

I had expected to head home right after the conference, but I didn't. On
the day before the conference ended, a woman sitting beside me at one of
the talks insisted on communicating with me. We chatted a bit; and then,
for no apparent reason, she asked me if I was going to hang out at the beach
for a while after the conference. The question struck me as odd, as it was
definitely out of context to the conversation. I thought it even odder that,
although she was attractive, I had no desire to prolong the connection.

I thought no more about the woman's question until after the last talk
on the last day of the conference I found myself driving not toward home
but toward Venice Beach. Venice beach is different from most beaches in
Southern California in that, before you reach the beach itself, there is a
grassy area lined with palm trees and before that an impressive boardwalk.
On the city side, the boardwalk is lined with stores, restaurants, food
vendors and some residential condos, while the ocean side is lined with
hundreds of vendors selling out of their designated stalls. This boardwalk
area covers quite a distance, well over a mile. Towards the south end, one
encounters various sports facilities, paddle tennis courts, basketball courts,
an outdoor gym boasting some famous past members such as Arnold
Schwarzenegger and, farther towards the beach, a skateboard park. One
cannot help noticing that the level of sports played at Venice beach sometimes rises to a very high standard. In past visits with the family, I have
witnessed amazing basketball games with players from the professional
ranks joining in. This was a weekday, so the beach was not as packed and
crazy as it is every weekend; but there were street performers of all types
and flavors on the boardwalk and many different kinds of people (some
of them *really different*) wandering around.

I just started walking along the boardwalk, heading nowhere in particular. The conference had put me into a deeper state than any I had ever experienced before, and the atmosphere on the boardwalk seemed only to enhance it. My senses were highly stimulated and my awareness, extremely sharp, so all the sights and sounds around me seemed crisper and brighter. I took it all in and soon found myself remembering how Ofir had always loved to come to Venice beach. He was a magician and juggler, so it was right up his alley. He was good at both those crafts, almost right from the start. When he was only twelve, he got to work as a sidekick to a magician, performing magic tricks alongside him at kids' parties and juggling up to five pins.

I walked the boardwalk lost in quiet contemplation for a long time and then decided to rest under a palm tree. As I rested, I looked around and saw I was surrounded by a sea of people of all ages also lounging under the palms. From the evidence of sleeping bags and mats lying about, not to mention the general state of personal hygiene, it was clear that they were homeless. Some were also clearly intoxicated, while others seemed high on something or another. After absorbing all that, I became a little nervous. Yet, I did not move.

After a while, I did feel ready to leave and stood up. At that moment, one of the throng spied me and called out a question, "Are you homeless, too?" I could have ignored the inquirer but instead answered no. Emboldened, he then proceeded to ask me for some cash to buy food. In an attempt to assure me that the money was indeed for food, he suggested I accompany him to make his purchase. I handed him some cash and told him that would not be necessary; it would be his choice how he spent the money. I walked off, but his question haunted me. I wondered vaguely if I had given him the wrong answer. Perhaps I should have answered, "Are we not all homeless?" That would have been a more honest reflection of my feelings.

I resumed my stroll along the boardwalk when, out of the corner of my eye, at the very edge of my peripheral vision, I saw a painting displayed in one of the stalls. For some odd reason, I stopped short and swiveled my head around to get a better look. This was very strange, as I had never been interested in art. Nevertheless, I was transfixed by this painting. Only when my brain was finally able to catch up, was I able to understand exactly what it was that I was staring at. It was a painting of an Inca warrior. He was large, strong, and powerful. But above all, he stood in a very intimidating pose, holding a knife in his hand, looking very threatening. Slowly my eyes lowered to some text beneath his feet. "As if through a glass and darkly the age-old strife I see. For I have fought in many guises, many names, but always me." General Patton, I remembered vaguely.

Suddenly, a feeling of nausea engulfed me, followed immediately by a flood of emotion, a powerful sensation, a kind of knowing and longing all at once. Standing motionless, overcome by these feelings, the oddest thought suddenly occurred to me. Looking at that painting, I felt like I was looking both into a mirror and through a window to the past, simultaneously.

I knew that I wanted to purchase that painting. No, I *needed* to purchase it. It was mine. It was as if I had just stumbled upon a long-ago-stolen family portrait. However, I was so overwhelmed with emotion that I was unable to engage the vendor. I did not know what to do, so I just stood there. Then, after a few minutes, I found myself walking down the boardwalk again, empty-handed.

I walked along, agonizing for maybe ten minutes before deciding that I had to go back and get that painting. If I did not, it would be as if I had left part of me at the beach. Was my decision-making being affected by the fact that I was very fatigued from the conference or that I had been walking the boardwalk all afternoon in the heat? It did not matter. I turned around and headed toward the painting.

On the boardwalk, bargaining is not only acceptable; it is expected. Yet, I paid the vendor his asking price, lest anything go wrong with the transaction. When he handed me the painting, I hurriedly walked off into the crowd, almost running, as if afraid the vendor might chase me

As if through a glass
and darkly the age-
old strife I see.

For I've fought in
many guises, many names.
But always me.

PAINTING PURCHASED AT VENICE BEACH, CA.

down and demand the painting back. It was crazy, I know, but that was how strongly I felt about owning it. To say I was confused would be an understatement; in fact, the whole thing actually scared me. Despite not knowing the first thing about art, I am able to say with a high degree of confidence that the painting was of a very poor quality. But to me, it was a Picasso.

By then, it was getting late. Time to return home. Walking to my car, I began reflecting. What I was feeling is difficult to describe; things were definitely stirring; and then I was riveted to the ground by an insight. I had always been highly intuitive, although I would not have thought to call it that. All my life before Ofir's passing, I had always just known what to do, even when there was no reason I should. But now, thanks to this conference, a different thought entered my consciousness. Perhaps I was being *guided*. Perhaps I'd been guided to attend the conference . . . and to buy the painting.

The more I thought about it, the more this guidance thing seemed undeniable. In fact, looking back at the day, I saw the genius of it. Whoever or whatever was guiding me wanted me to see that painting and also knew that I would need to be lured in by something I could understand and identify with. The quote by General Patton, also a strong male warrior figure, fit the bill perfectly!

So, I had a guide and a smart one at that.

If I could accept the concept of a guide, then it was not too big a step for me to embrace the idea of Spirit. Religion had always been problematical for me, but spirituality was different. The "measurement problem" in physics had opened the door to the metaphysical. The idea of God as a white-bearded man in the sky, that was just a human projection; but to my own amazement, I was beginning to consider that possibility of an unseen force, an Intelligence greater than our own. I could see that I needed a term for that. "Spirit" or even "Source" would do for now.

Not only was I investigating this new realm, but it was apparently reaching out to me as well. Contact! My search was definitely moving

along, not at the pace that I was used to; but then, again, I was not conducting business or communicating on my home turf, the physical realm.
I was being led at a pace that guidance was setting, and for once *I did not
need to be in control.* I accepted that and willingly followed along in a manner
very alien to that of my previous approach to life.

I felt I had begun to cross the Rubicon into spirituality, and the conference had served as a kind of baptism. In fact, I found myself thinking
how spiritual I was becoming and that maybe I had arrived! No sooner
had that thought entered my head than I came upon some people working out intensely at the outdoor gym. Even though I was eager to leave,
for some reason, I stood there for about fifteen minutes watching those
strangers vigorously pumping iron, accompanied by loud, deep groans
and dripping sweat.

The drive back home was uneventful; yet, by the time I arrived home,
I felt completely spent. I sensed I needed time to process everything I had
experienced; so, over the next weeks, I took time to reflect and let the
insights come. The first thing that happened was that one phrase, simple
but strong, kept echoing in my mind, "Things always happen for a reason."
I couldn't remember whether I'd heard this said at the conference or if it
had just come to me spontaneously, but it reminded me of something I
had read in a book by Carl Jung, a deeply spiritual man in his own right.
Jung had written about the concept of *synchronicity,* which says that there
are no simple coincidences, only meaningful coincidences.

Were there deeper messages and meanings in those experiences at
the beach? I sensed there had to be, but what? After puzzling over this for
quite a while, I had an insight. I was suddenly aware that I was not going
to be able to figure it out with my rational brain and that an answer would
come, but only when it was ready to reveal itself to me. I don't know how
I came to this conclusion or why I was so confident in it, but nevertheless
I was. And sure enough, days later I was at a coffee shop reading a book
when the insights presented themselves with absolute clarity. I put down
my book and recorded the following just as it all came to me.

Synchronicity 1—*The conversation I had at the conference, wherein my fellow attendee suggested I go to the beach.*
Meaning: Through a stranger, I was being sent where I needed to go to receive my next life lessons.

Synchronicity 2— *Sitting on the grass with people I normally would never choose to sit with and not feeling comfortable in their presence.*
Meaning: A lesson for me about not judging other people or their journeys.

Synchronicity 3—*The question asked of me: was I homeless, too?*
Meaning: A lesson to help me understand that we are all, in a sense, homeless and to understand that that is exactly why we need to do our work here: to earn the right to go home, wherever your belief system tells you that home is.

Synchronicity 4—*Being drawn to the painting of the Incan warrior.*
Meaning: The homesick/longing feeling I got from seeing that painting inspired me to remember that we live many lifetimes; this was a reminder to me of one of them.

Synchronicity 5—*Walking back to my car, eager to go home thinking that I had "arrived" in terms of my spiritual journey, yet stopping for fifteen minutes to watch some strangers do their workouts.*
Meaning: The metaphor of physical workout, which I can so relate to, helped me to understand that the spiritual journey requires a full lifetime of work just as physical well-being requires a lifetime of taking care of one's body. Further, this is not the work of only one lifetime, but rather many lifetimes as the painting of the Inca warrior so clearly showed me.

I concluded my writing with this:

I am grateful to my guides for all their help and I am grateful to my free will for accepting their guidance. One day I, too, will go home. One day I will meet Ofir again. One day everything that is will return to pure consciousness—GOD. We will all go home to be who we truly are—GOD.

Every day after that, it seemed, I felt my inner world expanding more. I was making all kinds of connections between things, and the web of understanding continued to grow. For example, I had joined an online support group for parents who had lost children. (I was the only father, the only man.) After reading all the emails, I had an insight. Thinking about some of Carl Jung's writings about archetypes and Rupert Sheldrake's work on morphic resonance and morphogenetic fields, I came to the conclusion that we parents who have lost children exhibit so many commonalities in our stories, feelings, behaviors, and thoughts that this must be an archetype, albeit one that had never been named. Perhaps we don't name it precisely because the experience is so horrific. The death of a child is one of humanity's most fearsome bogeymen, and we don't ever want it to feel familiar.

Whether or not the above hypothesis was valid did not matter so much. What did matter was that I was learning and growing. In truth, I had no choice. If I was to find Ofir, I had to be willing to traverse the length and breadth of the universe to reach beyond anything I had ever imagined. And it was happening; I could feel it. I was so convinced of this that I wrote about it in a letter to Ofir:

April 1, 2009

   Ofir:

Tough day, but I am making progress. Miss you so much. You would have been well on your way to getting your doctorate that you so much wanted and worked so, so hard for.

   I wish I could share with you my thoughts on all the books I am reading and get your feedback. In my search for you and the Ultimate Truth, I must confess that it is still, I believe, quantum theory that will get us there. The whole subject is very powerful and striking. My intuition

led me there and, as of now, I am more convinced than ever that I am
working and heading in the right direction.

 Consciousness is the key and I do not believe that is an epiphenomenon
of the brain/mind function. If I am right, then consciousness IS funda-
mental to everything that is: matter, energy, and all the four forces of
nature. This will then be the basis of the so elusive "theory of everything"
and will become the most fundamental feature of the unified field.

 If this is correct, then where are YOU? How does this all work?

 The good thing is, this will force science, psychology, philosophy, and
religion to work in conjunction with each other and not in opposition
or unilaterally. Hopefully then, we can put all this organized religion
nonsense to "bed." Thinking of you all the time. You will always be with
me; and, who knows, maybe one day we will meet again somewhere in the
unified field or something like that. Your light and legacy still shines bright.

 Love,
 Dad

I had hoped the sense of progress I conveyed to Ofir would help me
judge myself less, but it did not. When not actively searching for Ofir, I
would plummet right back into that immutable bubble of pain, sadness,
emptiness, isolation, and deep anger. Even as I was making what I thought
might be progress in my search, the experience of grief completely dominated.
The Beast, that dark, ugly monster, still had hold of me. And sometimes,
despite all I was learning, I still wanted to give up. A part of me longed to
dissolve into that deep, dark abyss that was always there waiting patiently
to swallow me up.

I told Ofir. He was the only one I could tell.

April 12, 2009

 Ofir, hi,

I am so sad and empty lately. I think of you so much and all the
destruction and devastation your leaving us has caused our family. There

*are days I deal very well with it, but there are days, like now, when it
becomes mind numbing and paralyzing. I hurt so much for Mom. I am
exhausted. No down time, no escape.*

*I joined an online support group. It is so helpful. I get to see from
the outside what "good" and "bad" grief looks like. Some of the moms are
so stuck in their grief. It is so sad and ugly. I am not judging them. God
knows I am one tear away myself.*

*There are others who are trying to move forward and those are the
ones I choose to communicate with. I have established a very close contact
with someone online whose son Russel died in a work accident. We talk
almost every day. Do you "know" Russel?*

*I wish I KNEW how all this works. Believing just does not do it
for me. I am caught in this paradoxical trap, a tangled hierarchy. My
brain wants to know you are okay, yet I am thinking the brain is what
prevents us from seeing reality and viewing the Ultimate Truth. Who
knows! This brain/mind thing is like drugs. We use it to feel good and
guide us, but what it reveals is all a fantasy and a lie. If there is something else, it must be beyond the mind/brain. I still feel your essence in
me, I do.*

*One of these days when I have the energy I am going to try and
carry on your passion of helping people and kids. I have been doing it
on a one-on-one basis and have been a great help and support to some
people. It is not me doing it, it is YOU. I am going to try and hit the golf
ball now. Talk soon.*

> *Love and miss you,*
> *Dad*

And so, I struggled to keep my energy up, to stay true to the search. I
was definitely gravitating away from putting all my faith in the rational and
trying to trust in spirit more. Yet, I was still not sure what the Ultimate
Nature of Reality was. I simply had a growing sense that something existed
beyond the physical realm; but I had no proof, no hard evidence.

Then, very early on a hot June morning in 2009, something occurred that I cannot explain. Before recounting it, I must first reiterate that this did, indeed, actually happen; every word of this story is true. I am emphasizing this because I know how fantastic it may seem. In fact, if I were to hear this same story from someone else, *I* probably would not believe it.

It was approximately 5:00 a.m., and I was lying in bed, wide-awake, when a tidal wave of sadness rose up and washed over me, preventing me from falling back to sleep. I stared at the ceiling for a short while and then suddenly turned to my then girlfriend, lying next to me. "I am going somewhere, do not be afraid," I said. I remember her looking at me with a confused, questioning look; so, I repeated my statement, saying "I have to go to Ofir," and then reiterated that she should not be afraid.

That was the last thing I remember.

I have no clue how much time passed, but upon my "return," I saw her raised up on her elbows, staring at me intently with a look of horror on her face. I, on the other hand, was very calm and inquired as to what had happened. The following is her account in her own words of what she witnessed.

> *All I can recollect is that you were going through another dimension. Ofir was calling you, and you were willing to go and leave this place. Your eyes went black, pitch black. It freaked me out. And you were gone for a time, not sure how long. You kept saying you had to go, and you left for a time and then you came back. It wasn't a place for you, for the living. It was a waiting place and you were only allowed a visit.*

I don't have any recollection of what happened after I announced I was going somewhere, and I don't know why I felt I needed to go, only that it felt as if I had no choice. Up until that point nothing "crazy" like this had ever happened to me, and nothing remotely similar ever occurred again; so, all I can say with certainty is that *something* happened. It is my belief that it is not by chance that I have zero recollection of what transpired. Maybe the experience was too traumatic to be processed here on this plane, so it was erased. By whom or what, I don't know.

What strikes me most about the incident is the utter calm with which I entered that other state. I seemed comfortable, not intimidated at all, as if this were the most natural thing to do, as if I were just going on an everyday errand. Another striking feature is that I never felt that something special happened. In fact, until this writing, I had never told this story before. I had never felt the need; I just felt it was between Ofir and me. That is interesting, in its own right, because I knew it was related to Ofir. I just didn't know how, and I still don't.

I understand that this story might test people and that most will want a rational explanation, so I offer the few I have come up with. I believe that in that moment I might have been so lost and depleted, my ego defenses so worn down, that I might have become more receptive to instructions arising from another dimension. Another, to my mind, less plausible explanation might be that I was so overwhelmed by the need to find Ofir that I simply imagined all this. In other words, I had become temporarily delusional. Based on the fact that there was a witness, this explanation would seem to make no sense at all, but I offer it as a placeholder.

✦

NATURE OF REALITY

They gaze through their lenses
Seeking the smallest
Reduce, reduce, reduce
So intelligent, so naive

They sit in their houses
Calling on the One
Reward and fear their tools
So intelligent, so naive

They teach in their institutions
They hoard and trade knowledge
Rational mind forever engaged
So intelligent, so naive

Will they open their minds and hearts?
Merge mind, soul and heart
For here the journey begins
In remembering, we go home

—M.C.

9. Doldrums

On July 8, 2009, I left for Israel to participate in the Maccabi games. I was not at all excited about the golf. Moreover, since I would be in Israel, I felt obligated to meet with family, which was always stressful because they did not understand my grief. Nevertheless, I felt that sitting at home would probably be worse. So, true to my pattern, I boarded the plane with only one purpose in mind, to escape the suffocating anguish.

I landed in Israel, went straight to the hotel and slept. The next day, jet lagged, I drove to the golf course to get in some practice. While I was in the chipping area, a player from the U.S. women's team showed up to get in some practice. Even though more than a hundred players had traveled to West Palm Beach last year to compete in the qualifiers, I clearly remembered seeing her there. She was strikingly attractive and stood out in a crowd. I knew immediately that this was a perfect opportunity for me to get my numbing fix.

I began chatting with her, and it did not take long for us to agree to have dinner together. In my confused and inappropriate mind of those days, even though the golf tournament had not yet begun and even though I had not yet met with a single member of my family, the trip was already a huge success—or it would be that night. As it turned out, we did spend most nights together, but not the days because we were too busy playing golf—a distraction as far as I was concerned. (Not her, the golf!)

When not playing golf, the U.S. team members typically hung out together. I, however, did not join them, preferring to find a quiet corner to read. The woman I had met did exactly the opposite; she was warm, friendly, and socialized with the group while I made no attempt to meet anyone. It amused me to watch guys flirt with her, knowing she was "mine." That is where my head was. A woman and books, that was all I needed.

Our team did well in the tournament. We placed second, no thanks to me, for I did not play well at all. Then I finally got to spend a little time with family, but things remained strained and awkward to say the least. They just did not get me, and at times they would look at me as if I were a Martian who had just landed in their living rooms. I flew home after a week, feeling empty.

Once back home, my searching never ceased. I read everything I could get my hands on, driven to understand the Nature of Reality. I began reading a book with a curious title; it was called *My Big TOE*.

The "TOE" in the title is an acronym for Theory of Everything. For mainstream physicists, this is the Holy Grail. They quest after it, believing it is possible to discover one, simple, elegant equation that will summarize everything we know about the physical laws governing the universe—and about the Nature of Reality. Einstein himself spent the last decades of his life looking for a unified theory (his TOE), but failed. So now, I had come across a guy who claimed to have accomplished what science had not been able to do since the dawn of man, and I was all ears. I read in the hopes that maybe the author had the answers I was looking for.

The author, Tom Campbell, is, by every measure, a fascinating man with an interesting background. He is a gifted physicist, having worked (maybe still) for NASA and the military developing missile defense systems and consulting on other projects. In the early 1970s, while at NASA, he helped Bob Monroe (*Journeys Out of the Body, Far Journeys*, and *The Ultimate Journey*) set up, design and build the Monroe Laboratories for the drug-free study of consciousness. Campbell ultimately became the subject of those experiments. In so doing, he learned both how to enter into altered states of consciousness and how to have out of body experiences. In sum, Campbell is a most uniquely accomplished individual, having waded deeply into both the subjective and objective dimensions of

Mom and me near golf course at ancient ruins
of Caesarea, Israel

reality with his forays into both metaphysics and physics. He was taking me down a new and interesting path that I had never considered or run into before—and it was making sense.

What I appreciated most about Campbell was the fact that he explicitly tells the reader not to accept anyone's ideas or theories about the nature of reality blindly, not even his. He states that it is incumbent upon each and every one of us to embark upon a search for our own "TOE" and to do so through direct experience, not necessarily via education alone. Secondly, there is no dogma in his book, no bias toward any particular field or discipline. He draws from all sources, incorporating physics, metaphysics, philosophy, mysticism, and more into his theory.

One of the basic premises of his Theory of Everything is that our physical reality is a digital, virtual reality. Consciousness, he says, is fundamental to all reality. Consciousness is sentient, self-aware, able to learn—alive. The goal of consciousness is self-evolution through experience. Therefore, evolution requires interaction. To facilitate interaction, a simpler, constrained environment is needed, so consciousness created a virtual reality—our physical reality—as a constrained environment made up of rules (i.e., local physics). In short, we're essentially living in the equivalent of a simulation, a virtual reality that's a subset of a much larger reality, the reality of universal consciousness, which is beyond human comprehension. We interact by making choices; we choose "this" or "that." That's why he calls it a "digital" virtual reality. Our choices are important because they shape how consciousness evolves.

I tried to wrap my mind around everything I understood Campbell to be saying. No doubt it resonated with me because I, too, had become convinced that consciousness came first and was primary.

I was learning a great deal by exploring what these brilliant minds were saying about the nature of reality, and I was starting to develop a very deep understanding of the nature of consciousness. This was what I wanted, but the journey was taking a toll. I was pushing myself very hard, hoping to have a breakthrough in my understanding. As a consequence, my own personal consciousness was itself going through a major shift. The search was continuously pushing me to evolve, to expand and develop an inner capacity to grasp what I was reading. It was asking me to grow in ways that were completely alien to the person I had always been, and I worried that I wouldn't be able to keep up, that I wouldn't be able to change fast enough, that I'd fail. By September, I had hit another rough patch. I felt so overwhelmed by the task, so out of my depth, that I lost all momentum. I confessed to this in a letter to Ofir.

September 29, 2009

Ofir, hi,

Me again. Tough day, actually very tough week. I am numb with pain and sadness again. I can't sleep or eat right. I was doing so well and then, crash.

I am not functioning. I know I need to function on a new and different level. I was making good progress; actually, no. I am making good progress. It is such hard work. It is like being reborn and trying to make your way from scratch again. I will do it, but it is going to take time and a lot of work.

I miss you so much; and, two-and-a-half years now, the fog remains very thick. Your leaving us has changed everything, everything. We are not the same family anymore and we are not the same individually. We have all changed. We will find our way and we will move forward and we will have a life, albeit a very different life. I continue my work looking for you and have made a lot of progress. I read and study every day, and use YouTube a lot. I have been able to listen to quantum physics lectures from Stanford by some of the world's premier physicists. One of them is Leonard Susskind. (He is the one who has an ongoing disagreement with Steven Hawking on whether information or anything, for that matter, escapes black holes.)

Now, more than ever, I believe that consciousness is fundamental to everything and that consciousness is not a construct of our brains and physical world, but our physical world is a construct of consciousness. I do not believe that any of this physical world we perceive is real. The only reality is consciousness. I believe that all conscious entities, no matter how dim, are all a small, tiny piece of the Source, the only thing that truly is. It is this huge ocean of consciousness that is the Source. There is no going back further and there is nothing more fundamental. The new multi-billion-dollar collider in Europe will never reach its goal. How can it, when what they are seeking is not part of this "reality," when what is real is creating and running this physical world and all the physical laws that govern it? It is like the players within the video game figuring stuff out and thinking that what they discover is real, not knowing that there are people who created them and control them.

So where are you, then? Did you go home? Did you come back to this virtual reality or some other one to continue your work to experience and grow your individuated piece of consciousness?

I have no doubt that you were so much further ahead of us in your work that you had to move on to different and more challenging experiences.

Believing all this helps in the big picture but not in the little picture of our physical virtual reality that I currently find myself in. The pain and sadness still feels so real, and that is what I must deal with and work on.

You have set me on a journey that I never dreamed I would ever take or would have wanted to take. I am on it and am going to travel it as long as I am still a player in this "game." We are all so exhausted by the sadness and could really use some relief. We are all dealing with it in our own ways and I KNOW that we are all going to be fine. My guide tells me so. I have really come to trust him/her/it, and I have really come to like him/her/it. We miss you and think of you every single day. I know we will "meet" again, not as Ofir and Martin but in the real sense of what we truly are. May your work continue and allow you to earn the right to go home.

Dad

In that letter to Ofir I tried to put a positive spin on the family situation, but the truth was that there was not an ounce of positivity in my mind.

The months passed. I read and read and studied and tried to learn and grow. Still, I struggled with the concept of consciousness and what it meant to my search for Ofir. Ofir was the only one who could understand, so I kept writing to him. I kept telling him that I was working on it and showing him how far I had come in my thinking. If I kept doing that, then perhaps he would not slip away.

December 18, 2009

  Hi Ofir,

It is our birthday today—like you did not know!! You are twenty-five years old. I mourn your future and a part of mine, too. I hope wherever you are and whatever it is you are doing is going well. This must sound so simplistic to you.

  I still think there are three options:

  1. You no longer exist.

  2. You have returned here or to some other local reality.

  3. You are somewhere in the unified field of pure consciousness.

  I believe it to be "3." I cannot begin to understand what that must look like because I believe it is what IS and what is fundamental to all that is. How could we possibly begin to grasp what this is? People tend to give it all kinds of names: God, zero point field, unified field, heaven, and on and on. My guide is really good to me and I try to listen and pay attention. My level of awareness has increased tremendously. I keep working on it and will not stop.

  This is your gift to me.

  My gift to you was life and it is gone. This is what makes it so difficult for me. This is why I search. I search to know that the life I gave you was only a stepping stone or leg in a process that is the work that your consciousness must do.

If I ever find a level of comfort in that knowledge then I will be at peace. Since you left us, there is no peace. I am not giving up either. My work goes on and I thank you for ALL you have given me. The part of you that I have incorporated into my being is simply beautiful and very spiritual. THANK YOU.

Dad.

My path, which at this point, was all about exploring the concept of consciousness, then took an unexpected turn. My guides, whom I'd come to trust, now led me to delve into what the major spiritual disciplines had to say relative to consciousness. Even though I had completely accepted the idea of being guided, my strong feelings about organized religion surfaced and I resisted. But then I remembered my vow to go wherever the path led, and I knew I had to pursue what they told me. So, setting my issues with organized religion aside, I began to read up on all the different spiritual disciplines.

I discovered that, in fact, consciousness played a key role in most spiritual traditions and was sometimes considered to be absolutely fundamental to everything. I read that consciousness is not matter; rather, matter is consciousness and that felt right. The following short exchange sums it up. A Western philosopher once asked an Indian guru, "What is mind?" The guru replied, "No matter." He was then asked, "What is matter?" And he replied, "Never mind."

It was at this point that I noticed a significant shift in my being. I was thinking considerably less and feeling more. I was finding that I could let the rational go completely at times and simply surrender. I was also beginning to feel safer in the knowledge that I was not in control. This was a huge difference and I was embracing it. Not only did I feel safe during those periods of surrender, but I felt more peaceful inside as well. Surrender does not work unless one also practices acceptance, so I was exploring that as well.

During those periods of surrender, I began so see that I was learning and evolving, albeit slowly, very slowly. The idea that consciousness was preeminent was opening me up; I could feel it. I became dimly aware that my search was evolving in a kind of pattern that was starting to look like a very intricate nervous system: one main path, the spinal cord with many different branches, the nerves, going in all directions to serve different purposes. My mind and soul were flowing in and out of one tributary, then another, and then another.

On the outside, however, my life was pure mayhem. I lived in chaos and in an ocean of pain. What I did not yet understand was that both of these journeys—the interior and the exterior—were necessary. In fact, they were symbiotic. The pain fueled me; it caused me to keep searching. The searching, in turn, helped to keep the pain in check.

The pain was sometimes so intense that it felt like I was stranded on the surface of some alien planet, being blasted by the equivalent of gale-force sandstorms. I was clueless about it then, but now I understand that this was part of a much larger process. Layer upon layer of tough armor that had built up over the fifty-one years before Ofir's death and that constituted the old me, had to be methodically and meticulously sandblasted away. As one layer fell, so the next below would be exposed. And then it, too, would need to be sanded down until it was gone. And, so, the process continued. It seemed unending.

And, yet, strangely – or so it seemed to me then, the more my outside layers were worn away, the more I seemed to be able to absorb on the inside.

It was now early January of 2010, in the fourth year after Ofir had been gone, and I had finally finished reading, *My Big Toe: The Trilogy*.

The book was unique and provocative in its ideas and concepts. Even though it was over 1,000 pages long, I never got bored with it for a moment, never tired of the subject matter. I was also warming to his thesis that we are living in a kind of virtual reality. The idea of a digital universe is not as crazy as it sounds. In doing further research, I certainly found much controversy and many contradictions, but I also came across many prominent physicists who promote this idea, including Nobel laureate Gerard t' Hooft, Archibald Wheeler, and David Deutsch, among others. In sum, I liked what I read and it felt right, so I held it as one possibility in my search for my own TOE.

Then, of course, as the guides would have it, I came across a workshop being given by Tom Campbell. I signed up immediately. After spending all that time reading his trilogy, I was really excited to hear Tom in person.

The workshop was, indeed, fascinating, but something happened there that I valued above all else. At one point, I stood up and asked Tom a question. I do not recall the question, only that it involved Ofir. I don't remember much about his answer either, but there is one thing he said that I remember with crystal clarity. He told me that, in all probability, *Ofir and I came from the same Oversoul.* Ofir and I had originated from the same source and, therefore, we would be connected always—connected for eternity. That idea resonated in my heart; it felt right. It was another straw to hold onto, more than enough to sustain me in my search.

And yet, by the next month I was itching to run again. I decided to go to Israel to attempt another visit with my family. I felt ashamed that I needed to run away so frequently. I didn't understand this until much, much later; but those escapes were not only necessary to give me a break from the self-imposed relentlessness of my search, they were also a part of the process.

I very much enjoyed the time I spent with my mom. Visiting with her was special, because she is an exceptional human being, and I developed a new appreciation for her. The way she conducted herself was amazing to me, especially given all the losses *she* had endured. By now, besides her parents, she had survived the loss of her husband, a son and then her grandson. Yet, meeting her, one would get the impression that life had been nothing but kind. Outwardly, she was always cheerful, kind and seemingly happy, but I knew otherwise. When I looked behind the veil, I could see that all her positive behaviors were also a means of avoiding the sad and tough truths of her life. Was I the only one who could see it?

With the rest of the family, though, there was very little movement. I still felt they did not get me. The thing that made that so very clear was their propensity for denying the pain I was in. They made constant, insensitive declarations about how great it was to have grandkids; and they went on and on about how wonderful it was that the family was spending time together, blah, blah, blah. I could not listen to it, so I spent most of my time reading in coffee shops.

And writing to Ofir.

March 18, 2010

    Hi Ofir,

I am sitting at a coffee shop in Israel and just had an epiphany. I told someone this morning that I am not sure why I continue reading and studying so much. I even asked what is the point? I am now sitting reading my book and writing and suddenly it hit me what the point of my work is. I don't know how to explain this; but, in one sentence, I am trying with all my being to create a place for you to go on, not in my mind, but in a "real" place.

I was reading my book, trying to get more insight into what happens after death, if anything. I have taken a very scientific approach because I want to get as close to the truth as I can. It suddenly hit me while reading that maybe I am being somewhat biased towards the idea that there is something after death because I want to know in a soul-wrenching way that you are not just simply gone. I suddenly felt a little cheated by myself that I was not being as honest and scientific as I originally set out to be.

Well, I just sat with this thought for a while and then it hit me. In quantum mechanics it has been shown and proven that the act of observing or measuring is what collapses the wave function and that then a probability function becomes a given reality. It is the consciousness that observes or measures—this is the key point; it is the ONLY point.

Well, then, at a very deep level, that is exactly what I am doing!! I am (my consciousness is) working as hard and ferociously as I (it) can to create a reality wherein YOU do have a place and venue to go on and are not simply gone. I am consciousness. I do create reality, so I am not spending all my time doing what I do just to comfort myself or for some other esoteric reason. I AM NOT HELPLESS AND OUR RELATIONSHIP STILL EXISTS AND I CAN "BE THERE FOR YOU."

So, understanding this and utilizing the knowledge that you have granted me, I will continue with my work to not only find but CREATE a reality that is for you to continue in and exist.

This thought gives me great relief. I still feel the deep need to be there for you as I always tried to be. I don't know any other way to explain this but I WILL continue my work because my instinct (my guides) tells me I am on the right track. I will always believe my guides and will not allow my brain to fool me into believing what it perceives to be reality.

This may sound strange, but if we do go on after we die, then "I" is not my body and NOT my brain, so they cannot be real. The only thing that is real is my consciousness. My guides are pure consciousness; I have felt them all my life.

Love and miss you more than anyone can imagine. I went to a lecture a few weeks ago and for the first time I actually talked about you in public. The lecturer after listening to my question did not even answer it, he simply said that you and I share the SAME Oversoul, so we are connected in the most fundamental way possible. It was strange he would say that just based on listening to me because he did not even address my question. What does he know??

LOVE YOU and please know you are not alone or should I say I am not alone???????????

Dad

Besides the time spent with my mother, I felt the trip had been a total waste of time. I returned home in the spring and spent a listless summer. Nothing occurred of any note. The days just passed, one after the other, a colorless string. Outside, the temperature climbed and climbed. By August, one could barely go outdoors without feeling scorched, so I retreated inside like all the other desert denizens and ventured out very little. I felt very isolated, and my grief was beginning to get the best of me, yet again. Sometimes it seemed like the Beast was more real than I was. I was so used to him hanging on my neck that he had become a part of me and I of him; I could never imagine him leaving. It was much easier to imagine myself disappearing. And so it went.

Then, about midway through the month, I realized that I was again in serious trouble. Once again, my journey had come to a standstill. Lost, I poured my soul out to Ofir.

August 11, 2010

> *Ofir, hi,*
>
> *I have been really struggling the past few months. I am not reading much, not feeling my guides at all and basically just existing.*
>
> *I am trying very hard to continue my search for you and the Ultimate Truth. Even though I do understand that finding you is not so much an academic or information-gathering function, I cannot help but continue with the pursuit of information and knowledge-gathering. I do understand that the brain and the physical are NOT the answer, but here is where I exist and this presently is my reality: the four-dimensional, physical, space-time.*
>
> *In the past, my guides have told me that pursuit the Ultimate Truth can only be done through subjective experiencing. Unfortunately, our reality—or perceived reality, I should say—is what we know, what our brains interpret for us. I am very "hooked" on this perception of reality and objective data and that is why I am frustrated and disillusioned. This*

whole situation just compounds itself and is a vicious circle like when we feel bad because we are fat; so, we eat to feel better, get fatter, eat to feel better, and so it goes. I get frustrated, try harder to gain knowledge, get even more frustrated and so on.

The answer has to be the exact opposite—to just LET GO, not to analyze, not to even think, just allow the truth to be felt and experienced. The Truth cannot be found; The Truth cannot be learnt; The Truth is fundamental and The Truth just IS. The subset cannot identify the set; it can only be the other way around. In simplistic terms, an atom does not "know" what its higher self is, but a molecule certainly "knows" what atoms it is made from.

The best I can come up with, with my brain, is that consciousness is the only "thing" that can identify itself and all that Is, because consciousness is fundamental and at the same time the highest self of all that Is. I do feel and sense this. I just want to experience it.

This is so confusing because when I say "I," what do I mean? My brain and physical being or my consciousness? I must mean my brain because, if consciousness is the highest self, it already knows. If I mean the brain, then it can never know the Ultimate Truth.

I must conclude, then, that what I am trying to achieve is not possible, the subset cannot identify the set. All I am then left with is the belief that my consciousness knows and is the Ultimate Truth.

Maybe that is why we perceive life to be so tough: our brains are trying to accomplish and interpret things that, in effect, are not real. What are we supposed to do then? I guess the answer is we are here in this reality and must "play the game" by its rules. Only after we leave this reality, as you have done, then possibly some form of ourselves gets to experience and feel the truth. It is just so hard in this reality—in this subset, trying to understand without knowing the set. I am not sure what the purpose of all this is, then. We must just live it out and believe that is the best we can do.

*LOVE AND MISS YOU EVERY SINGLE DAY. IT DOES
NOT GET ANY EASIER. ALWAYS THINKING OF YOU,*

Dad

I was asking the same questions that had been asked, researched, and
meditated upon by many throughout human history including the wisest
and most brilliant. These were the questions people ask themselves in the
quiet of night, in those moments of inner stillness. Yet, in my life Before
Ofir, I had *never* considered these questions. Why would I? The material
world was so much easier to master. Why venture out of the bubble?

I had stretched so much; I had gone so very far in my search. Yet, I
was still very much the man I had always been, and I could feel those
forces calling me back.

Look deep into nature, and then you will understand everything better.

—Albert Einstein

10. Into the Light

ANIEL WAS NOW ATTENDING COLLEGE in San Francisco and Tal was working. Rachel and I would talk from time to time, but her anger and resentment towards me would never allow any kind of forward movement between us. Every time I attempted to share with her, my words hung empty in the air. Our conversations never reached a point where I felt able to share with her what I was doing. Even though she had acquiesced to my leaving, she was still so angry with me that I had become like the devil in her eyes. Who wants to hear what the devil has to say? How could anyone blame her? I certainly did not.

The deeper truth is that I never told her that I was searching for Ofir because I was afraid I might fail and let her down again. The only thing Rachel knew was that I was reading ferociously. In fact, absolutely no one knew what I was doing. I never discussed my inquiry with a single soul. Most people probably figured I was just going through one mega-huge, red Ferrari-convertible kind of midlife crisis.

As that summer wore on, my somber mood didn't lift, but it began to fade into the background as I resolved to soldier on in my search. By now, I again felt a strong urge to go somewhere. After returning from the Tom Campbell workshop, I had felt so uplifted that I had sought out more conferences to attend and had made a list of them. I decided to take a look at the list to see if there was anything interesting coming up soon.

A conference in New Mexico offered by an organization called Source for Educational Empowerment and Community Development (SEED) caught my eye because it would be held in a couple of days. But initially the title, "The Language of Spirit," put me off. I had no particular interest in language or linguistics. Then I read the small print, "A dialogue exploring the Nature of Reality from Indigenous and Western science perspectives," and got a feeling I can't adequately describe, something like a warm shiver. I immediately signed up.

I flew out to Albuquerque in mid-August for opening day. Upon entering the conference hall, I was surprised to see the chairs set up in concentric circles with a gap forming a pathway into the center. This looked odd and it certainly was impractical, taking up way more space than necessary. I wondered what the reasoning was. If not obviously running the show, the old rational me was still always lurking in the background never acknowledging guides or anything spiritual, for that matter.

The invited guest speakers were beginning to take their seats in the innermost circle. Some represented Western culture, others indigenous ways of knowing, and some were conversant in both. Many were professionals in various fields and disciplines, scientists or linguists or philosophers; a few were even world-renowned in their respective fields. The Indigenous people were elders for the most part, who came from different indigenous nations in North America and other continents. It was a very impressive group of people, to say the least.

These dialogues had a history, I subsequently learned, going back more than a decade. The first dialogue of this type had been convened in 1999 for the purpose of its attendees exploring together a very intriguing phenomenon: the worldview or perhaps more accurately the cosmo-vision being revealed by quantum physics. While that cosmo-vision was foreign to most Westerners, it actually had much in common with traditional indigenous understandings of the nature of the universe. The book *Blackfoot Physics* by the physicist David Peat, a past attendee of these conferences, elucidates the purpose of the conferences very well. The idea was to convene representatives of both cultures to delve into the differences and commonalities between Native science (Native ways of knowing) and Western science, using a very specific kind of, and format for, inquiry known simply as dialogue. To reflect this, some years later the organization changed its name to Source for Educational Empowerment and Community Dialogue.

The form of dialogue to be used here was a hybrid of two other dialogical configurations. One source was the traditional Plains Indian talking circle; the other source was known as "Bohmian dialogue," named after the late physicist/metaphysicist, David Bohm, who developed it. Together with Leroy Little Bear, Native elder and facilitator for this SEED dialogue, Bohm had helped organize the first-ever dialogue of this type, bringing scientists together with Native elders.

This did not surprise me. In my research into quantum physics and the Nature of Reality, I had read enough about David Bohm to know that, if I were ever obligated to choose a guru, he would be my first choice. The obvious reason was his genius. Einstein had seen Bohm as his intellectual son and the Dalai Lama had considered him one of his scientific gurus. But there were other, deeper reasons. He seemed to be both compassionate and humble, rare virtues, especially in his line of work. He was not dogmatic in his views and seemed to be open to a wide variety of ideas including those that transcended physics.

Bohm's theory of the implicate/explicate order says it all. He saw that, beyond physical reality there was another order, an invisible order, complex and intricate, that moved in accordance with its own transcendent laws. This struck a chord with me; it seemed to speak directly to the Ultimate Nature of Reality that I, too, was seeking. Many of his writings allowed me, over time, to embrace the idea that the physical and the non-physical are both part of experience. Thankfully, I had arrived at the conference also having some basic understanding of the spirit realm, though I knew I had barely a clue as to what it was. I simply knew it existed because of my own experience. I had "come to know," as the indigenous people like to say.

In Bohm's journey, I saw a parallel to my own. He began life firmly embedded in the rational mindset of science, but then his awareness expanded to encompass the spiritual or at minimum the metaphysical. I, too, had once believed that the material/physical world was all that mattered, but ever so slowly it seemed, I was being cracked open wider and wider. I was expanding from the inside out; perhaps so that I, too, could see more, could develop a more all-encompassing view. And sometimes, as I read and searched and thought, I felt Bohm's presence, almost as if he were walking beside me on my quest. I once wrote a letter to a colleague of his, airing my thoughts about Bohm. The reply I received confirmed everything I had come to believe about him. She wrote, "First I would say that, apart from the content of your conclusions, Bohm would certainly support your approach—to read carefully, both 'objectively' and 'inwardly,' and then come to your own working sense of what it all means. That seems to me very close to the spirit of truth."

As the time for the dialogue approached, the paying guests, myself included, took seats in the concentric circles surrounding the inner circle. Then, opening prayers were offered. These were followed by traditional Native chants. One of the chants was to be performed by a Diné (Navajo) called "Woman Stands Shining" (Pat McCabe). When she was called upon, I remember thinking what an incredibly beautiful name she had been given. I had never been among Native American people before, and I could not have found a better representative of indigenous culture than Woman Stands Shining. She truly stood shining, and I sensed something special about her. In conjunction with the SEED dialogue, she would be my introduction to a world and a way of being I had never before encountered— bringing me to yet another milestone in the journey.

Something then occurred that I did not understand. Before she began her chanting, Woman Stands Shining asked us to close our eyes. She gave us a few seconds to adjust before continuing. She then asked us to "imagine seeing buffalo passing through the room" and proceeded to begin to talk us through the experience. I remember just sitting there, dumbfounded, thinking *Is this woman nuts?* My initial inner response was ridicule, *No problem, you go ahead and play with the buffalo. I am going to Starbucks to get a coffee . . . and, oh, by the way, when you are done playing, come get me.* Such was my primitive mindset, a product of my limited awareness and level of understanding.

When we Westerners direct the word "primitive" towards another people, surely we are speaking of ourselves. In all honesty, what saved me that day, as on many other days of my journey, was my suddenly remembering the commitment I had made at the very beginning of this journey. I had made a contract with the Universe, promising that absolutely nothing would be out of bounds, that I would discount no possibility, and that I would listen openly to everything that was presented to me, no matter my initial reaction. According to that contract, everything would get a chance to be heard—even imaginary buffalo. It took a lot of discipline for a Neanderthal like me to accept all these new (to me) concepts, but I slowly began to compose myself. I told myself to let go and release all my judgments and preconceived beliefs and just give it a chance—a real chance. I closed my eyes, felt my ego dissolve away and sat there, empty and vulnerable.

That simple action was to change my life forever.

In a few moments, I found myself in this place of ... I have no language for it. What I am able to say is that, no, I did not experience the buffalo passing through the room. But what I did experience was *Woman Stands Shining seeing the buffalo passing through the room.* I don't even want to begin to try and explain that one. Suffice it to say, it happened; it was a real, vivid, and genuine experience. It was as if she had safely led me to the edge of her experience, knowing that I was not capable of my own ... yet.

Woman Stands Shining will always hold a special place in my heart for leading me in this most gentle and compassionate way into that space of "no language," to Neti Neti—neither this nor that—as the Hindu Upanishads say, meaning one can only say what it is not, never what it is.

We returned from our visioning experience and awaited the beginning of the dialogue.

The Bohm form of dialogue has a certain protocol. When the moderator feels the time to be appropriate, he or she opens the dialogue by

Woman Stands Shining speaking in a Dialogue Circle

asking a kick-start question, typically in the form of a koan, a sort of riddle or puzzle like that used by Zen Buddhists. This question sets the direction of exploration for the dialogue. The next step is for the facilitator to ask everyone in the room to empty themselves, to let go of their most cherished and firmly held beliefs, assumptions, and cultural biases. These are the things that make up our *tacit infrastructure*, that is, our mental model of the world and how it works. It is tacit because we are rarely, if ever, consciously aware of it; it is an infrastructure because it is the mental foundation from which we operate and function. Like a physical infrastructure, it supports our everyday navigation of the world. It is also like physical infrastructure in that it can become inadequate; it can get rusty and old and become outmoded. But because it is tacit, we don't see how our mental model routinely filters out information that doesn't fit our pre-conceived notions. Legend says that the natives of Tierra del Fuego could not see Magellan's ships anchored in the harbor because their mental models of the universe did not include enormous galleons. Modern humans think we are too sophisticated or intelligent to have such blind spots, but how likely is that, really?

In a sense, when we are asked to release our tacit infrastructure, we are also being asked to give up our identity, which we are usually reluctant to do. We tend to be very attached to our identities, believing them crucial to our being and survival. After all, who are we without all those mental concepts?

During the dialogue, the idea is to empty one's mind totally so that thought might flow freely through a cleared mind. Behind that, there is another, even more profound understanding: the deepest form of thought arises not from humans, but from Source, from Origin—from Spirit, if that word is not too scary. To allow these thoughts to come through us, we must get out of the way. We must become conduits for this sacred information, allowing thought and meaning to arise from Origin and to manifest in the physical world through us.

For this to occur, the dialogue space must become a safe container. This was stressed over and over; the dialogue space needed to be a space where people could be vulnerable, free to express whatever came to them without fear of judgment, shame, or embarrassment—without all those negative consequences we are taught will result if we ever deviate from our learned roles and express our authentic selves.

Even though those of us seated in the outer circles were to be observing and not speaking, we were also asked to do the same: empty our minds. And so now, with my eyes closed, I tried again to release all my thoughts and judgments, just as I had with the buffalo. This time, though, I was much more conscious of what the task was. I was being asked to suspend the tacit infrastructure that had taken me decades to construct and firmly cement, to release all the biases, judgments, and beliefs that made me, me. This felt like an impossible task because I was not aware of what my tacit infrastructure was. I had never even considered that I had a tacit infrastructure, let alone understood what it looked like. I was me, end of story. No, I was not going to accomplish this in just a few moments, so I simply told myself not to think. I asked my ego-mind to take a time out and let me *just be.*

We sat in silence for some time as everyone did his or her inner work. Then, the dialogue began. When someone in the inner circle indicated that he or she was ready to address the question, the person was handed the talking stick. This, too, has great relevance; the talking stick represents the connection to the non-physical world, the place where everything originates. When holding the talking stick, the speaker with an empty mind transforms into a conduit through which information can flow from Source into the material plane.

So, there I was, witnessing yet another example of the material and spiritual realms being interconnected with and accessible to each other. I stopped to reflect on this. I had been introduced to this possibility in my exploration of quantum physics, particularly through Bohm's notion of explicate and implicate orders, which says that there is a deeper, more fundamental reality underlying the one we commonly perceive. Bohm's concept reinforced the idea that the material and non-material realms were not separate, but profoundly intertwined. This possibility had first suggested itself to me as I was traveling the path of the intellect, but now it had been reinforced by personal experiences with my journey to the "other side" and my sense of being guided. So, the evidence was building. Now I knew, for certain, that the spiritual realm existed. It was no longer just a belief, a hope or projection; at last, I had an inner knowing. I hoped desperately that I could hold onto that conviction, that my strong rational streak would not override it again.

The goal of this form of dialogue is not to reach any conclusion or agreement through rational means but rather to simply allow thoughts to flow freely so as to ultimately reveal a much deeper level of meaning. All this was more than foreign to me; but as the dialogue proceeded, I began to get a better understanding of the process and more and more began to fall into place. The chairs being arranged in concentric circles replicated the Talking Circles of the Plains Indians, and the opening path through all the circles faced the East, the direction of the rising sun. The opening in the circles was symbolic, but it also represented a sincere intention; it was an invitation for Spirit to enter. These symbolic gestures helped humans connect with the spiritual realm.

If one experiences life like an indigenous person or like an open-minded Westerner such as David Bohm, then one knows at a very deep level that we truly are all connected. Not only are we all connected to each other, but we are also connected to the Source of all that is—name it as you like. When we acknowledge this connection, thoughts can arise from Source and flow through us, in this case at the conference with each speaker serving only as the conduit for that flow from Spirit into the physical/material world.

When Spirit is truly present, you can feel it. Information, thought, and meaning flow freely in the flux of universal energy to which we are ALL connected. Because of this connection, this Implicate Order, thoughts are in free flow and they can take many paths. One of those paths appeared to be from a person in the outer circle to a speaker in the inner circle. It was not unusual to think something only to find that very same thought being expressed aloud by someone in the inner circle. When that occurred— and it did for me, more than once—it was beyond magical.

This happened when Woman Stands Shining spoke about a time when her daughter was in the hospital. She had brought with her a buffalo robe, which she put over her daughter. She touched her daughter tenderly and sang to her all through the night. As I listened to her speak, I began to understand something very profound. When my son was lying in a hospital bed, I had put all my faith in doctors and machines. The machines were everywhere with what seemed like miles of wiring, dozens of blinking lights, and a continuous, rhythmic beeping. And as my son lay there, all I could think was that I wanted even more machines; I wanted even more doctors. That is what my culture had taught me.

With that awareness, I was so envious of Pat/Woman Stands Shining and also so sad because I realized that I had had no clue about how to really engage the situation. You see, Western science does not teach us what we really need to know, the real science, the science of living and dying. So, in the end, the machines did nothing, I did nothing, and he left us. He left behind a cold empty space and me struggling to comprehend what had happened. Worst of all, everyone and everything I had been taught to rely on and submit to had failed me, including me. I had failed myself and worst of all, I had failed my son. I felt betrayed and violated. If only I had known the true science, the authentic science, the Science of Life.

The dialogue went on for three days, and so much was happening inside me that I had great difficulty sleeping between sessions. It was on one of these evenings that I wrote my first essay ever as an adult. It was called "Authentic Listening." I wrote it because, by then, I had concluded that the SEED dialogue was not about talking; it was about Listening. I purposely capitalize the word to pay respects to a process that I have come to see as sacred. As I wrote, I remembered these lines in a poem by Rumi:

"Out beyond ideas of wrongdoing and rightdoing, there is a field.
I'll meet you there."
The poem continues:
"When the soul lies down in that grass, the world is too full to talk about.
Ideas, language, even the phrase 'each other' doesn't make any sense."

I recalled how I'd puzzled over those lines when I first read them. Now, to my amazement, I realized that I understood them or, more accurately, I *felt* them, I knew them. When one engages in Authentic Listening, the speaker and listener slowly fuse into one, meeting up in that field Rumi spoke about, that place of deep knowing, memory, knowledge, and everything else. I thought about how it is difficult to engage in Authentic Listening in our day-to-day world. With all the distractions and intense behaviors we humans choose to engage in, we very rarely really engage with people. How often do we feel safe enough to do so? It is hard to let go totally and be in a fully vulnerable state of being. We actually fear it, as if letting go might cause us to become irreversibly poisoned by some invisible deadly radiation or, worse yet, lose our hard-earned identity, even if it is just for a moment.

On the final day of the dialogue, during one of the breaks, I happened upon the founder and chairman of the board of SEED and we immediately entered into a dialogue of our own. He delved into the history of SEED, while I shared with him some of my journey of the past few years. At some point I mentioned that I was beyond angry at the Universe for taking Ofir from us. His response stunned me. He began by sharing something that one of his mentors and dear friends, who had recently passed on to the spirit world, had said. Grandfather Leon Secataro, a Navajo elder and leader, enjoined us "to always be thankful to the ancestors and for everything that has happened to bring us to this moment in time." By this reasoning, he said, my anger was not merely inappropriate, it was plain wrong. I did not know whether to laugh or punch him. Was he actually asking me to reconsider my feelings or, worse, be thankful that Ofir had passed on? Confused, hurt and angry, I immediately ended the conversation and moved on. And yet, a seed had been planted (no pun intended).

I left the dialogues feeling extremely blessed to have had the opportunity for the first time in my life to spend time in the presence of indigenous people from all over the world. It was through them, led by Woman Stands Shining, that I was able to stumble my way toward Authentic Listening. The dialogue experience was, I sensed, an initiation of sorts; it had introduced me to Rumi's field, eternal and unbounded.

After the conference I decided to spend a few days in Santa Fe. I was strolling around the Plaza area when, oddly, I decided to enter an art museum. I say "oddly" because, again, art had never interested me. Once inside, however, I walked around looking at the artwork, attempting to enjoy and appreciate each piece. It was not working, but I forged on anyway. After about fifteen minutes, a small painting on the opposite wall caught my eye. I do not know how it could have, because it was too far away for me to see it in any kind of detail. Nevertheless, it was as if that painting were holding a fishing rod and with a hook firmly implanted in my lower lip, reeling me in.

The next thing I knew I was standing directly in front of the painting, which turned out not to be a painting at all but a photograph. As I studied it, I saw an elderly woman with a heavily wrinkled and worn face sitting in a chair on a patio staring out into the yonder. Behind her stood a young woman, her hand resting on the elderly woman's shoulder. In the foreground were open lands for as far as the eye could see. What struck me about the elderly woman was that she was not, in fact elderly, but had lived a very difficult life. She also had a sad, almost distraught, look in her eyes.

Beneath the photograph was written a caption. I moved closer to read it. The elderly woman was addressing the younger one, explaining (I paraphrase) that their people had once lived upon these lands, but then the white man had come and taken them. Then the lands had then been mined for many years, but when the mines stopped yielding, the lands had been abandoned.

I felt an unfathomable sorrow shoot through me. In that instant I felt a glimmer of what that woman must have felt as she looked across that expanse. I did not know what it felt like to be so deeply connected to a certain land. Like many westerners, I was rather rootless. I had been so desperate to leave my homeland that I had buried away any sense of connection. But if one is truly connected to one's land and one is then forced to leave it, it must feel like an amputation. And then, if that land is subsequently abused, it must feel like a rape. As insanely preposterous as the following may sound to us Westerners, it is most relevant to the Native way of being: extracting "valuables" from the ground is like a rape. It is a brutal and savage rape of their and, YES, our great common mother, Mother Earth.

I remained standing there almost in a trance and lost track of time. When I came to, I realized that there were tears streaming down my cheeks. The gallery was not empty, so I felt embarrassed. I made a beeline for the exit.

When I was finally out of the view of others, I stopped and began a serious inner dialogue that went something like this: Yes, the photograph was sad in its content, but why did I have the extreme emotional response? My history is not from this country, so my ancestors could not be directly responsible. Why, then, did I feel guilt? Neither am I indigenous of this land, so my relatives and ancestors were not part of this tragedy; why did I feel her pain? I was neither perpetrator nor victim, so what was going on?

The dialogue in my head continued for a while but without reaching any resolution. The next day, I flew home and resumed my life of reading and searching. Then, a few days later, while I was doing something totally unrelated, the meaning came to me with total clarity. *We truly are all connected—on a level deeper than we are able to comprehend.* The inner narrative went on, delivering fully formed thoughts, as if I were downloading wisdom from somewhere in the Cloud. *If we truly are connected at a very deep level, then it does not matter what one's role or circumstance in life is, be it victim, perpetrator, neutral bystander, or whatever. If we are all connected, then we are both victim and perpetrator. We have all inflicted injustice and we have all suffered.*

What?

In that moment, I could actually *feel* that connection; I could feel both sides equally, the pain *and* the guilt—that was why I was so completely overwhelmed. We *all* come from the same Source, we are all connected, and *all truly* is one. I could *feel* the full truth of it.

Never before had an idea been driven home to me so powerfully. I knew then, without a doubt, that this conference had been a significant turning point. It had opened me in a way I had never experienced before. If I had found Tom Campbell's Big Toe a plausible candidate for *explaining* the Nature of Reality, the dialogue took me even further to genuinely *experiencing* it. This realization took my breath away. I knew in my being that this was true, but my mind hadn't yet caught up. It took me several weeks to begin to piece everything together; but as I did, this is what came to me:

Authentic Listening is only achieved through the surrender of control. Only when we release control can the heart-mind take over from the ego-mind. This way of being was the exact opposite of how I had lived for fifty-one years, but nevertheless, I had managed it, at least for a few days. For the first time in my life, I had experienced the beauty of *true* power, which went by the name of surrender. My warrior mind was confused to say the least. To it, surrender was a dirty word, never to be contemplated; yet here I was flipping it a full 180 degrees to represent beauty, strength and, yes, power. I raised my eyes to the heavens fully expecting to see pigs flying!

Having left the SEED conference with the newly acquired ability to Listen, I began to see things differently, which was good, yet painful in many ways. The reality that appeared before me now looked nothing like anything I had understood or believed in all of my life. First off, indigenous people are not primitive. *We are.* Our culture lacks understanding of the true Nature of Reality. Second, my understanding of Nature itself was wrong or, at best, shallow. I, like most Westerners, had always believed that Nature was separate from me, different in every way. But now I saw another view; indigenous people believe that they *are* Nature, that there is no separation. And that made me think about my own experience. I had always felt a special connection with plants, even though my rational mind had dismissed it.

Beyond that, I had learned that we humans are not alone isolated in our solitary consciousness but immersed in a living Universe that is also alive and aware. The world-renowned physicist Archibald Wheeler stated it very clearly, "We live in a *participatory [italics added] universe.*" In so saying, the Western scientist was confirming what indigenous peoples have known since the dawn of existence: our lives are dances, dialogues, with Nature and beyond. Wheeler arrived at that conclusion through quantum mechanics; indigenous people know this by looking deeply into the sky or a stone or the eye of a wolf. Both ways lead to the same truth.

Coming to know our place in the universe and specifically our relationship with Nature was beginning to give me answers to questions I didn't realize I had. If I really looked at my life, I would have to acknowledge the many times I had this underlying feeling that something was not right. That feeling had been secretly gnawing at my being for much of my life. In fact, there had been moments throughout the years—secret moments—when I would burst into tears for no apparent reason. I never told a soul.

As I thought about this, I began to get in touch with something beyond my personal grieving. I came to understand that all of humanity is grieving. We are grieving for many reasons, but most of all we grieve our banishment from Nature. We are a part of Nature, but we believe we are not. And, so, we are separated from ourselves, from who and what we are at our very core. Our umbilical cord has been severed from the womb of Mother Earth. We are sad, confused, disorientated, lonely, and lost;

we wander a landscape that is foreign and frightful to us, and we do not understand why. It is because we are grieving. We are mourning the loss of our true identity. We are grieving not being able to participate with Nature and not being nurtured by Nature, our original teacher. This grief is not dissimilar to a force field. We are not able to see it, feel it or hear it, yet it is pervasive and powerful.

In that moment of realization—and only for that moment—I felt the Beast release his hold on my neck. For an instant, we looked each other in the eye. And I saw in his eye everything; I could not even distinguish between it and myself. The concept of human and Beast was meaningless; the difference, non-existent in that beautiful moment.

Those three days of practicing surrender were now proving to be the catalyst for an even more profound change; I could feel it. I felt like a caterpillar in a chrysalis. Before a caterpillar can transmute into a butterfly, something has to give; the being it was has to disintegrate—and that process has to be damn scary for the caterpillar. I knew the thing that had to give in my case was my tacit infrastructure, that whole conglomeration of beliefs and assumptions that made up my worldview and my sense of myself. In many ways, it felt like I was being asked to let a part of myself die. I had to give up my tacit infrastructure. But to let go, to relinquish it, I'd need to know what it was.

Perhaps, to figure that out, I needed to go back to the beginning.

✦

*It has always been a mystery to
me how men can feel themselves
honoured by the humiliation of their
fellow beings.*

—Mahatma Gandhi

11. The Crucible

On January 24, 1956, *Look* magazine ran a piece entitled, "The Shocking Story of Approved Killing in Mississippi." In the article, J.W. Milam and Roy Bryant tell the story of how they kidnapped, tortured and murdered Emmett Till, a fourteen-year-old African American boy from Chicago, who had been visiting his uncle. While in a grocery store owned by Bryant, Till supposedly flirted with Bryant's wife, a white woman. In a rage, Bryant and his half-brother, Milam, kidnapped Till, beat him, gouged out an eye, shot him in the head, tied him with barbed wire to a cotton gin fan that Till had been forced to carry to the site, and threw his body into the Tallahatchie River.

The case drew national media attention when Till's mother decided to hold an open-casket funeral to expose the brutality of the murder. On September 19, 1955, the trial of Bryant and Milam began in a segregated courthouse and in under an hour the all-white, all-male jury came back with an acquittal. Later, *Look* magazine paid the defendants $4,000 each to recount their story of the murder. The shear racism and injustice of the act helped spark the Civil Rights Movement.

On the same day the *Look* article was published, I was born into a similar but even more extreme culture halfway across the globe, that of South Africa.

South Africa, too, was characterized by racism, hatred, and inhumanity, but our country's power brokers had given it a sanitized name, *apartheid*, to disguise the ugly truth. I will not dignify the word with a capital "A."

The term apartheid is an Afrikaans word that means, literally, aparthood. Afrikaners, also known as Boers, are white South Africans whose ancestors were mainly Dutch colonists with a smattering of German, Belgian, and French Huguenot. The Afrikaners hated every class, color, creed and religious group other than their own. Thus, when the National Party, which was presided over almost exclusively by Afrikaners, came to power, apartheid—forced segregation—became the law of the land. The National Party governed South Africa from 1948 to 1994, almost fifty years.

To be born into the apartheid system was to be born into a world of tortured separations. For the racist regime in power in South Africa at the time of my birth, these separations were banal; they were but "the truth," only the most logical and natural way of looking at and addressing life. From there, it was only a short distance to demeaning tyranny.

The apartheid system classified and graded people by color, creed, and even religion. It used this classification to sort us into a hierarchy. The hierarchy was very clear and, sadly, it was overtly accepted as the norm. There were four distinct ethnic groups: Whites (10% of the population), Blacks (80%), Coloreds of mixed race (8%), and Indians (2%). Whites, of course, were at the very top of the pyramid, but not all whites were equal. Whites were further categorized, first by ethnicity. The Boers or Afrikaners led in the ethnicity "race," followed by the English with Jews running a distant last.

Then, each racial group was sub-divided based on socioeconomic status in keeping with the values adopted through the rise of Western culture over centuries. For example, an ethnic English or even a Jew could elevate his or her social status if they were born into or acquired, financial wealth. In other words, money tended to buy status as it does any Western society. In this regard, there was some social mobility, but among the Whites almost exclusively. Status could also be elevated through achievement. But, to be totally clear, the most socioeconomically depressed or immoral White was still many, many, many rungs above any and every Black person, no matter how wealthy, distinguished, or educated. In other words, all

Whites were deemed better and more worthy than any and every Black. In fact, if a Black person were to show any initiative in contradiction to the White philosophy or laws—or even worse, a level of intelligence or wisdom exceeding that of the White regime—they would be removed from society. They would be sent to some distant prison, Nelson Mandela being the prime example, or put to death.

This worldview was imposed on each and every citizen. It was preached and reinforced from cradle to grave in every facet of life. One's survival depended upon one's clear understanding of where one fit into that hierarchy. If one forgot, it was not long before one was reminded through either verbal or physical retribution.

The messages of the apartheid regime were so insidiously successful in that regard that the white minority, just 10% of the population, was able to control the other 90%.

Separation was not only preached it was enacted. For the most part, Whites and Blacks lived in separate worlds as was the intention of apartheid. The government segregated virtually everything from education to medical services to housing. When the National Party first came to power, it forced 3.5 million Blacks to move from their homes into segregated neighborhoods. Whites enjoyed privilege and convenience while Blacks had their own transportation, medical, educational and civil services and facilities, restaurants and townships, all of which were grossly inferior, if not subhuman, by any decent measure.

To maintain this grossly distorted societal structure, the apartheid regime ruled by fiat. They passed a spate of discriminatory laws, rules and regulations based on their own designated hierarchy of classes of people and mercilessly enforced them with extreme efficiency and dedication. For example, if a Black needed to enter a White neighborhood or commercial area, he or she was obligated to carry a pass. That pass had to be in the Black's possession at all times as proof of legitimacy. Blacks also had to abide by curfews. I remember in my town a siren would go off at night warning all Blacks that it was time to be off the so-called

TYPICAL HOMES IN BLACK TOWNSHIP

IN CONTRAST, ME (FRONT), BROTHER NORMAN AND BROTHER RAYMOND
POSING ON THE LAWN OF OUR FAMILY HOME IN TYPICAL
WHITE NEIGHBORHOOD

White streets. Police vans patrolled White areas regularly to round up any Blacks who were either found to be without passes or who had disobeyed the curfew hours. Blacks did not have the right to vote; in fact, this had been so since 1905. It was illegal for Whites to intermarry with *any* of the other ethnic groups, and the Immorality Act of 1950 made sexual relations with a person of a different race a criminal offense.

In sum, our entire culture was based on division, separation, divisiveness and alienation, resulting in dualities within dualities. And so, from the very beginning, my psyche was mired in separation and duality.

Growing up a white kid in that era and that place, I received one overarching message. Rather than learning that all humans are all equal members of a human family, I was indoctrinated in how to evaluate and grade people—including myself.

Despite the rampant conditioning, it was still possible for a few of us to see how repulsive and abhorrent this system was. Yet, even if one did not buy into it consciously, the conditioning was so strong that one could not help but be shaped by it, at least in part. At a minimum, a young adult would begin his life as a divided self and would continue throughout his life to constantly measure, evaluate, grade, categorize—and ultimately discard or repress—anything "undesirable" including aspects of himself.

I began life in a small town called Kempton Park about forty-five minutes outside of Johannesburg. Having two older brothers, I was the youngest in a family of five. We were a typical middleclass family of Jewish decent with Lithuanian roots. Because of the vitriol and hatred that many Afrikaners exhibited towards Jews, our family never, ever, associated with non-Jews. I attended a Jewish day school and all my after-school activities and friendships were strictly with fellow Jews. In fact, overt anti-Semitism was so rampant that I grew up believing that everyone who wasn't a Jew hated Jews.

I had a good family life in many respects; but perhaps because of the formality of our social structure, there was never any real warmth. There was no hugging nor were there any other expressions of love, even within family circles. It wasn't that the love did not exist, because it did; it was the expression of that love that was so lacking. Like everything else in our lives, the expression of emotion came with rules that had to be strictly followed. Adults, for example, had to be addressed as "Aunty" or "Uncle" followed by a name. Never, but never, was an adult addressed by their first name exclusively. It was also mandated that kids should be "seen and not heard." Typically, we had very little direct interaction with adults unless directly solicited. I clearly recall being intimidated and afraid of my friends' fathers; they were strong, standoffish rulers of the world. It was much easier to be in the presence of mothers, but that, too, was uncomfortable.

I did not experience a deep emotional connection with my parents, especially my dad, which may be typical for most kids of my generation. He was a good and honest man, providing well for his family, but work was his priority. He owned a pharmacy and insisted on working six days a week, plus two hours every Sunday. Mom reluctantly worked alongside him, helping out.

When I was twelve years of age, my maternal grandmother was diagnosed with leukemia. She came to stay with us so that my mom could take care of her. It was a difficult time for all of us, especially my mom, who was very close to her. When Grandmother died it was about a month before my Bar Mitzvah, and so it was decided that there would be no party or celebration of any kind. Thus, I missed out on what might have been a highlight. Otherwise, childhood within my family was mostly benign. I went to school, played sports, and hung out with friends.

Almost every White family had Black servants and ours was no exception. We had three servants who worked full-time in our home. By the standard of those times, my mom treated the help very well, with respect. This would never excuse our family for being a part of that system, but I did witness many events in which my parents made ethical choices. One event sticks out in my mind. One evening, when I was about ten years old, we heard a lot of commotion outside the dining room window. My parents ran outside to investigate with us three boys following behind.

What I witnessed can only be described as horrific. White policemen were mercilessly striking a Black man while shouting hysterically, "We are going to beat you to death, kaffir!" (In Afrikaans, "kaffir" is a derogatory and contemptuous word for a Native African.) Without any regard for her own safety, my mom jumped in between the policemen and the man they were beating up. The policemen instructed her to leave the scene; but she refused, protecting the man with her own body. After much back-and-forth the policemen stopped the assault and took the man away in their van.

Only God knows what they did to that poor man at the police station. What was the crime that demanded such a severe beating or even death? Not having a pass that permitted him to be in a White neighborhood. These kinds of events were all too common in that world of ours. The atmosphere so disturbed my parents that, right after I was born, they researched the possibility of migrating away from South Africa, but that did not occur until much later.

There was another dark component to the apartheid regime. Most of the White minority was devoutly religious in the sense that they believed that God was on their side, condoning their belief system. Their self-proclaimed moral superiority provided a justification for their actions; it was their duty to protect society from Blacks, Coloreds and Indians and from whatever they deemed to be immoral. Thus, the regime banned television programs, magazines, and all literature that portrayed any level of equality among races. In short, they forbade any outside influences that might have opened the public to alternative ways of thinking including about sexuality. Ironically, this repression reached its height in the 1960s and 1970s, exactly the time when the lid was coming off sexuality in the United States. I remember going on a school field trip to what was then Rhodesia (now Zimbabwe) when I was about fourteen years old. Instead of being excited about visiting the Victoria Falls or other beautiful and interesting places, my friends and I were more eager to see television for the first time—and most of all—a *Playboy* magazine!

This relates to another way in which I experienced separation. My only real exposure to the feminine came from my mother and, less so, from the girls at the co-ed school I attended. Our home was male-dominated with three boys and my dad calling all the shots. And, my dad's role—providing for the family—trumped everything else. Similarly, in the larger society, the men ruled while women took a back seat. At school, boys and girls had clear and distinct roles; they were treated differently in every way, ranging from sports to forms of discipline. Boys played rugby, cricket, soccer, and tennis. Girls played only netball and tennis; they never even contemplated participating in any of the boys' sports. Boys were disciplined by being "flapped" or caned, but I honestly do not remember if girls were disciplined at all! I think girls were expected to be girls and to behave perfectly, so they did.

I attended a Jewish day school so authoritarian that it fell right in line with the unforgiving government system. Stringent rules and regulations governed everything including a strict dress code. In the wintertime our uniforms consisted of a white shirt and tie, slacks, black jacket, and a red cap—no exceptions and absolutely no deviations. In the summertime we wore safari suits, which frankly looked ridiculous. One would have thought that our school was located in the middle of the bush and that we were hunters. Reality was the opposite. We kids were the hunted—in school and at home— with robocops at every turn, ready to enforce at any time. So, we were expected to be in bed and asleep by eight o'clock. And even in bed we were not exempt from uniforms; we always dressed in pajamas with matching tops and bottoms.

I went to high school in the late 1960s and early '70s, when the hippie movement was at its peak. All the boys longed to look cool and grow their hair as long as possible, but that was not allowed. At any moment, a teacher or even the headmaster himself, might barge into our classrooms, patrol the rows of desks and check each student individually for inappropriate appearance, hair in particular. God forbid if even one hair on our head was outside the designated parameters.

My best friend Benny (left) and me (right) – Age 6

In sum, we were living in a military-style system. Relentlessly and inexorably, both in school and out, we were being indoctrinated into a worldview that applied to every facet of our lives. Everything was classified. Everything was either black or white, literally and figuratively, with no grey areas. Right and wrong were absolute; there was only one right way, and it was never, ever, left to us to make that determination. Beliefs might be inculcated in ways that were often subtle, but they were reinforced in the harshest way possible. Punishment could come at any time, whether because we had been caught not following the rules or just on a whim. Being hit with a cane or some other sort of stick was the standard form this so-called justice took. I noted that our headmaster seemed to really enjoy himself while physically disciplining a young boy. He would use a cane of sorts, while our woodwork teacher preferred a folding ruler made of steel. Being a smart ass, I was definitely leading the pack in "cuts," our word for caning.

And so, as a young boy, I came to believe that life consisted of *one right way* and that making a wrong decision, no matter how trivial, would have severe consequences. I remember an example that is so vivid that I expect I will take it to my grave. One day the entire high school was seated in our assembly hall watching some kind of performance. After the performance ended, everyone clapped loudly. Some of the seniors, myself included, whistled in addition to clapping. As we returned to our classroom, sure enough, we heard the voice of "the boss" (what we called the headmaster) coming through the PA speaker hanging on the wall.

He ordered, "Those people who were whistling in the assembly hall, come immediately to my office."

My buddy looked at me and whispered, "We are not going." I signaled back, "Yes, I would." A back-and-forth exchange ensued in which he begged me not to, but I simply could not help myself. Without saying a word, I got up, left the classroom, walked over to the boss's office and knocked on the door. A voice told me to enter. I did, and I found myself alone with him.

We waited in silence; but as the minutes ticked by, it became clear to me that no one else was showing up. My anxiety level rose exponentially. The boss was a short, slender man but very intimidating, nonetheless, as he stared at me from behind his black-rimmed eyeglasses.

Not willing to show the fear that I was experiencing, I stood casually, supporting myself with my hand on the chair beside me and waited for him to speak. He stared at me like only he knew how, elevating my apprehension even more. Then, after glaring at me for what seemed like hours, he finally spoke. Some forty-five years later, I can still hear his words in my head.

"Chesler, I was not going to cane you because you are the only one that owned up, *but look at you* . . . leaning on *my* chair with your shirt partly hanging out your pants. *You are a slob.* Go stand in the middle of the room and bend over."

I received four of his best and left his office with my butt stinging like it had been sliced to pieces. I went straight to the bathroom, where I waited until the stinging subsided to the point that I could walk normally and then returned to the classroom. As was always the case, the first words I heard from my classmates were "How many, how many?" (I should mention that the PA system worked both ways. Many times, the boss would listen in unbeknownst to us and inevitably request that some "rat" be sent to his office because he "did not like what he was hearing.")

It is important for me to mention that I had voluntarily submitted because *I actually believed that I deserved to be punished.* Reflecting on this also takes me back to something that happened when I was ten years old. My parents had bought my brothers and me a pellet gun. We'd go out to our small one-car garage and shoot at cans for target practice. One day, my brother Raymond and I decided that it would be a great idea to go out on our street and practice on the streetlights. By then we were really good marksmen, so we shot out a number of lights.

The next day as we were coming home from school, we noticed a police van parked outside our house. Obviously, shooting out streetlights was not legal, and the cops wanted to know who was responsible. Raymond and I owned up, as we always did, and informed them that we were the "vicious hardened criminals" they were looking for. Again, just like in school, I found myself standing before, and having to answer to, authority, this time in the form of not one but two very intimidating male figures.

After a few long minutes of intimidation, they were kind enough to suggest that only one of us need take responsibility. Since Raymond was the elder, it was he they led out of the house and into the police van. When he was returned home later that day, he immediately dropped his pants and revealed six thick, dark blue welts. Our finest had taken a thirteen-year-old boy and whipped him mercilessly. To this day, I feel terrible that he alone paid the price for something I, too, was responsible for.

From that moment on, I always took full responsibility for my actions, which explains how I ended up in the headmaster's office. If I didn't, I knew I would live to regret it. And if I ever failed, I knew I had to be punished. It never even entered my mind that the headmaster had the option of forgiving me; that was utterly inconceivable.

Looking back at these incidents, I saw a deep paradox. On one hand, I was by nature fiercely independent, so I was often defiant. Yet, I was also compliant. I was so conditioned to follow orders and respect authority— no matter how cruel or suffocating—that the pressure to conform always seemed to trump my true nature.

This was evidence that my malleable young mind had adopted the very operating system that I had so come to resent. I had managed to resist the overt racism of the apartheid worldview, but I had indeed succumbed to the idea that life was black or white with no grey areas. I guess that is how brainwashing works. One is taught to ignore, even fear, one's own inner voice so that a foreign infrastructure can be installed. All the while, it is being insidiously sewn into one's psyche, one stitch at a time, until one's indigenous psyche is overwhelmed and one's inner voice grows ever fainter to the point of being all but extinguished.

Despite all this indoctrination, something in me resisted. It bided its time, quietly waiting for the right moment. That moment came one day during my senior year of high school. I'd been in the library, studying hard, preparing for finals, when I decided to take a break and go to the park to study in the fresh air. I was sitting on a bench when a Black man approached and sat down next to me. This was against the law; a sign on the bench made that crystal clear. But I was in no way bothered by it, and we began to engage in a friendly conversation. After a while, I went back to my studies while he also remained seated, enjoying the serenity of the park setting. Suddenly, I heard a man's voice screaming from a distance. When I looked up, the screamer was headed directly towards us. When he reached the bench, he verbally assaulted the man sitting next to me in a hateful and barbaric way. Of course, this outburst was all about a heinous crime: he was a Black man sitting on a Whites-only bench.

As the Black man got up and left, a miasma of strong feelings enveloped me like a thick fog rolling off the ocean. I felt so sad for the Black man. Only moments before, we had been engaging in some good human-to-human conversation; then, he had been spoken to as if he were less than a wild animal. I felt sad for the White man as well, sad that he was capable of behaving in such an inhumane manner. This was a sick system, and the fact that I was a part of it flooded me with shame. I knew that feeling would never leave me.

That's when I made the decision.

I completed my senior year of high school but refused my parents' offer to pay for college. Within weeks of graduation, I was on a plane, bound for Israel. At seventeen years of age, I left South Africa and put it all behind me. I thought.

Life isn't about finding yourself.
Life is about creating yourself.

— George Bernard Shaw

12. Freedom in the Holy Land

ARRIVED IN ISRAEL IN JANUARY 1974, armed with the tools of my culture: I was a strong male possessing a dominant ego, a warrior-like aggressiveness, and a very rational and linear thinking mind. I felt right at home in rigid, rule-oriented environments that were rife with conflict and built upon materialistic values. This was my context; this was all I knew. This was how I had been equipped to begin my adult life. Without my knowledge or consent, the rest of my being—especially my spirit—had been relegated into insignificance. At the time, I was not even aware that such a thing as spirit even existed. How could I? Even the old-man-in-the-sky concept of my childhood religious education never meant anything to me and certainly didn't lead to my paying attention to the spiritual.

From the airport, I made my way to the home of my eldest brother, Norman, who had migrated to Israel three years earlier and now lived on a kibbutz in the Jezreel Valley, just south of Nazareth. I was received by his pregnant wife, whom I was meeting for the first time. She was alone because my brother, who was on reserve duty with the military, had not yet returned from the recently ended Yom Kippur War.

I spent a few weeks helping my sister-in-law around the house while my brother was away; but very soon after he returned, my desire for independence began to assert itself. I wanted to forge my own way. So, after doing a little research, I found a different kibbutz on the Northwest coast of the Mediterranean Sea bordering Lebanon and moved there. The setting was spectacular with the homes of the kibbutz sprawling out and overlooking the warm waters of the Mediterranean. The whole area was surrounded by agricultural fields, mostly banana orchards, stretching out as far as the eye could see. The green of the fields running alongside the blue of the sea was a captivating sight.

I was experiencing freedom of choice for the first time, and it was so welcome that it was almost intoxicating. But what did I do with that freedom? One might think that a young seventeen-year-old, raised in such a restrictive way and now unleashed into the world, would have engaged in experimentations of all kinds. Wrong! I had been programmed to be disciplined and dutiful and that had become my operating system. So, I immediately set about learning the rules of the game in my new home. I wanted to succeed, to make something of my life, and I was ready to apply myself with great focus and energy. The idea of experimenting, exploring or inquiring into other ways of life—or just having fun—did not even enter my mind.

On the kibbutz, jobs were assigned. The first job I was given involved working in those banana orchards nestled along the shores of the Mediterranean. Since I had no prior experience with the growing of bananas, I was only qualified to perform the most menial of tasks. During harvest, only the more experienced workers could determine which bunches were ready to be cut down. My job, then, was to carry the harvested banana bunches out to the road, where a tractor-drawn trailer stood ready to be loaded. I was willing and eager, but those banana bunches could weigh up to 120 pounds. Throw into the mix the fact that I had to trudge through mud to get to and from the trailer and it was a pretty tough go.

I never let it dampen my enthusiasm, though. I was eager to go to work every day, and the harvesting process was actually quite fascinating to me. The harvest crew was divided up into groups of four, each led by a senior worker. Wielding a machete, he would walk through the rows, inspecting, choosing, and ultimately chopping down the ripest bunches. If it was your turn to carry a particular bunch out to the trailer, you had to stand under the bunch and catch it as it fell. The senior guy on my team was very hard-working man, quiet and stoic. Small in stature, he barely reached up to my shoulders. Without saying a word, he would point to a bunch. That was his way of saying "get your shoulder under that bunch now because in the next few seconds it is coming down." When it was me he was addressing, I would maneuver in, stand underneath the bunch with the bottom resting firmly on my shoulder and wait for him to swing his machete. In an instant, the full weight of all those bananas was resting squarely on my shoulder.

For the most part, things went fairly smoothly. Yet, under the best of conditions, this process was both delicate and grueling with just a dash of potential danger. However, for me, there was somewhat of a problem. This man was so short that at times he had to jump in order to reach the stem with his machete. His height made me very apprehensive, as I worried that he would miss the stem and chop my head off. Thus, every time he swung that "Samurai sword" of his, I would instinctively duck. This would irritate him, either because he saw it as a sign that I doubted his expertise or perhaps because he felt it was a dig at his height (or lack thereof). I can't imagine what the two of us, continuously jumping and ducking, must have looked like to an observer.

This was hard work, but it was also rewarding. I always derived a sense of satisfaction at the end of the day from seeing all those beautiful bananas stacked so symmetrically in the trailers, forming a huge pyramid. To me, those pyramids represented perfect order. No, it was beyond metaphor; it was the way life was meant to be. Each day's work concluded with a visual that confirmed my understanding of life. What could have been better?

My upbringing had prepared me well for work, but I was decidedly lacking in the social realm, as I soon discovered. One day after work I headed to a spot only we locals knew. Just below the kibbutz very close to the border of Lebanon, there are some beautiful grottos. We would go there to sunbathe on the huge boulders above the grottos. The ocean waves would end their journey by crashing into the grotto walls with a thunderous collision. On that particular day, on the way down, I met up with two European girls also heading to sunbathe on those boulders. It was very common for a kibbutz to host volunteers from foreign countries. Mostly, these were young kids traveling about the country. They would work in trade for food, lodging and the opportunity to experience kibbutz life and Israeli culture while incurring almost no out-of-pocket expenses. The girls invited me to join them; and I agreed, happy to have some company.

When we arrived at our chosen spot, I began prepping to spend a few hours soaking in the sun. When I finally looked up, both girls were removing the tops of their bikinis! I was horrified—no, I was terrified. Having grown up in a family with only brothers in a repressed, male-oriented society, I had zero experience to draw upon. I hadn't even been exposed to nudie magazines. The sight was all too overwhelming for me, and I needed to extricate myself immediately. I declared out loud that I was going for a swim and leapt over the edge of the boulder into the water thirty feet below. I swam away and did not return, not for my towel nor any of my belongings. Once on shore, I went straight back to my room to process and recuperate.

This situation was quite comical, yet, also sad, for it showed how my upbringing had stunted my social and sexual development. Relative to the rest of the Western world, I had a lot of catching up to do. I took this on as yet another goal and attempted to socialize with the other volunteers. I was successful in making friends with two girls, one American and the other Canadian. I really liked the American girl, but did not know how to go about telling her. To add insult to injury, she and her friend treated me like their little kid brother because of how "naïve" and "cute" I was. This view was hopelessly cemented one night when they came to look for me in my room. It was about 8:30 p.m. and there I was, dressed in my pajamas, fully prepped for bed. The instant they saw me, they halted with a look of shock and disbelief on their faces.

"What's wrong?" I asked, but they could not answer because they were laughing uncontrollably. I was at a total loss as to what was so funny. Finally, after regaining their composure, they very gently explained to me that no one in America and Canada wore matching pajamas at our age, and they certainly did not get prepped for bed, let alone, at 8:30! It wasn't a total disaster, though. That night, they decided to take me under their wings, and I became the subject of an intense and accelerated cultural deprogramming and reprogramming project. This meant spending most of my free time with them, which was great. However, to my disappointment, it never evolved into anything more.

With a confidence that belied my tender age—I had just turned eighteen—I was fearlessly committed to exercising my newfound independence. It was going to manifest in my making every decision for myself from that point on. So, it was then that I decided that I wanted to become an Israeli citizen. What better way to start anew than by choosing the country in which I would begin my new life?

Despite my being green and untested, I possessed the clear understanding that my freedom came with responsibilities and consequences and that I, and I alone, would answer for all my actions. I also understood that there were clear distinctions between right and wrong and that doing right would always be rewarded and wrong would always be punished. My mind was so well trained that even when my independent nature longed to express itself, I only allowed it to do so within the rule set I had learned in my youth. Perhaps that explains why I decided to join the military.

Military training is compulsory in Israel for all citizens. Even though I was not a citizen yet, I decided to volunteer and get my service behind me as soon as possible. I also figured it was a good way to forge my new life. I was sent to a unit made up entirely of new immigrants. We did the same basic training as all the other units, the only difference being that we were taught Hebrew. I blended in well and took my training seriously.

After completing basic training, I volunteered for advanced training as a paratrooper. After completing that training, I then volunteered to train to become a squad leader. After finishing that course, I served on one of the country's three borders.

The fact that I had run away from a country rife with conflict just months earlier only to come to another country steeped in intense conflict might be perceived as ironic, even tragic. But if so, the irony fully escaped my young mind. For me, the idea of living in the midst of conflict was just a given.

On one of my leaves, I met a high school girl named Rachel. I was very attracted to her warm and nurturing personality. Even though she was a girl, I was somehow able to identify with her. Most girls intimidated and confused me; but she did not, perhaps because she was as innocent as I was. And so, over the ensuing months, we became very close. Without being consciously aware of it, we each gave the other what we needed most. Being around her gave me a sense of peaceful calmness that my restless mind could not obtain on its own, while I was for her the strong, rational, protective male figure. At the time, I was still only eighteen and she, only sixteen. How could I have possibly known that we were so right for each other?

Wanting to spend all my leave time with Rachel, I decided to move to her kibbutz while I completed my military duty; but unfortunately, our timing was off. As soon as my military service was done, Rachel graduated from high school. She began her own military service not long after. So, again, we found ourselves apart.

I took a job working in the cotton fields. Cotton was a very lucrative crop, so my job was stable. But beyond that, I loved it more than I could have ever imagined. On a kibbutz, personal finances were never a motivating factor in one's decision-making process because all members received the same benefits, regardless of the kind of job they were doing or the hours they were working. This ideology never bothered me because I loved my work so much. I never cared about others' work performance;

I just focused on doing the best job I possibly could. During the summer months, for example, I would set my alarm for 3:30 a.m., work till 2 p.m., go home to rest, then return at 4:00 p.m. and work until at least 7:00 p.m.

I became passionate about my work and threw myself into learning anything and everything I could about growing cotton. I paid close attention to every detail of the growing process and diligently studied the various cultivation practices involved. Mastering the technicalities was gratifying, but there was another dimension that meant even more to me—I seemed to have an inexplicable connection to the plants. In fact, up to that point, I had never before felt so connected to or felt so much love for anything in my life as I did for those fields of cotton plants. In their presence, I would experience a sense of oneness and peace that is impossible to put into words, and when I was away, I would actually pine for them.

I fell in love with those plants, purely and unconditionally. I felt responsible for each and every one of them, and it pained me to imagine that a plant was not being taken care of. Those plants were my family. They nurtured me in a way that my family never had; and I, in turn, would have done anything for their well-being. I can clearly remember running through the sprinklers daily, the mud oozing between the toes of my bare feet, passing through row after row until I was satisfied that every plant was receiving its share of life-giving water. I gave them all my attention and care, and in return I was blessed to witness their growth into maturity and then the production of their offspring.

All of this took place out-of-doors, out in the vast open spaces, out in Nature under the watchful eye of the warm sun and the relentlessly blue sky. And yet, I never gave a thought to the larger context. I just went about my work with a highly focused devotion. Looking back, however, I think this might have been my first introduction to the idea that life is not linear, as I had been taught, but profoundly circular. This was manifest in the seasons and in the stages of crop growth from seed to sprout to bloom and harvest, culminating in death and re-seeding. At the end of the season, the spent plants were plowed under, returned to the land, incorporating the old crop into the soil only to be reborn as a new crop the following year.

Witnessing all this, I got to experience a full spectrum of emotions, which also cycled around—the sadness I felt at the passing of the old crop transmuted into rejoicing at its rebirth, and then back again. But steeped in rationality as I was, I was largely oblivious to the deeper significance of the visible cycle. I could only acknowledge experiences if I could translate them into something rational.

In those fields, I felt that I had found my calling, and so I dedicated myself to it wholeheartedly. I wanted to understand as much as I could about growing cotton, so I devised my own version of an education, which meant throwing myself completely into an experience and then analyzing that experience, probing it for what it could teach me. For example, I would go home at night and draw involved maps of what had gone on in the field that day. I also formulated questions and then read the pertinent literature on my own and at my own pace to answer my own questions and hungrily soak up anything and everything I could find about plants—not just cotton—agriculture, cultivation, et cetera. I spent most of my free time at home educating myself in this way. I dove into this reading because it was relevant to what I was experiencing in my life. This new knowledge wasn't abstract or sterile like the knowledge I'd received in school. This knowledge was *alive*; it had meaning to me. I was never against learning or gaining knowledge *per se*, but I was against being *force-fed* knowledge in some sterile classroom, removed from life and then being asked to regurgitate it. In contrast, every fiber of my being confirmed that this new path was a real and complete education. I was being educated in the school of life.

Four months into Rachel's compulsory military service, we decided to get married, which automatically exempted her from having to complete her two-year term. We wed on the sixth of June, 1977. I was twenty-one and Rachel, nineteen. It was a typical kibbutz wedding, simple and beautiful.

Kᴵʙʙᴜᴛᴢ ᴏᴠᴇʀʟᴏᴏᴋɪɴɢ ᴛʜᴇ Jᴇᴢʀᴇᴇʟ ᴠᴀʟʟᴇʏ

Harvesting cotton

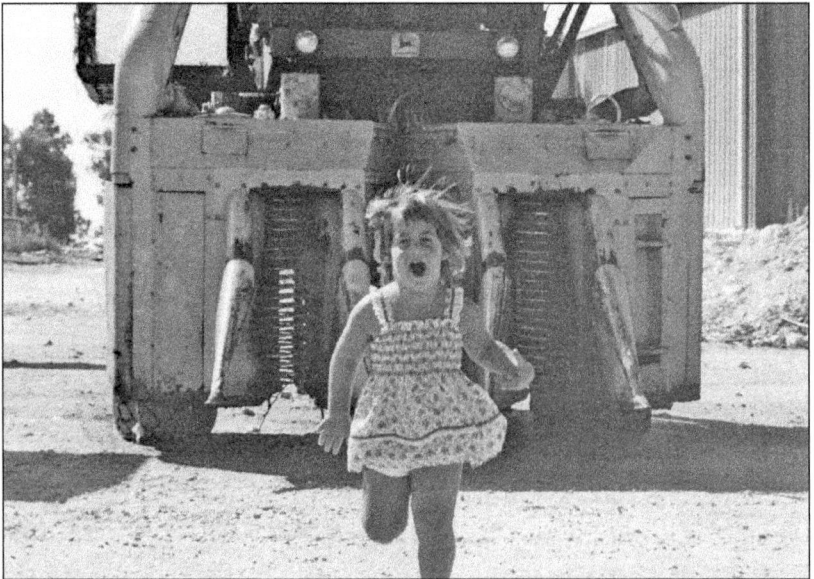

My niece running in front of cotton harvester

My parents flew in from South Africa and my other brother, Raymond, who had recently immigrated to Israel with his family, drove up from the kibbutz where they were living in the southern portion of the country.

The question of a honeymoon arose, but it was quickly settled. It was the height of the growing season, and my strict conditioning told me that if I had a job to finish that should take precedence over anything personal. Rachel, being so young, agreed, and so we quickly settled into married life with work progressing well for both of us. Rachel was working as a dental assistant and I in the fields.

Not long after we were married, the head of the cotton growing operation resigned, and a replacement could not be found from among the older, more experienced employees. The scope of the job was huge, and it came with a heavy responsibility. Cotton was the largest source of income for the kibbutz, and the value of the crops was well north of seven figures. It was probably for these reasons that no one was stepping forward for the job.

With no other remotely qualified takers in sight, I was approached to head up the organization, even though it would have been no easy feat for a kid of then twenty-two. Unlike everyone else, however, I did not immediately shy away from the offer. Instead, I asked for a few days to think it over. That granted, I went to seek advice from one of the kibbutz elders who acted as a mentor to our branch. After a lengthy conversation, he said, in parting, that he thought I would not be a good choice because I was too impetuous.

With a somewhat bruised ego, I ran home to find a dictionary. I could not open it fast enough; what the hell did impetuous mean? After digesting the meaning of the word, I came up with a question. Yes, he was correct that I made decisions very quickly—but was that necessarily bad?

True to my nature, I accepted the challenge. I would do it. However, that night, sleep did not come easily. I wondered if, in fact, I *had* been too impetuous. Still, I didn't let my doubts stop me.

During my years leading the cotton operations, we all did a great job. We made substantial contributions to the financial wellbeing of the kibbutz and ultimately went on to win a national prize for quality and overall yields. At the age of twenty-two, fewer than four years after I had set out alone, I was enjoying great success. I was productive, and I worked hard and got along well with almost everyone. I was courteous and respectful. In other words, I was following my conditioning with efficiency, precision, and a laser focus. I was exercising my understanding of how to operate and function in the world, and it was working. And I was executing all this by wielding the multipurpose tool that went by the name of control. I was using that tool so efficiently that it reinforced even further the idea that this was how one should live one's life.

All this success at work was, however, exacting a cost on the Chesler household. Because of the copious amount of time and attention I was investing in the fields, Rachel was growing unhappy. By 1980, three years into our marriage, she had had enough. One evening, she gave me an ultimatum: either we would leave the kibbutz together or she would leave alone. Rachel did not make such statements lightly, so I did not take it lightly either.

Faced with a decision, I felt as if I were being forced to choose between the two loves of my life. Yet I understood, intuitively if not consciously, that Rachel was the antidote to all my conditioning. While I was capable of extreme focus, my highly indoctrinated mind was always moving; it was always busy analyzing, thinking, forecasting and anticipating. In contrast, Rachel was an oasis of calm. She gave me a sense of stability and peace. I needed that. I knew I could continue my life's education anywhere, but it had to be with Rachel. And so, with mixed emotions and a very heavy heart, I chose to say goodbye to my cotton plants.

Now free, Rachel and I wanted to take some time to travel. We were grateful to receive $2,000 from the kibbutz for all our hard work. And so, with that hard-earned cash in hand, we decided to buy two tickets to San Francisco. Although we weren't aware of our real motives at the time, we were going to America not just on vacation but to seek a new life.

Why America? I didn't understand it then, but now it is so obvious. I wanted to go to the United States to prove myself. America was the most powerful and materialistic country in the world—that made it the perfect place to put myself to the test. I was like a young gladiator, itching to plunge into the arena, convinced of my own capacity to win at battle. Thus, to me, America was Rome, home to the best and most well-trained gladiators in the world. I was hungry to challenge them, to challenge myself. If I could succeed in America, I would be validated as a human being. It would prove that my worldview—control through rational thought—was the right way. (And, therefore, of course, every other way had to be wrong.)

The truth is, we really knew nothing about America. We didn't even have a clue as to where San Francisco was. We only chose it because a friend of a friend lived there. Were we brave, naïve or just plain stupid?

Unfortunately, it was while we were making our plans to leave that my parents finally immigrated to Israel. I hadn't seen them much since I'd departed South Africa seven years earlier, and now I was poised to miss them yet again.

It is no use saying, 'We are doing our best.' You have got to succeed in doing what is necessary.

—Winston Churchill

13. If I Can Make it Here

RACHEL AND I LANDED at the San Francisco airport in the evening, took a bus into the city and spent a night in some kind of youth hostel. I believe we paid $5 just for the room, but we also got cockroaches, druggies, and turmoil; the price was all-inclusive. We tried to sleep, but the shock factor kept us wide-awake. Morning could not come fast enough.

When daylight finally did arrive, we quickly found a way to make contact with that friend of a friend. He invited us to spend a few days with him, and we gratefully accepted. With his help, we began getting our bearings and organizing ourselves for the next part of our journey, which involved some vague plan to drive south to search for work in the agricultural industry.

At this point, we were still telling ourselves that we had come to America on vacation; the idea of trying to stay permanently was still too scary to say out loud. But that changed one day when I was going about doing some errands. I walked into a dry cleaning store, expecting only to drop off our friend's jacket. Making my way toward the counter, I noticed a glass case in the center of the store. Inside was a pair of old, worn-out shoes. Curious, I walked over to take a closer look. Next to the shoes inside the display was a placard saying that the owners of the dry cleaning store had come to America with nothing, just those shoes. I was transfixed. I remember looking down at my flip-flops and thinking how good they'd look in a glass case. If these people had done it, why couldn't I?

I was on fire now to start our new life. I told Rachel of my plan and she was right on board, so we dug into our meager resources, bought a

169

1958 Volkswagen bus for $800, and took off heading south. We soon discovered that the vehicle used almost as much oil as gas, but it didn't dampen our spirits. We stopped in San Jose and searched for work, but it seemed impossible to come by. We were frustrated and a little scared, but after a couple of days we heard a rumor that a company in the Coachella Valley was hiring kids to work in their vineyards, so we stocked up on oil, climbed back in the VW, and made our way further south. Luck was with us; the rumor was true, and we began work soon after arriving. The company provided housing too, so we moved into a double-wide trailer, sharing it with some other kids, who also worked in the vineyards.

We had some stability now as far as income was concerned, but that wasn't going to be enough for me. I wanted more, so I kept my eyes and ears open. After only a few weeks, I heard about an Israeli consultant who was working locally, advising growers on the use of the then new technology of drip irrigation. This sounded interesting, so I contacted him and we set up a meeting. The meeting went really well; and by the end, he had hired me as his assistant. This new job enabled Rachel and me to move to a place of our own. We found a tiny farmhouse surrounded by vegetable fields. The house consisted of one room with a shower in one corner and a small kitchenette in the other. We were miles away from civilization, but the isolated location and meager living conditions did not bother us; it allowed us to be alone at last and we were grateful.

Things began to happen after that, almost as if by magic. I had been working with the consultant in the vegetable fields for only a few months when the son of the owner of the vineyard I had worked for previously stopped by my worksite to ask me if I would be interested in a managerial job with their company. I was more than interested and told him so, so we set up an interview for the following day. But before he left, he turned and uttered these parting words, "Make sure you get some new jeans and a haircut before you show up." As I watched him drive off, I thought back to my days on the kibbutz and how I had become accustomed to working in the fields in shorts and sandals, not caring much at all about my

appearance. Apparently in America things were different; the require-
ments for a managerial role included looking good. That very afternoon I
had my hair cut and bought a new pair of jeans.

The transformation of my appearance must have worked because,
even though I had no experience growing table grapes, I was hired. My
new job was geared towards infrastructure development and the maintenance of new vineyards with an emphasis on drip irrigation. In conjunction
with the latter, I was also to help with all cultivation practices during the
different growing seasons. This was a great opportunity to learn, and it
meant forward progression for Rachel and me. I was to be paid a salary,
drive a company pickup truck and live in a company house. We would
still be living far away from civilization, but we were closing in. Best of all,
it meant job security and a steady income; I would work every day, not
just on call when needed.

So, Rachel and I moved again, to another double-wide trailer.
Compared to anywhere else we'd ever lived, this place was huge with a real
kitchen, bedroom, and living room. Best of all, we had it all to ourselves.
We thought we had died and gone to heaven.

Things progressed very quickly for us. I was integrating well at work,
and the company was sponsoring me for my green card. For the first time
since arriving in the States, we began to feel at home. Up until then, we'd
still thought about going back to Israel; but as we began to feel more settled
in America, our desire to return home waned. At least, that was how it was
for me. I had come here to do battle, to prove myself, and I was enjoying
being tested. Rachel, on the other hand, would have much preferred to be
closer to her family. I didn't share that same feeling about my family; in fact,
I felt that I was on a mission and that thinking about my family would only
get in the way. But I felt empathy for Rachel, and so, true to form, I took
control and set about fixing the problem. In short order, Rachel became
pregnant and we were on our way to creating a family of our own.

During this period, many ranches were converting to drip irrigation
because it was a more efficient watering system. These new systems were

fairly complex to set up; so, because of the magnitude of the job, our company hired an outside contractor to perform the installations. My job was to oversee the work being performed by the contractor. I took my role very seriously and closely monitored every move from the moment they began in the morning until the moment they stopped. As a consequence, I was learning a lot about the technical aspects of the job. Then I also became curious about the financial aspects. Since I was present when we reviewed bids and negotiated with contractors, I was well aware of our costs. Over time, I also got a good feel for the costs to the contractor. With all this data at my disposal, I decided to do an analysis, looking at everything from the contractor's side. I was shocked to realize how much profit he was making. At the time I was earning just $1,500 a month while working ten to twelve hours per day, six days a week. Something began to percolate.

A few weeks later, right before I was due to go on my very first paid vacation, I was asked to sit in on a company meeting in which we were deciding about the next drip irrigation project. After much consideration, a decision was reached to convert two forty-acre blocks. As the meeting was concluding, I blurted out something that shocked even me. I suggested that, rather than hiring an outside contractor, they let me install the system during my two-week vacation. I told them confidently that I could do it at a lower cost.

The owner of the company, a tough, but fair, businessman, sat back and silently contemplated my suggestion. He remained mute just long enough for me to begin a frenzied conversation in my head. It went something like this: *Are you nuts? What prompted you to come up with that crazy idea? Do you want to jeopardize your job, idiot?* On and on the chatter raged. Then, though barely audible over the noise in my head, I detected my boss's voice fading in. He asked me if I really thought I was capable of getting the job done. Almost as if someone else were talking through me, I immediately replied yes.

He looked me square in the eye and, without hesitation, said, "Okay, do it," and walked out, leaving me seated alone in the conference room. I was in a state of shock, which was quickly accompanied by a growing feeling of nausea as I realized that there were many very practical questions to address, questions that I had not even considered prior to my outburst. Did I, indeed, have the expertise? Could I finish in two weeks? Where was I going to find the heavy equipment to dig the trenches? And those weren't even the most serious questions. Was I jeopardizing my name and reputation and the job security I was so fortunate to have? Was I putting Rachel and our baby at risk? *Am I indeed too impetuous?*

But fate was with me again. By the end of my "vacation," during which I worked both day and night, the job was completed, and everything was functioning perfectly. Not only that, for the first time in two years, Rachel and I had a little cash in the bank.

The time was nearing for Rachel to give birth, and on May 8, 1982, Tal Chesler came into the world. The first few months with a new baby were interesting, to put it mildly. We had no clue about how to take care of a baby; but we fumbled our way through, employing a process that was largely trial-and-error. In time, though, we got the hang of it, Rachel, especially. She proved to be the best mom any baby could have wished for. I, on the other hand, wasn't quite sure how to nurture, so I left most of that to her.

In short order, I found myself again getting restless at work. My independent nature and my need to be in full control of my life were beginning to gnaw at me again. I knew what was churning beneath it—I wanted to run my own business and since we'd received our green cards, this was now a real possibility. I knew there was a high demand in the marketplace for good contractors. My recent success had proven that I could do it, so I decided to leave my job to become an irrigation contractor. In short order, my new business was flourishing.

I was tremendously busy up until the hot summer months, when work ground to a halt. We decided to take advantage of the forced break and take our first vacation in three years. We purchased a small, used travel trailer, hooked it up to our "new" car, an antique Chevy pick-up, stopped by AAA for a case full of maps and set out on a road trip across country. By now, Tal was almost a year-and-a-half old, and being that he was an exceptionally good and easy baby traveling with him was not a burden at all.

We drove to the East Coast, covering close to 10,000 miles over three months. We kept expenses down by sleeping in and eating out of the trailer. We had the most incredible experiences visiting many different cities, national monuments, parks and museums. The only blemish on the trip happened towards the end. We'd gone to an amusement park in Seattle, and Tal was on a merry-go-round with me by his side and Rachel was out on the grass taking pictures. I desperately wanted to show that my boy was a "man" (at not yet two years old??). My plan was that when the carousel came around the next time, Rachel would see Tal riding the horsie all alone. So, I let go of him, confident he could handle the "horsie" just fine. Of course, I made this genius move when out of sight of Rachel. The last time she had seen Tal, I was supporting him. Well, to my horror—not to mention Rachel's—just as we came into view, Tal went flying off that wild horsie and came crashing down onto the metal floor, cracking open his lip. We rushed him to the emergency room, and I will never forget the sick feeling I had watching the medical team strap that little screaming kid down, so he would be still while they stitched up his lip.

Needless to say, any parental points I might have accumulated with Rachel up until then were immediately revoked with some stiff penalties imposed. This reinforced my conditioned understanding of the strict division of parenting roles. As the mother, Rachel's role was to nurture; and as the father, mine was to provide and protect. I also felt it was my responsibility to teach my son how to function like a real man. I felt an urgency to do this as soon as possible, but I also had to protect him while he learned. Unfortunately, as a twenty-seven-year-old father, I had my priorities backwards; I had chosen the "real man" thing over the "protect" thing. The lesson was seared into my brain; I vowed to never again fail to protect my child.

Meanwhile, my business continued to grow. I was solidifying relation-ships with others in the business world; and bit by bit, we kept moving westward until we finally made it to the most desired city in the valley, Palm Desert. Then, on December 18, 1984, our second child, Ofir, was born. When the doctor handed him to the nurse, she raised him head-high so that we could see him. What happened next was Ofir's "hello" to the world. The nurse held him firmly in the air and said something like, "You are so cute." Ofir, wanting to be polite, I'm sure, but not yet able to talk, responded the only way he knew how: he peed in her face!

Everyone in the OR burst out laughing. My son had not been in the world for more than two minutes, and he was already peeing on it! It was like he was saying, "Dad, I am independent and very aware that I am. I can handle myself. I have this." And that was entirely true! He did know how to handle himself, even as a baby. When he would wake in his crib and cry for us to come get him, we would get there only to find that he had somehow already removed his diaper. And I don't mean he'd torn it off; he'd carefully undone the little glued strips on each side! From the very beginning, he genuinely seemed to know what he needed better than we did. I liked that because it was so different from how I had been in my first seventeen years. As a parent, however, it was also tough to swallow.

We took Ofir home, and we were now a family of four. Family life was great, but I was getting somewhat bored at work again. Having installed hundreds of thousands of feet of underground piping by now, the work had become routine and I needed a new challenge. However, I didn't want to leave a business that was doing so well, so I decided on the next best thing; I would get a hobby. But, what? It came to me almost instantly. Planes had always been a passion of mine and learning to fly was a lifelong dream, so I decided it was time. After doing some research, I decided to learn to fly an ultralight.

I searched for a local flying club and discovered one that operated out of an old, abandoned military landing strip. According to the map, it was isolated and only accessible by dirt roads, but I set off to find it. Finally, I reached the facility, which consisted of two small trailer homes, a hanger and a runway, all surrounded by nothing but wide, open desert for miles around. I was given a tour and sales pitch and within a half hour I had signed up for lessons. My instructor turned out to be none other than the brother of James Cameron, the director of *Terminator*, *Aliens*, *The Abyss*, *Titanic*, *Avatar*, and many other movies. Mike was a different kind of a guy; he was also a very good pilot. I enjoyed his company, and it did not take him long to get me fairly proficient on the stick and rudders.

Then one day, after we'd returned from a routine lesson, he walked over to the hanger and, without saying a word, pulled out a single-seater plane and left it on the runway. Then he walked up to me and said in a matter-of-fact voice, "It is a great day for a solo flight."

I was sure he meant that he was going to go flying alone, so I responded politely, "Okay, enjoy," and walked away.

But he came after me and turned me around to face him. Looking me in the eyes, he repeated his prior statement, this time with one minor change, "It is a great day for *you* to solo."

Had I been able to move a muscle, I would have bolted into the desert like a wild mustang; but when he asked me if I thought I was ready, that someone-else-who-lurked-inside-me blurted out a very unconvincing, "Yes." It was the voice of my male ego and all my conditioning; I was not going to show weakness! And so, before I knew it, I was strapped in the pilot seat all alone.

Mike did a last-minute, pre-flight check and, when he was done, came over to give me some final instructions. I saw his mouth move but heard nothing except his parting words, "You will do fine."

I sat in the seat motionless, my entire world now reduced to the interior of this tiny, open cockpit. Had the day finally arrived, just like that? After what seemed like an eternity, I pulled myself together. The worst that could possibly happen was that I was going to die that day. With that thought comforting me, I fired her up, pushed the gas throttle all the way forward, waited to reach take-off speed, waited a little longer to exceed that speed, and then slowly, very slowly, I pulled back on the stick.

Once I was up in the air, flying straight and level, I calmed down considerably and actually began to enjoy being alone in the skies. Thinking back on it, I was probably experiencing true freedom for the first time in my life. I felt free in both body and mind—especially mind. Somehow, I had left the weight of my upbringing on the runway, and I found myself floating in a realm where endless responsibility and duty did not exist. For maybe the first time in my life, my mind was empty, and I felt free to just simply be. I had escaped!

With each full revolution of the prop, my confidence grew. After about fifteen minutes of exploring the blue yonder, I looked to my left and saw Mike flying fairly close to me with another pupil sitting in the same seat I had occupied myself just half-an-hour before. He gave me a thumbs-up and peeled off to continue on with his lesson. I flew twice more that day and drove home beaming with pride.

After that, it did not take long for me to order my own plane, one of the highest performing ultralights of the day. These planes are ordered in kit form, so I built it myself and then customized it, putting in a much bigger engine and a three-bladed adjustable prop. I gave it a custom paint job and added a few more bells and whistles. I had a lot of fun with that plane and over time even performed a few light aerobatic maneuvers. My hobby was providing a lot of enjoyment, not the least of which was the opportunity to hobnob with other pilots. One day stands out. I was sitting at the club chatting with the boys including two pilots from out of town who were very well known for their insane stunts. This was a pretty fearless bunch, guys who lived to fly and flirted with danger constantly. In fact, one of them had been severely crippled by a crash that he was lucky to have survived.

The beer was flowing, the atmosphere was loose and wild, and stories were flying (no pun intended). Being a fairly new pilot, I hadn't accumulated any stories of my own; so, I mostly listened, saying very little. Their stories were making quite an impression on me, so I began asking all kinds of questions. My curiosity about aerobatics was so obvious that one of the guys decided to throw down the gauntlet. Why don't I go up and try a full loop? It was a simple maneuver, he said. A full loop is achieved when you take your plane all the way around in a vertical circle. For a few moments in the full loop you, the pilot, are upside down.

I felt my adrenalin rise. This was just the kind of challenge that got me going, Then the owner of the school weighed in; he strongly discouraged the idea because I was too new a pilot, but the first guy kept prodding me to give it a shot. Now there was a cacophony both inside and outside my head. Since these planes were single-seaters, hands-on lessons were out of the question; if you were going to learn to do it, you had to figure it out for yourself. The fact was, I hadn't yet. *The owner is right*, I thought, *I'm too green*. Then, just when I thought sanity had prevailed, my tormentor leaned toward me and told me exactly how to do it.

"Dive the plane," he said, "and when optimal speed is reached, pull the stick back all the way and keep holding it there. Do not panic and let go. Just keep holding it all the way back until you reach level flight once more."

That was all I needed. I had to try it. I jumped up, fired up my plane, climbed to two thousand feet, dove the plane until it was going almost 100 mph, pulled back on the stick, prayed hard—and survived a beautiful, tight loop.

Soon, I was spending most of my time either working or flying. And again, Rachel was getting lonely; she was homesick for family and wanted to return to Israel. I was too busy at work to leave then, so we arrived at a compromise. She would go to Israel now, taking the boys, and I would join them there as soon as possible.

Early the next spring, I reunited with my family in Israel. I expected to be there just for a vacation, but by then Rachel had decided she did not want to return to the States. Reluctantly, I agreed and began looking for work. We were living in the city, so it was not easy for me to find agricultural work. Perhaps that was fortuitous because it was during this time that my dad fell ill with cancer. Although I was still looking for work, I tried to spend as much time with him as possible. My dad had never shown much emotion towards me while I was growing up; and, sadly, this was the case even during his illness. We did have some good chats, but our conversations were mostly devoid of emotion and definitely not commensurate with the circumstances.

Then, as the cotton-harvesting season was about to begin, I found work operating a cotton harvester. I had some prior experience from the kibbutz days, so it was not difficult to land the job. The harvester was a highly sophisticated machine, expensive to run and difficult to operate. I worked very long hours, but I enjoyed it. I felt at home working outdoors again.

We gave ourselves a year to see if we could build a life for the family in Israel, but it soon became obvious to both Rachel and me that we wanted to return to the United States. We arrived back in the winter of 1986 and, over the next few years, again settled into our American life. I quit flying to spend more time with the family and slowly got my business back on its feet. The following winter, Dad died. I was on the first flight back to Israel to attend the funeral; but knowing that both my brothers were there to support my mom, I soon flew back to America, hoping to eventually process his life and death.

My contracting business was doing well. I had secured a substantial new account with a local vegetable grower, and I was spending much of my time on his ranches with my crews overseeing the installation of the irrigation systems. Each day, in order to reach the blocks where we were working, I had to pass through fields filled with watermelons, bell peppers, squash, green beans, asparagus, eggplant, tomatoes, and more. I soon found myself paying rapt attention to the crops and to the various cultivation practices taking place throughout that season.

To this day, I will never understand how or why, but I zeroed in on bell peppers. In fact, I became rather obsessed with them. By the fall, despite the fact that I actually had no knowledge about growing vegetables, I decided that I was going to become a vegetable grower and, more specifically, a bell pepper grower. Even though the idea seemed very natural at the time, it was actually nothing short of insane for many reasons. For one, growing any kind of crop is extremely costly. Also, finding land to rent was difficult enough for established growers and virtually impossible for a novice such as myself. Thirdly, one needed some very expensive and specialized equipment to prepare the land. Oh, and then you needed a good, experienced sales force to bring your harvest to market. The obstacles went on and on. I could write an entire book about why that particular business was the most idiotic idea of all time for a young man in my situation; and, yet, the idea would just not go away.

So, over the next few months I tackled each of the obstacles in turn, like the gladiator I was. Magically, solutions presented themselves. After everything fell into place, we planted our first crop. It took many a sleepless night and much sweat and anguish, but we went on to have a good and profitable season.

Then I began to dream again—this time in color.

Colored peppers were the crown jewels of the pepper kingdom, but they presented even more challenges to growers. Thus, at the time, most of the colored peppers in the US market were imported from Holland, where they were grown in greenhouses under perfectly controlled conditions. If, however, a grower in the US could successfully grow colored peppers in open fields, the market would be almost exclusively theirs. The challenge was to find a variety of colored peppers that would grow outside in the desert. I made it my job to find those seeds. Within a short period of time I had become one of only two growers of colored peppers in the valley. My intuition did not fail me, and the venture proved to be extremely lucrative.

As the years went by, everything continued to progress well. My businesses grew, and so did the boys. Soon, Tal and Ofir went off to college. Rachel stayed at home with our youngest, Daniel, while I worked and played golf.

It was in this context of continuing prosperity that Rachel and I decided to design and build our dream house. Friends recommended against the project, warning us that "building a house together was the quickest route to divorce." But, trusting in our bond, we moved ahead anyway. We spent many a weekend pouring over different layouts. Once we had a good idea of how we wanted the house to look and function, we hired an architect. Plans in hand, we began construction with me serving as the general contractor. With the house measuring in at 8,000 square feet, plus landscaping spanning an acre, this was not a simple project. I supervised everything closely; it was rare for me to leave the site. Finally, in the spring some fourteen months after we began, the inspector signed off on the final inspection, and we moved in. The house, in conjunction with the pool, paddle tennis court, and landscaping was a stunning site.

It was only a few months later that I received a phone call from my eldest brother, Norman, telling me that our middle brother, Raymond, had been diagnosed with terminal cancer. Raymond and I were not close and over the years we had had very little contact. Yet, only minutes after putting down the phone, I was making arrangements to fly back to Israel. Within days, I was at Raymond's side and did not leave for two weeks. Knowing that he was an Apple fanatic, I had purchased the latest and best Mac for him as a gift. He was ecstatic. I took him to all his doctor appointments, and we spent most of the rest of our time chatting on his patio.

That was when I really got to know Raymond.

When someone is dying, sometimes all the unimportant, petty stuff will fall away. If that occurs, what then shows through is who that person truly is at their very core. This hadn't happened with my dad, but it did happen with Raymond. At least that was how I experienced it. I was able to see right through to the very essence of his being and what I observed was simply beautiful and good in every way. He had a naive, child-like way about him. When I showed him pictures of our new home, his face lit up with boyish wonder. He became so excited that he insisted he would post the pictures on a website so that, as he said, anyone could view the pictures. I have no clue if he ever did. I suspect he didn't because, during that time, he was slipping into unreality. He repeatedly talked about coming to visit us to see our home in person and chirped on about other plans he had in store for us all. Each time he did this, it would tear at my heart. In response, I would simply nod and say how much I looked forward to it, knowing full well that it was one huge fantasy, that he was not going anywhere other than his final resting place.

When my time there was up, I said my final goodbyes and flew home, carrying with me much sadness but also much gratitude for the gift I had been given. Having the opportunity to be in the presence of such a brave, kind, and selfless being was an incredibly profound experience, the full meaning of which I would not begin to comprehend for years to come.

Within a month of returning home, I received a call from Norman telling me that Raymond had passed on. I flew back for the funeral to pay my respects to my brother. Then I flew back home, and our lives continued on as before—up until May, 2007, when sitting outside my newly constructed palace of a house, awaiting our guests, I finally realized that my dream had actually happened. I had made it in America; the evidence was all around me, all 8,000 square feet of it. Yes, I had been validated; and my worldview, corroborated. I had controlled everything to perfection, like a world-class conductor in front of his orchestra.

I sat back and waited for the standing ovation that surely must be coming. I waited and waited, but all I heard was silence.

The house that ostensibly "validated" me

A girl phoned me and said, "Come on over, there's nobody home."
I went over. There was nobody home.

—Rodney Dangerfield

14. Pilgrimage

AFTER RETURNING FROM THE SEED CONFERENCE, the soul-searching review of my life had brought up a lot of material, things that I had experienced but hadn't thought about for decades. I needed to integrate it all somehow. But how? I didn't know what else to do, so I just started hiking again. Two mountain ranges rise up starkly from the flat desert floor, the Santa Rosas and San Jacintos. They seemed to call to me; so, I went to them, sought refuge in them.

I hiked almost every day all through that fall, walking and walking and walking to tire myself out, to get myself so exhausted that even the pain had to quit. I pushed the boundaries of my physical strength, perhaps because I was becoming dimly aware that only when I was totally spent were my defenses rendered weak enough to allow a true insight to break through.

Somehow, I had the wisdom to turn to Nature, to surround myself with wild beauty and give myself over to Her. I sensed that through my exposure to indigenous ways, beginning with the SEED conference, I had come upon yet another tributary that was leading me to Spirit. I had been re-introduced to Nature, and I saw Her so differently now. Nature was not something to be used, harvested, consumed. She was the protagonist in the beautiful dance we call life and beyond. This changed everything. On my hikes, I was able to feel everything around me. I knew Nature was no longer something separate or apart; Nature was becoming more and more a part of me and vice versa.

I didn't know exactly how, but I was convinced that my new understanding of Nature was significant to my search, so I had to tell Ofir.

December 19, 2010

> *Ofir, hi,*
>
> *It is your birthday. You are 26 years old. I mourn your future and celebrate your past. I celebrate my past, too, and mourn my future. You were a huge part of it, as is Tal and Daniel. We miss you so much. The pain is paralyzing. There are many days that I don't want to or can't get out of bed.*
>
> *I am still in the process of finding the appropriate venue in which to honor you. We have done some work and have sent many kids to summer camp in your Name. This is good and satisfying but this is NOT my life's work. I am looking for something bigger, something that will touch many young lives and go on forever. You never had the opportunity to finish your legacy, but you had accomplished so much at such a young age that it will be easy for us to continue on your path. I have some ideas, but it is going to take time. I have been working on an idea, so I have not had much time to read. I feel like I need to because it grounds me and keeps me focused on my journey.*
>
> *I am not letting my guides in and need to change that. It is so difficult trying to remain focused on taking care of you and all the other responsibilities I have. Please just know we are trying.*
>
> *I started hiking again and did the seventeen-mile hike from Palm Desert to Palm Springs over the mountains. I get such clarity when I hike, and it has prompted me to start writing again.*
>
> *When I hike and am away from the distractions of everyday life, I am able to disconnect and reach my higher self. It is beautiful. When I walk alone in the mountains I become part of and one with my surroundings and it is simply incredible. I feel the rocks, the plants, and the*

animals. We are all one and the same. I thank you for that gift. I thank
you for allowing me to reach a higher level of consciousness.

I attended a conference between Western scientists and indigenous
people from all over the world. I learned so much from the Native
Americans. When the Western scientists spoke, I listened intently. They
are so knowledgeable and brilliant, but I just heard them. When the
Natives spoke, I not only heard them but felt them. It was an incredible
experience. I spent some one-on-one time with them, too, and learned so
much. It was spiritual. The Westerners fed my brain and the indigenous
people fed my soul and entire being. The institute that put on the con-
ference is where I hope to get YOU involved. You are a perfect fit. I will
write again soon. Miss you so much.

Love and honor you always,
Dad

While I hiked, I thought about my life thus far, about all the experiences that had shaped me. The loss of Ofir and then the loss of my
marriage had filled me with such grief. Those losses were so primal that
I was wracked with mourning, further compounded by anger and self-
recrimination. My inability to protect my family and to protect Daniel,
especially, had so shattered my sense of myself that after a lifetime of
more than fifty years, I wasn't sure I had any idea who I really was. At
times this brought me to my knees and I was tempted to let the Beast
finally take me. Yet, a tiny light flickered in all that bleakness. Because
of what I'd learned at the conference, I had a sense that understanding
more about my tacit infrastructure was somehow very important. I had
gotten a start by considering my childhood, but I longed to discover
more about the patterns and structures that shaped me, that made me
act and think as I did. Yet, I didn't have any idea how to begin. Once
more, I was stalled, so I just hiked. I gave myself over to blue sky, to
spiked cactus and dust.

Sometimes there were moments on those hikes when I would feel something moving through me. It was almost as if something was attempting to comfort me. A part of me craved healing, I knew, but I could not acknowledge the need because it implied weakness. Still, that part of me—the part that knew better, the part I was just starting to think of as my "higher self"—was petitioning the heavens on my behalf.

And the heavens answered. I know because sometime in the winter of 2010, the phone rang and called me back, back to my homeland, back to the beginning.

On the other end of the phone line was a very good friend whom I had met while serving in the Israeli military. Without even greeting me, he merely said in Hebrew, "I have someone here who wants to talk to you." A brief pause followed while he transferred the phone, and then I heard a voice speaking in a very thick South African accent: "Howzit Chezzie, how you doing, boet [brother in Afrikaans]? The speaker chattered on, peppering his speech with phrases I had not heard since my school days; but I had no clue with whom I was talking. And then, suddenly, I knew. It was Benny, my best friend from childhood! I was catapulted back across the decades. We had met on the first day of school in first grade, and from that moment, we were inseparable. In many ways, he had been the closest friend I ever had, but we lost all contact when his family decided to emigrate to another country. He had been thirteen when they left and by the time he returned to South Africa, it was I who was long gone.

Our friendship might have been cut short, but it was unconditional and pure. I recalled vividly how much we would laugh. It was an uncontrollable laugh, the kind that starts in the tummy and then just goes on forever until it hurts. It is that laugh kids know only too well, the kind that life tends to chip away at until as adults we almost forget it even existed. It never took much to get us to the point of no return; it was as if the laughter was always right beneath the surface, waiting to burst forth. The only catalyst needed to begin the chain reaction was the silliest, most benign thing. This laughter was also time sensitive; it had to happen as often as possible. So, if there was no outside catalyst, then one of us would self-detonate and the other would follow suit.

The circumstances surrounding that phone call prove that we really do live in a small world—or was there something else at work? My Israeli friend was in South Africa visiting his brother, who happened to also be friends with my old buddy. During the visit, my Israeli friend, for some unknown reason, mentioned that he had served in the military with a South African guy named "Chesler." Bennie, my childhood friend, immediately responded, "I went to school with a Chesler." It soon became obvious they were talking about the same guy. Hence the call.

The phone conversation went on for a long time and ended with my old friend saying—no, demanding, "You have to come visit. I am not taking no for an answer."

With that, a new opportunity to run away from the grief presented itself and I jumped at it. But as the days passed, I began to see the trip very differently. It was an opportunity to better understand and possibly even come to terms with everything that had recently been revealed to me during and after New Mexico. It was a chance to go back to the source of my tacit infrastructure and perhaps finally understand it.

I knew the trip would be a real eye-opener in more than one way. I had not been back to South Africa in almost forty years, not since 1973, when, as a confused, ashamed and disgusted boy of seventeen, I had run away. Over those forty years, the country had gone through incredible changes on all fronts, culminating in possibly the most profound change any country could possibly undergo. It now had a new constitution, a new national anthem, and a new national flag—a dramatic metamorphosis. To me, this was akin to a person having both a personality and body transplant and then also changing his or her name. I had no interest in politics *per se*, but the fact that apartheid was no longer the law of the land was good enough for me to consider returning. This was to be my return to my homeland.

I was going home, and I had questions. I vowed to hold my own personal version of the Truth and Reconciliation hearings. The Reverend

Desmond Tutu might not be presiding, but that didn't mean these "hearings" weren't important, at least to me.

I had made plans to go visit my mom in Israel before flying on to South Africa, and this in itself was gratifying. For some reason, perhaps mostly because something had changed in me, during this visit my relationship with the rest of the family shifted in a much more positive direction. I believe we all came to understand that, even though neither side could go all the way to embrace the other's perspective, we could all move toward the middle.

On March 10, I landed in South Africa, where my old friend met me at the airport. I guess Einstein had it right: time *is* relative. Many years had passed and we both had aged considerably, but relative to our friendship, time had not budged. We recognized each other immediately and within minutes we were giggling little boys again.

But that was the only thing that was the same. Everything else had changed—and drastically. As we drove to my friend's house in Johannesburg, I gaped out the car window. The sense I had looking out was similar to the feeling one gets when running into an adult that one has not seen since he or she was a young boy or girl. With the memory of the child firmly embedded in the brain, the sight of the adult can be startling, and the brain has a tough time adjusting. That's what happened to me and South Africa. The whole country had molted, exposing new skins. It started with the airport. When I was a boy, it had been named for Jan Smuts, an Afrikaner; now it was named for O.R. Tambo, founder of the African National Congress (ANC) Youth League and a compatriot of Nelson Mandela's. The next things that struck me were the infrastructural changes. I was amazed at how close the airport was to Johannesburg and how quickly we reached my friend's house. How could that be? The airport had not moved and certainly the city had not, either. Well, now we were speeding along at eighty miles per hour on freeways, not ambling along on single lane roads the way we had in the sixties and seventies.

As we approached my friend's neighborhood, another strange sight met my eyes. His house was totally surrounded by a high masonry fence topped off with two layers of barbed wire, giving the appearance of a compound. There were also cameras along the entire perimeter. Most houses we passed had a similar look. When I queried him about this, he told me in a very matter-of-fact tone that, in Johannesburg, it was not uncommon to get hi-jacked at gunpoint when arriving at or leaving one's home. In fact, this had happened to his wife on multiple occasions; hence, the heightened security. To me, living in an affluent neighborhood was not worth exposing one's family to that level of danger nor was it worth that kind of oppressive protection. My friend and his wife seemed to accept the situation as normal, however. It was just the cost of doing business, so to speak.

I spent ten wonderful days with my friend and his family, who were all exceptionally kind and hospitable towards me. During that time, we visited many of our old stomping grounds. We began with our middle school. The school had changed very little. In fact, as we entered, the headmistress happened to pass by and, incredibly, she recognized me. She, too, was an old classmate of mine. Seeing her as headmistress struck me as odd, but encouraging. Growing up, I had never seen women in positions of power. All my school principals had been male.

The experiences and sights of old were so familiar yet so distant that the overall effect was surreal. Typically, food was not an important factor in my life, but being back in South Africa, the place of my childhood, brought it to the forefront. I had to taste all the foods that I loved as a kid, especially those that were indigenous to South Africa: biltong, slupp chips, and chocolates. Biltong is made from beef or a variety of different kinds of wild game. It typically comes either sliced or in sticks about 12 x 3 x1 inches. The closest thing like it is beef jerky, but it is never as thin as beef jerky. It also does not taste at all like beef jerky. How could it? It is biltong!

One finds chips—or French fries as we call them in the United States—really all over the world, but they are nothing like South African slupp chips. *Slupp* in Afrikaans means droopy. Slupp chips are served

L-R: Benny, principal and me with a picture of "the boss" (my school principal) in the left background

with salt and vinegar—well, that is simply the best and tastiest config-
uration of a potato possible. What makes them slupp chips is that they
should be absolutely drowning in vinegar. I was delighted to find they
tasted the same as when I was a child. The only difference between the
chips I ate on this trip and those I ate as a kid was that they used to
be served in old newspapers. The newspaper thing was very important
because after eating the last chip, sucking the vinegar from the newspaper
was the "coup de grace." Eating slupp chips with the family was never as
satisfying as with my friends because I was not allowed to suck the vinegar from the newspaper. I never understood why. (I am sure the dirty old
newspapers, plus the ink and chemicals mixed in with the vinegar had
nothing to do with it!)

Finally, there were the chocolates. The supermarkets had entire isles
dedicated to chocolates and huge stands touting Cadburys slabs, exclusively. It was amazing to see and taste the broad variety of flavors.

One of the highlights of my stay in Johannesburg was the opportunity
to visit a private game reserve. When I was growing up, there were no
private reserves. Our family had gone to *the* game reserve, The Kruger
National Park. We would stay in straw thatched bungalows, sleeping in
something that only vaguely resembled a bed. Showers and bathrooms
were in a separate location across the campgrounds. It was as close to
living in the bush as one could get without actually living in the bush.

This time, we went in a group of seven, which was the perfect number
to fill up a jeep. When we arrived at the camp, we were shown to our
rooms. I was stunned by the opulence. In any city anywhere in the world,
these suites would be considered five-star accommodations. These were
certainly not the bungalows I remembered from my youth, not to mention
the fact that they were in complete contradiction to the surrounding bush.
Plus, I had a room by myself. Well, almost. A huge lizard was my roommate,
for a while anyway.

We ate first-class meals together on a huge patio overlooking the
bush. Many times, during dinner, we would hear the roar of lions or the

sounds of other animals close by, a thrilling experience. Then, one evening at dinner, another event took place that gave me food for thought—no pun intended (well, maybe). Dessert was being served, cake to be specific. Not paying close attention, I took a bite. As soon as the first morsel hit my tongue. I knew that taste. The taste was distinct and overpowering, but what was it? I had eaten this cake many times as a boy. I could not contain myself any longer and asked my friend if this cake had a name. "It certainly does," he answered. "It is called a Lamington Square."

Immediately, everything fell into place—my taste buds, brain, sense of smell and memory all agreed; this was my favorite cake as a child. After I had finished what seemed like my 500th piece, I got to thinking. What had just transpired was a great lesson in why it is so hard to let go of one's subconscious and tacit infrastructure. Traditions, attitudes, behaviors, places, events, tastes, everything from our early life are so firmly recorded, stored and ingrained in our very beings through our five senses that we simply *become* them. The simple smell and taste of a cake I had not seen or eaten in forty years were able to evoke the strongest of memories and very pleasant ones at that. They resonated with my nose, my taste buds, and my brain so fully that I did not want to let them go. If this cake and the memories it evoked were not part of my tacit infrastructure *per se*, then didn't they surely have to be, at a minimum, building blocks?

Every morning both before and after breakfast and for a third time at sundown, we would pile into the jeep and go out into the bush seeking wildlife. We saw a wide variety of animals. On one outing we came upon a couple of lions. Our guide stopped right next to them; they were on the side of the jeep I was sitting on. To say that I was uncomfortable is an understatement. If I had leaned over and stretched down enough, I would have easily been able to pet them. It did not take long before someone blurted out, "Let's move on, we have seen enough!" Guess which of the magnificent seven that was! Of course, I had not seen enough; but on the other hand, I also was not eager to become lunch.

The highlight of the trip came totally unexpectedly. One morning before breakfast we were privileged (or not) to witness a sight apparently so rare that our guide described it as a one-in–a-thousand chance. We had been driving around for a while in drizzling rain seeing nothing of interest, so we told our guide we wanted to return to camp. He agreed, and we began heading back. On the way, we encountered a herd of wildebeest. This was the most common animal in the area, and we had seen literally hundreds over the past two days. But for reasons not clear to me, our guide stopped and waited.

He must have had a deep intuition because we were all becoming irritated, wanting to get back. Suddenly a huge explosion of energy burst along the right side of the jeep. Out of nowhere, a cheetah leapt out of the long grass and at lightning speed began to chase the herd of wildebeests. Our driver hit the accelerator and followed right behind the cheetah in hot pursuit. The cheetah very quickly zeroed in on a calf that was running in the middle of the road directly in front of us. The herd dispersed and disappeared from sight. The only ones remaining in the picture were the calf being chased by the cheetah and us following a very close third.

One thing that was so incredible about all this was that this entire chase took place on the road, directly in front of the jeep. That poor calf was no match for the fastest animal on the planet and it did not take the cheetah long to bring it down. Our driver maneuvered the jeep within feet of the calf and cheetah, both seeming to be totally oblivious to our presence. We witnessed every detail of the kill. She grabbed the neck of the calf in her jaws, clamped down and asphyxiated it. There was no blood, and it was over in what seemed like seconds.

What followed was even more incredible. The cheetah abruptly left the kill, wandering back off into the grass on the other side of the jeep. That was very strange. Animals do not kill for sport; that is something only we humans seem to enjoy. Everyone in the jeep had a theory as to why the cheetah had left. Then, just as the debate was getting heated, the cheetah reemerged from the long grass followed by two of the cutest cubs. They

measured maybe eighteen inches in length and were not very tall. Mom
and her two cubs walked past the front of the jeep, back to the dead calf.

The mother stood watch, sitting up on her haunches surveying the
area while the cubs tried to chow down. They were desperately trying to
penetrate the skin, but no matter how hard they tried, they could not. It
seemed extremely odd to me that the mother never seemed threatened by
us, not even when she had returned with her cubs. I do not remember her
ever even looking at us. She only surveyed the grass for other predators.
The only thing I can think of is maybe her tacit infrastructure told her
she lived in a game preserve. Eventually, she went over to assist her cubs.

It was a very graphic display of how nature functions in the wild;
and as I watched, riveted, my emotions were running high. I felt sorry for
the calf and its mother, but also exhilarated from watching the kill. Then,
witnessing those young cubs trying to feed filled me with tenderness. We
remained at the kill site, observing, for at least an hour and then departed
for our not-so-well-earned breakfast.

Later, I would see those three days in the bush as being connected to
what I had experienced in New Mexico the previous summer. It did not
matter that the experiences had occurred on two different continents; the
language of Nature was universal. Chaos theory tells us that many things
that appear chaotic are part of a larger order, and this can generally only
be seen when the big picture ultimately reveals itself.

I was beginning to sense that what we had witnessed was a very com-
pressed example of this phenomenon. By far the most profound lesson
concerned my understanding of Nature. I had lived my life until recently
with the typical Westerner's arrogance toward Nature. I once viewed Life
and Nature as many Westerners do, as separate and necessarily so. To live,
to survive, we believed we had to separate ourselves from Nature, subdue
and dominate her. Then, at the dialogue, a new understanding had begun
to permeate. I began to see how Nature and Life were inextricably connected, interdependent. They are the "DNA" of our planet, intertwined in
a helix, co-creating and co-existing. And now, in the bush, this experience

Mother cheetah on the lookout while her cubs attempt to eat the fresh kill

showed me how full of meaning Nature really was. I saw why indigenous people view Nature as the Original Teacher. Nature teaches us to look beneath surface appearances to see the deeper meanings, the larger patterns. On the surface, it may look to us like Nature is about individual characters taking part in an often chaotic and sometimes cruel existence; but beneath that, there is One Whole. Every living animal and plant is an intrinsic part of that Whole; each has a purpose within the Whole, which it serves for the benefit of the Whole. This is the beauty and harmony of Nature: the perfect consonance of the parts. This is the heart of life, life's heartbeat. The mother cheetah rejoiced for her cubs while the mother wildebeest grieved for her calf. In these two different experiences, I saw the two halves of the Great Circle, Life and Death. In that instant, they came together, united, to make one complete Whole. Without the one, there could not be the other; both were essential.

That day, I knew I had been given a glimpse of the Ultimate Truth of Reality. It was there in Nature, if only we cared—or dared—to Listen. That day, I was able to Listen. I learned that if one Listens through the ear of Nature, one experiences, even above the noise of death, a sense of equanimity. I feel it now, pervading my being. One was not to be sad over the killing of the young Wildebeest for the calf had served its very important purpose and had moved on to its next experience. Furthermore, its death was not meaningless. It was not killed for the shallow thrill of sport; rather, its death was necessary, essential to the continuance of life. One did not need to mourn it, but one did need to pay respect to it, honor it and celebrate it for participating in the composite of the Whole.

And what of the mother of that wildebeest calf, she who was left behind? What was her experience? What would her life's purpose be after the death of her calf? Did she also learn this great lesson, I wondered, or did she already know it? Did she sense it instinctively? My guess is yes, definitely yes.

And with that, I knew I had to take the next logical step and pose a question to myself. But it wasn't just *a* question; it was *the* question—and

I didn't want to face it. In fact, I needed to coerce myself into addressing it. So, I did. I put myself in a corner from which there was no escape and posed the question I did not want to hear: *There is a lesson here relative to my journey and my grief for Ofir. What is it?*

I had forced myself to ask the question, so then I owed myself an answer. I came up with the following: I grieved deeply for Ofir, but the Whole of Nature, of Life, did not and could not. At that level, at the level of Nature, even Ofir's death was part of the Great Whole; and, perhaps, it had even been essential in a way that I, an all too fallible human, could not yet understand.

The second this thought formed in my mind, it took my breath away. Where had this thought come from? Surely it was not *mine*. I was not evolved enough to have such a thought; I was still immersed in pain and grief and anger. I still had a dark Beast hanging around my throat—not a merciful cheetah but something preternatural. No, no, this thought could not have been mine. It must have come from another source.

And then another thought came. As much as Nature was again rushing in to comfort me, this time by letting me know that Ofir's death served a spiritual purpose, it was also delivering a message. She was telling me that it was okay to grieve but that I, too, still had a purpose in Life. When I was ready, there was a task waiting for me. Within that vast, indeterminate and incomprehensible web of the Whole, there was something I needed to do for the benefit of the Whole.

But I wasn't ready yet. There were still more lessons to be learned.

> *The weak can never forgive.*
> *Forgiveness is the attribute of the strong.*
>
> —Mahatma Gandhi

15. Truth

THE DAY AFTER RETURNING from the game reserve, my friend drove me to my hometown, Kempton Park. To my surprise, I was able to navigate the town with ease; I knew my way around as if I had never left. Many of the landmarks were no longer present, but that did not matter; I was totally at "home." I write "home" in quotations because, although I grew up there, I have never considered South Africa home. Still my connection to Kempton Park was strong and I was eager to revisit it.

My dad's old pharmacy used to be located in the small downtown area, and I had fond memories of hanging out there and at the train station close by. It was a real treat for us brothers to get on a train and take a trip to the big city of Johannesburg, typically to see a movie and eat a Wimpy burger. But as we approached, it was clear that this area, which had meant so much to me in my childhood, was now nothing more than a neglected slum. The store still existed in some form, but I was not able to get out and investigate. My friend advised strongly against stopping "for any reason," so we quickly left. I returned from that outing very sad.

The next day, we headed out again, this time to view my boyhood home. I had to see it one last time. I had departed South Africa so abruptly, still a kid, closing the door behind me and never looking back. I had walked away from my family, my culture—my childhood. I longed for a sense of closure, and I thought that seeing the house, going into the house, one last time might give it to me.

Along the way, we passed by the former homes of all my buddies and relatives, and I realized that this area, too, had become rundown and poverty

CHILDHOOD HOME WITH MEN PLAYING DICE IN FOREGROUND

ridden. Finally, we came to a stop just outside 20 Bosch Street, where a group of Black African men were sitting on boxes on the lawn, playing dice and drinking.

Even though I had been born into the apartheid system and had never known anything else, I had been revolted by it as a kid. No matter what I was told, every cell in my being had told me it was wrong; humanity should not behave like that, casting out and abusing other human beings. Everything about it sickened me, and so I had escaped as soon as I was able. All that being true, because of what I was coming to understand as my tacit infrastructure, the sight of those African men on the lawn of "my" house was confusing to the senses. Not only had our neighborhood been all White when I was growing up, but every city and town was all White. The Blacks lived in what were called the "townships," which were nothing more than shantytowns, cauldrons of misery. Clearly my eyes and mind were observing through the lens of the child who had once played soccer on that very same lawn some forty-five years ago; and anger, sadness, and fear were taking over.

While all these thoughts and feelings were racing through me, I heard this faint voice in the background begging me not to get out of the car. I re-focused on my friend's face and heard him repeat his plea with a real look of concern in his eyes. He was reminding me of all the residual resentment and anger that Black Africans had towards Whites. Those feelings still ran extremely strong, resulting in many horrific acts of violence. My friend knew the reality of the situation, and he was genuinely concerned for my safety. He wanted us to leave, but it was way too late. The decision had been made. I was going in.

It was at this point that my symbolic Truth and Reconciliation process began. I tell the story now from two perspectives, as I experienced it in the moment and as a witness. I tell it like this because I feel it is the only way to do it justice.

From the outside, the house had not changed much. Nor had the landscaping changed, besides being somewhat neglected and overrun. I walked up to the group and, in a friendly manner, introduced myself and explained to them that I had grown up in that house. I received no response, only silence. *The perpetrator of the racist, oppressive and inhumane behaviors of the past is reaching out, but apparently the victims want no part of it.*

I tried to appear affable and confident, but I knew what a volatile situation this potentially was. I was on hyper-alert; and internal questions were coming faster than my ability to process them. *What are the victims thinking? Do they despise the perpetrator so much that his life is actually in danger? What did he ever do to cause them to hate him so—or is it enough that he is White?*

I stood looking at them, waiting. They did not meet my gaze, but only looked down or at each other. They went about their business, ignoring me. Minutes ticked by. I held my ground even as paranoia was running rampant through my mind.

Someone had to break the standoff.

In disbelief, I heard my own voice asking if it would be possible to walk through the house. *The perpetrator reached out for the second time. In so many words, he is saying, "Look, this used to be my house; but now it is in your hands, and rightfully so. I fully understand and accept that. Justice has been served. I am asking only that you allow me some closure in this way. Please acknowledge this need."*

My request was greeted with more silence, this time accompanied by an icy, angry, group stare-down. *The perpetrator's presence triggers memories of the pain, suffering, anger, and resentment of the past. The fierceness of those emotions is confusing and overwhelming to the entire group, who are victims of those crimes against humanity. This is why they have remained silent and defiant.*

As I awaited a response, a furious debate was taking place within me, as if there were two different people occupying the same body. One side was resolute about what had to be done, and the other was chastising the first, raising all kinds of questions and warnings: Are you nuts? Shut up and leave! What are you doing, idiot?

As the silence continued and the pressure built, my resolve began to falter. It was time to give up and return to the car, to concede that my friend was correct, that I had no business being there. *The vibration of suffering is so strong in the air that the perpetrator cannot hold the gaze. He has turned away and begun to disassociate from the situation. The perpetrator was just about to walk off when the victim takes a transcendent action.*

One of the men stood up and gestured for me to follow him. The tension in the air was palpable, but I had to see it through. I stepped over the threshold into my boyhood home. Inside, nothing felt the same. I was allowed to enter only the main rooms because the rest had all been rented out. It had been turned into a hostel of sorts. This was not a large house, but there must have been fifteen to twenty people living inside.

I knew I was not welcome, so I never paused and only spoke when spoken to. Very soon, I decided that I had gotten the most I could from the situation and that it was time to exit. I thanked everyone and quickly, very quickly, made my way back to the car. I jumped in and told my friend, "Drive, just drive." My heart and mind were racing faster than the car. *The process of healing is not an easy one, and the strong emotions resulting from a history of oppression are not going to evaporate in an instant. The perpetrator drives off feeling that he has done the right thing for himself and hopefully for the other, and that is all he can do. The victim feels. . .?*

We headed back to Johannesburg to make our last stop. My friend felt more comfortable about this destination, saying it was in a safer part of town, whatever that meant. By the time we got there, my breathing had finally returned to normal.

I saw that heavy security surrounded the building complex I planned to enter, but that didn't deter me from sneaking in. I knew exactly where I was going and how to get there. I was heading up to 301, the apartment our family had moved to when I was fifteen. I exited the elevator, walked to the end of the corridor, and knocked on the door. A young Colored teenage boy opened the door partway while his sister stood behind him, peering over his shoulder. They seemed to be alone with no adults present. I explained to them that I had lived in their apartment when I was their age, back when the dinosaurs still roamed the planet, and asked if it would be possible to do a walk through. Fully expecting to be rebuffed, I was pleasantly surprised to hear, "Come in," as the door opened wide.

They were both friendly and warm, talking in turns and showing a real interest in me. They also seemed very close to each other. When we passed what had been my bedroom, I stopped and pointed that out to them. The boy smiled and with much pride, informed me, "Now it is mine." Because of the way he said it, I felt like he was looking to bond with me, which touched me. I remember wondering how often they saw their parents. They seemed happy, yet very alone in the world and eager for outside company. I spent another ten or fifteen minutes chatting with them, then bade them goodbye. What a contrast this visit was compared to the previous! Those two kids left a strong impression on me. They were incredible beings, warm, smart, and projecting nothing but goodness. *Apparently, all hope is not lost. The new generation is receptive, welcoming the perpetrator with kindness and warmth. As he leaves the building, the perpetrator feels his guilt, fear, and shame lessen considerably. The future looks much brighter to him.*

Before returning to South Africa, I had made the decision not to contact any other old friends or even relatives. I had told my friend about this decision; and although he found it curious, he agreed to abide by it. But fate—or my guides—had other ideas. The day before I was to leave Johannesburg, my friend and I went out to do an errand at a nearby shopping center. On the way, he happened to mention that a friend of his worked in one of the shops. When he told me his name, I immediately recognized it. As kids, we had lived next door to each other! This was a small world, indeed.

Of course, once my friend learned this, he tried to convince me to go in and say hi, but I demurred. With my grief ever present, I just did not have the emotional energy to engage. Even at my host's home, I would often slip away to my room to be alone, not wanting to socialize. But my friend was

BROTHER AND SISTER NOW LIVING IN
MY OTHER CHILDHOOD HOME

insistent; and after much back and forth, I reluctantly agreed. I exited his vehicle and walked over to the shop where my ex-neighbor worked.

It actually felt good to see him. We reminisced for a while, and I was about to leave when he told me that a first cousin of mine worked right upstairs. Instantly, memories flooded in. When I was a kid, I had spent a lot of time with this cousin. Our two families had been very close, and we visited often, spending many weekends together. I thanked my old neighbor for the information but didn't intend to do anything with it; just hearing about him had been enough to fill me with emotion. Upon returning to the car, however, I made the mistake of telling my friend about my cousin; and of course, he tried to convince me to make contact. The more he pressed, the more irritated I got. He was beginning to feel like my dad, lecturing me on the rights and wrongs of proper social behavior. But the truth was he was a very warm and social man by nature, and he just could not understand my hesitation. "I have not seen him for forty years," I protested. "It can wait another forty." In response, he just glared at me intently, refusing to start the car. After five long minutes of this, I realized resistance was futile. I got out of the car, walked back to the building, climbed the stairs and went in to see my cousin.

The first moment we saw each other, we just stared. I think we were both in shock. He looked to me like a ghost, and I must have looked the same to him. We just stood gazing at each other. Finally, the spell broke and we embraced in a long, tight hug. This was too much for me, and I burst into tears.

Before Ofir's passing, I could be stoic in the face of almost any event, but that was no longer the case. Tears were always right beneath the surface, and any kind of emotional input could cause the floodgates to open. So, I shouldn't have been surprised that just seeing my cousin was sufficient to trigger a cascade of emotion. Still, something about it puzzled me.

My cousin did not cry, so I felt I needed to compose myself quickly. I did and apologized profusely. He assured me that he understood, and we then began chatting about our families. At some point, he mentioned that his mom, my dad's sister Bella, was in a home for seniors and suggested that we visit her later that day. This time, for whatever reason, I had no hesitation; I readily agreed.

When he picked me up later that afternoon to drive out to the home, my cousin warned me there was a good possibility that Bella, who was in her nineties, might not recognize me, but I knew otherwise. I just knew.

We arrived at the facility and walked through the dayroom, looking for her but not finding her. Finally, my cousin spotted her. She was sitting outside on the patio, staring off at the horizon. From inside, I regarded her closely. The look in her eyes told me that she was gazing out into the yonder beyond the yonder, into the great yonder with no name, way beyond anything the rest of us could see or understand. As crazy as this may sound, I knew she was already visiting the "other side."

I went out onto the patio and sat next to her, while my cousin drew up a chair on the opposite side. Sensing my presence, she slowly swiveled her head towards me. She gave me a puzzled, almost suspicious, look and immediately began babbling about inconsequential things. It suddenly occurred to me that the last time we had seen each other she had been my age now or a little younger. And then in that instant, I knew Bella was very close to crossing over to the next world. It was going to happen soon; I had no doubt. I felt it. I reached over and held her arm.

As soon as I touched her, her whole demeanor changed. The babbling slowed, and she became peaceful and quiet. I began to stroke her arm and soon we were meeting in that field that Rumi wrote about, the one I had experienced at the dialogue. My cousin is typically very talkative, but he did not speak for the entire visit. He simply observed. I think he too realized something very special and profound was taking place.

We did not stay long; we did not need to. Everything that needed to be communicated was; it had happened in a place beyond time and space. My cousin took a picture of us, I kissed Bella goodbye and left.

AUNTIE BELLA AND ME

Looking back, it has become abundantly obvious to me that the chain of events that brought me to my aunt could not have been merely coincidental. My newly evolving self was engaging in higher states of consciousness, listening deeply to guides. I may not have developed an intellectual understanding of the Ultimate Nature of Reality, but a part of me was participating in its Superstructure. What transpired between Bella and me is best explained by the email I sent my cousins the day after that visit.

March 30, 2011

    Me to cuzzins:

". . . We are ALL part of one another, and we will carry our common experiences for our entire lives and beyond. Aunty Bella confirmed that for me. Just in the same way that a very young baby recognizes its mother and always does, Bella in her deepest being felt me as I did her. The gifts that she gave me I will cherish forever and will carry with me for eternity. I could have walked away and felt that I had just spent time with a senile old lady who just blabbered on, BUT she made sure that I got the deeper message she was conveying to me, and I did. I almost felt like there were two separate entities that were addressing me. The here-and-now old lady and the deep, profound, all-knowing spirit that resides within the vessel we call Bella. She moved me deeply.

At times I felt that my Uncle Robert, my dad, Raymond and even my mom were present in Bella. The fact that I did not feel Ofir present tells me that the messages I was getting were for me, messages relating to my past and specifically to my childhood and, in some way, to how that past connects to my present and future, too. I must now go home and process all of this.

I will stay in touch and write again soon. I look forward to hearing from all of you. Be well. I wish you and your entire families health and happiness. I leave

    With a LOT of love in my heart,
    Pikkie

Pikkie is a nickname I was given as a young boy. I believe it to be an Afrikaans word. It is difficult to translate directly to English. It has multiple meanings but mostly little guy or inexperienced guy, which makes sense. I was the youngest cousin by many years.

In several loving and validating letters, my cousins let me know my visit with Aunt Bella, as shared in my email to them, touched them deeply; and it became clear that our cousin relationship had been not only renewed but strengthened and broadened.

And then, on April 28, 2011, after a life-altering, post-Johannesburg trip to Cape Town and my subsequent return home, I received the news that my Aunt Bella had passed on.

The emails continued.

April 28, 2011

> *To the entire Bookatz family,*
> *I just received the news from Norman regarding the passing of your beloved mother and our very dear family member, Bella. Please know I am thinking of all of you in this very difficult and sad time. I can only add how thankful and blessed I was to have been given the opportunity to spend the short time I did with Aunty Bella. Time IS an illusion because that short time to me was a lifetime. I carry Bella's spirit with me on my journey, as I know you all do. Be well, and you are all in my thoughts.*
> *Love,*
> *The Cheslers in the U.S.A.*

May 11, 2011

> *Hi Marty,*
> *Thank you for your beautiful email and your words of comfort. My mother loved you, Mart, and you gave her something very special when you visited her. It was almost the beginning of her journey into the past and into the next world . . . How are you doing and how are all your family??*
> *Sending lots of love,*
> *Your cuz, Norm xx*

May 11, 2011

> *Norma, hi,*

> *I am happy you brought up the subject of the "next world." I recently told Etya that when I was speaking to your mom, I felt like I was talking to pure spirit and that she had already transitioned.*

> *I know this sounds strange, but in my belief system this is very possible. I believe anyone can attain this state, but most don't because it is too difficult to let go of physical existence. Letting go does not mean to die (that is, to die physically), but only to quiet things down and recede into the field or void. I have attached an essay I wrote recently. This may help you to understand me and to what depth I was LISTENING when your mom spoke.*

> *I felt like your mom had accomplished this only because she was ready and totally willing to let go of this physical world. This is the second time in my life I have experienced this. I do have the ability to feel beyond what presents itself in front of me. This may not resonate with you, but the important thing is that your mom, my aunt, is at peace. We will all miss her physical presence dearly.*

> *My family is well, thanks. This is a difficult time for us. The fourteenth of May marks four years since Ofir's passing, and for us it seems like and will always be yesterday. It was also Mother's Day and that does not make it any easier on Rachel. The boys are fine. Tal just turned twenty-nine on Sunday and Daniel turns twenty-one in June. I am reading and writing a lot and attend many conferences on spirituality and the like. I hope all is well with you and your family. Please say hi to cuz Raymond.*

> *With gratitude, blessings and love,*
> *Your cuz, Martin*

Rest in Peace, Bella. And thank you for meeting me in that ineffable field of no language.

There is no easy walk to freedom anywhere, and many of us will have to pass through the valley of the shadow of death again and again before we reach the mountaintop of our desires.

—Nelson Mandela

16. Reconciliation

WHEN MY TIME IN JOHANNESBURG came to a close, my time in South Africa did not. I had wanted to visit more of the country and spend some time alone as well, so I flew on to Cape Town, which sits on the very bottom tip of Africa. I spent three days there, during which I had two incredible experiences. The first involved Robben Island in Table Bay. Robben Island has an infamous history going back centuries. It has been used as a leper colony and an animal quarantine station, but mainly as a prison. Many African political prisoners of the apartheid era were imprisoned on the island, the most famous being Nobel Prize laureate, Nelson Mandela. Now a tourist attraction, it has been kept much as it was when Nelson Mandela was imprisoned there at the hands of the apartheid regime.

After a journey by boat, I joined an organized tour of the island and prison. We visited the cell where Mandela spent eighteen years of his twenty-seven-year incarceration. I found it unimaginable that this man not only survived in such inhumane conditions but actually grew in resolve and character. It is beyond comprehension the pain, misery, and humiliation Mandela must have endured, not for personal gain but for an ideal, an ideal that should be the most basic of human rights. Each and every human being should have the right to equal treatment and equal justice, no matter . . . anything. No conditions or exceptions, none. What is it about humans that they resist this idea?

I remember standing on the ferry returning to the mainland and beaming with pride. I had just been afforded a rare opportunity to feel proud of being human. Nelson Mandela's struggle is a profound example

Robben Island as seen from the top of Table Mountain

Entrance to the jail on Robben Island

The cell where Nelson Mandela spent 18 years of his life

Solitary confinement cells on the Island

of the righteous and honorable prevailing over the most incredible evil, and I feel every child should take the trip to Robben Island for it represents the worst and the very best of the human spirit.

I remained standing on that deck all the way back till we docked, allowing the cold ocean air to penetrate my being. I felt so alive. Never before had I felt so strongly that *anything* was possible. What a message the avatar Nelson Mandela left us. Will we listen? Are we inspired? Are we paying attention? Rest in Peace, Nelson Mandela. May your spirit help humanity to evolve and adopt your essence as its own. God bless.

My second incredible experience in Cape Town took place on Table Mountain, the most recognizable landmark in the area, where it overlooks the bay and the city. It earned its name due to its top being as flat as a table. The mountain is truly majestic to behold; and when it is surrounded by clouds, it becomes an even more stunning sight. As far as I was concerned, however, the mountain did not exist only to be looked at and admired. It needed to be climbed. That's what the mountain wanted, and I was more than happy to answer the call.

I left the hotel early in the morning. I had arranged to be dropped off on the eastern side of the mountain at the Kirstenbosch National Botanical Garden. I walked through the gardens to reach the trailhead that led to the top. What a treat it was! I saw some of the most spectacular indigenous flowers I had ever seen, not the least of which was the Protea in all its varieties and colors. (The Protea is the national flower of South Africa and the nickname for the country's national cricket team.) I spent as much time as I could, admiring the beauty of the gardens, then continued to the trail.

The first portion of the hike was exciting as I had to climb ladders and rocks through some dense, green brush. The hike was very satisfying because of the diversity of both the plant life and the terrain along the way. The higher I got, the less green I encountered until the vegetation became quite sparse. About halfway up, as I stopped to eat a piece of fruit that I had brought along, a tsunami of sadness rushed over me and

I began weeping uncontrollably. It was so sudden that it caught me off guard. *What had triggered my grief?* I sat alone on that mountain asking to understand. And then it came. I was appealing to the Universe for one last time to hand me back my boy; or if not that, to please tell me where he was. I did not want to be on that mountain and I did not want to be looking for him, anymore. The task seemed impossible, and I was physically and emotionally spent. I just wanted to go home to my family, to all five of us.

After calming down, I tried to put things back into a more positive perspective and I arrived at the following thought: Maybe once again I was being guided. Maybe this was all a metaphor. Perhaps, standing alone on that huge mountain, I was being shown how small and insignificant I was. Maybe I needed a lesson in humility. Just as it took time and energy to reach the top of the mountain, the search for Ofir was proving no less demanding. I needed to take heart, remain focused, and have patience. Only with heart, focus, and patience would I be able to find Ofir.

I decided that this was an accurate assessment, and so I continued up the mountain with a renewed sense of purpose. At last, I reached the top, which sits about 3,500 feet above sea level. As advertised, the topography there was, indeed, very flat, just like a tabletop.

I was feeling great and began to think about my hike down the opposite side of the mountain. As I surveyed the situation before beginning my descent, I noticed that the trail was very different from the one I had ascended. In fact, the contrast was quite stunning. I had come up a trail initially lush with green shrubs and colorful flowers, but the trail down looked barren, very much like a desert.

Before I had started the hike, I had realized that the descent would need much more of my attention, so I had stopped at the cable car station to make inquiries about different trail possibilities, distances and the projected time the hike would take. Based on what I was told, I had gauged the amount of water to carry. Yet, being from a desert, I am always conscious of my water supply; and it was a very hot day, so I checked to make sure

I had enough water with me for the hike down the dry side and decided I did.

And so, I began the trek down. Almost immediately, I realized how vastly different things were on this side of the mountain, even more than I saw from the top. On the upward climb, the views had been pretty, but not all that special, so I did not stop much. But this side of the mountain owned truly spectacular views. One could see the entire bay and the ocean beyond. Robben Island was clearly visible, looking like a small boulder in the middle of the sea. The newly built soccer stadium, an amazing architectural achievement, was also distinct standing between the mountain and the bay. The stadium had seen much action in the 2010 Soccer World Cup; but from where I was standing it, appeared lonely and deserted, in need of some action.

There was an even more significant difference in the two sides of the mountain. Not only did this side feel like a desert, it *was* a desert. While I was hiking up, heat had never been an issue. During the descent, however, it was not only hot by the thermometer—and I know what hot is, having experienced summer temperatures in my home valley as high as 128 degrees in the shade—but the sun was beating down fiercely, adding reflective heat off the mountain. I knew that I was not a slow hiker, but I began to ration my water anyway.

The directions I'd received before starting down the mountain had told me I needed to make a left turn about an hour from the top. Because I was moving fast, I began looking for the turn forty-five minutes into my descent. Nothing. An hour came and went, and I had still not reached it. I knew that it was at least a half-hour from the turn to the bottom—if I ever found the turn. I was now running low on water, and I was beginning to become concerned.

I walked and walked, but still the turn did not come into view. Despite my rationing, I did not have much water left. Plus, I had not been drinking enough ever since I'd begun to ration it., and it amazed me how fast I was dehydrating.

RETURNING FROM ROBBEN ISLAND WITH TABLE MOUNTAIN
IN BACKGROUND

By the time I finally reached the turn I was completely out of water. This was nuts. I was always the one carrying extra water for others in the desert! How many times had I run into tourists who were ill-prepared for the desert heat and given *them* water! Clearly, I had not had nearly enough water with me to begin with. I had broken my own cardinal rule: never trust other people's judgments when it comes to decisions regarding safety. There are just too many variables involved. So now it was me who was desperately hoping to run into someone with water. Unfortunately, there was no one else around. I was alone. When I reached a point where I began to stumble I knew I was in deep trouble. At one point, I saw a cable car on its way down, and hoped that maybe someone would notice that I was struggling and send help.

I kept going until finally I saw two people hiking in my direction. Later I would learn that I was pretty close to the bottom by then, but it did not matter because now every step seemed like a mile. When I reached the other hikers, as thirsty as I was, I was feeling so ashamed that it was actually difficult for me to ask them for water. I could not believe how irresponsible and stupid I had been! Again, the messages of my youth showed up: there is only one right way and being wrong must be punished. Thirst won over, however, and I did ask for a drink. They handed me a full bottle. Water had never ever tasted so good. At least I still had the where-withal to understand that these guys were just starting out, so I did not drink too much, certainly not as much as I wanted or needed. Fifteen minutes later, I reached the bottom. People stared as I drank and poured bottle after bottle of water on myself.

A few days later, I was still processing the climb. I thought about how different the two sides of the mountain had been in almost every way— landscape, climate, and vistas. One side was cool, humid, and green with dense, abbreviated views of wide-open rolling hills, while the other side was hot, dry, and desolate, but with magnificent views of the ocean and city that went on and on. It struck me that even though these two climbs were extremely different, they had one element in common— the destination. *Two distinctly different routes led to the same destination.*

For a person who had been taught his whole life that there was only one right way, this was a truly remarkable revelation. And yet, there was no discounting it. A person climbing one side of the mountain could rightfully insist that the climb was easy because the trail was lush and green, the air cool and fresh, and for that reason they might look down on a person struggling to climb the other side. But then that second person could legitimately claim that the trail they were ascending was harsh and bleak, due to the excessive heat and desert environment. Both were right. Furthermore, both might tend to be righteous about how right they each were without ever seeing the Ultimate Truth—which was that they both were right. And that the route didn't matter; what mattered was the destination. And that was the same for everyone.

This metaphor seemed to apply to almost everything but most of all to religion. How many wars have been fought to prove that one way up the mountain is better than another? The toll has been staggering. One day, when we all reach the top, we will see that we were all talking about the same destination and that our journeys, though so very different in every way, were irrelevant in their differences. We were all correct. Our understandings of God or Source or Spirit and our practices in honoring Him or Her or It were only concepts, just ideas. The spiritual paths represented something so much greater, which in the end analysis belonged to all of us. How ignorant and sad that we fight over something that we actually agree on. If only we could see the big picture or more accurately the whole picture!

The hike had humbled me, and it had also brought me greater awareness for which I felt very grateful. I felt I had been given another glimpse of the Ultimate Nature of Reality. What I saw was that It was Oneness and Multiplicity both.

I had been raised in a paradigm of dualities set in opposition to each other with one becoming so rabidly authoritarian that it almost extinguished the other but for the flame nurtured by valiant spirits like Mandela. Then I saw that version of reality—that story of duality—was an illusion, a smokescreen, a lie. And it was a crafty lie. It had many disguises and lurked everywhere, not just in South Africa. Most often, it disguised itself as "The Truth" and invoked religion to rationalize and legitimize the hateful acts committed in its name. But I was on to it now. Because of Table Mountain, I had seen through to the core, and I would not forget. That mountain taught me more about life, human nature and self than I could ever have learned in any of our academic institutions.

I needed time alone to digest everything that had happened, so for the last part of my trip, I planned to follow the Garden Route, a drive along the coast that extends for hundreds of miles. I spent seven days on that road, and because I zig-zagged all over the coastline, I drove close to a thousand miles. My days were long and full of activity, and the trip was spectacular in every way, rich in scenery, views, towns, activities, and animals, and more. I hiked every day, to waterfalls, over a suspension bridge crossing a sliver of ocean and along many other trails following the coastline. In Tsitsikamma, I canoed across a portion of ocean to the mouth of the Storm River. I had with me an inflatable Li Lo, which was nothing more than a pool air mattress. Once I reached the river I hiked upstream with the Li Lo, inflated it, and drifted lazily back downriver to the kayak. Before leaving I deflated the Li Lo, put my safety jacket back on, and kayaked back across the ocean to where my car was. I visited ostrich, crocodile, and wildcat zoos and farms and toured the Cango caves in Oudtshoorn. These caves are spectacular with fascinating limestone formations in a variety of colors. On one of my hikes, I was surprised to find the Spathiphyllum (Peace Lily) plant, growing wild. It's a common houseplant back in the United States, but I had never realized it was native to South Africa. I hiked among these "houseplants" for quite a distance.

None of my days were planned, but there was never a dull moment. I slept in places of all shapes and sizes, varying from nice bed and breakfasts to austere youth hostels, whatever was available. Most days I would leave at six o'clock in the morning and not find a place to sleep till eleven

CANOEING OVER OCEAN TO STORM RIVER

On Li-Lo cruising down the Storm River

o'clock at night. My only companions were two songs that played multiple times a day on the radio, "S&M" by Rihanna and "Price Tag" by Jessie J.

During that final week I spent traveling alone, I did my best to make peace with the country of my birth. I visited and paid homage to some of her most beautiful and exciting places. In return, I was hosted with acceptance and kind hospitality. On the seventh day, I arrived in Port Elizabeth and boarded a plane for Johannesburg. The next day, I left South Africa for the long plane ride back to the USA.

As we took wing, I looked down, watching the land mass recede into the distance, I once again felt reflective. It had taken me almost forty years to do so, but I was flying home feeling that I had finally created some closure for myself around the early chapter of my life. Even though I was still not at peace with myself, I felt I was at peace with South Africa; I felt I had forgiven her. South Africa was no longer my home, but I left this time with a sense of pride, respect, and admiration for her. I believed that, as a country, despite her ongoing problems, she has made the right choices. At the same time, I imagined that it would take me months— maybe years—to process everything I had learned from returning to the crucible of South Africa, the place that forged me. It was probably only through the medium of time that I would be able to piece it all together. Maybe that is how it is for all of us: the past undresses slowly; she only reveals herself over time, and one's life is only understood in rear view mirrors even though you have to live it face-forward.

There can be no keener revelation
of a society's soul than the way in
which it treats its children.

—Nelson Mandela

17. Apartheid of the Mind

L ULLED INTO A REVERIE by the drone of the engines and with many empty hours to fill, I began to look back.

In the beginning of my journey, as I had come to think of it, I thought this was to be an intellectual journey, so I turned to science—to quantum physics, specifically—which then led me to an exploration of the nature of consciousness. Consciousness still seemed key to my search, and this had provoked a curiosity about my own consciousness. Then, by chance or, more likely, by synchronicity, I'd encountered events, situations, and ideas that intrigued and humbled me and made me question my deepest convictions. I'd felt the interconnectedness of all things and even embraced the idea of being guided, which made me see my intuition and so-called impetuousness in a whole new way.

As far as consciousness went, I'd been shown that we all possess a tacit infrastructure, an internal web of beliefs and assumptions that shape what we perceive and how we think and act. It was in New Mexico that I was first introduced to this idea. In preparation for participating in an intercultural dialogue, we'd been asked to set our tacit infrastructures aside so that Spirit might move through us. I'd found the former challenging because I wasn't quite sure what a tacit infrastructure was, let alone what mine might be. As far as Spirit was concerned, well, I never got that far.

Somewhere along the way, I had begun to realize that Ofir was sending me messages like a homing beacon, but my head was so full of noise that I couldn't hear them. That's when I began to understand that *I needed to change, that I needed to function differently*; I just wasn't sure how. To my amazement, no sooner had I realized this than I was called back to South Africa, to the country of my birth, to the culture and experiences that had shaped me, to the very source of my tacit infrastructure.

My experiences there had been profound, but what did they mean for my journey? That's what I was struggling with on my flight home. It felt like I had a lot of the pieces, but I couldn't figure out how they all fit together.

I'd been following this train of thought when I noticed a shift in the way the plane was navigating through the skies. Over the open sea, we'd entered into some choppy air, just enough to feel some invisible bumps. In that moment, every ounce of energy seemed to drain out of me, and I was overcome with exhaustion. I'd slumped in my seat, lulled by the drone of the engines and the rhythmic rocking. Closing my eyes once more, I gave in to fatigue and to a waiting dream.

As I drifted into a deep sleep, a vivid image began to take form. I see myself back in my mother's womb. I can even feel myself floating, weightless and buoyant, in a sac of warm fluid. There, in a state of joyful freedom, I alternate between drifting and conducting a multitude of graceful aerobatic airplane maneuvers: rolls, somersaults, lazy 8's, Immelmans, Lomcovaks. Safe and cozy, I waft, blissfully oblivious to my being on the verge of entering into a completely different world, the next stop on my soul's journey.

Then, suddenly, that other world appears before me and I feel apprehensive. My fluid world is without restriction, but things seem very different in the world I am about to enter. For one, in the next world there is something called "time," and it is time now for me to transition from my watery cocoon into that next world.

My arrival is greeted with much excitement, and I see many smiling faces looking at me, all of whom I recognize as family and friends. I am the object of much attention and am rarely left alone because the physical vessel that houses my spirit being is actually quite fragile. My womb world is gone now, and without its protection, I am vulnerable and helpless.

The attention and care given to me is most welcome, and it continues unabated throughout my infancy. I am grateful and yet, even in my very immature state, I sense that something is missing. Only now do I see: my physical vessel is being nurtured, but little regard is being given to the soul inside.

Sadly, due to abject neglect, my spirit begins to fade away. By age seven or eight, the memories of my time in the womb have all but disappeared into an ocean of darkness. I have forgotten almost everything, and anything I haven't completely forgotten is relegated to the bone yard of my subconscious. Occasionally, memories surface, but those are only vague, dreamlike fragments. They are not given any credence.

My life suddenly fast-forwards, and I see that I am a youth now; and throughout this also vulnerable period, the objective is to program my malleable brain and discipline my body so that I will become a productive member of society. I am being conditioned to fit without resistance or question into the system.

I am a good student. Quickly, I absorb the lessons from what I see and experience. The essence of life here is conflict, opposition, duality; it is always something versus something else. For the most part, there is no flow, no natural way of being as in my watery world, only harsh, deterministic choices. I learn that everything in South African life is to be separated and put into categories arranged in a strict hierarchy of value, the parameters of which never waver. In this system, everything is divided into black or white, with no shades of grey. "White" means good, better than, and privileged; "Black" means bad, worse than, and non-deserving. All this is decreed with no room for free voice or free choice.

My education continues, unrelenting. There are many rules and regulations and the overarching message is that there is one—and only one—right way. Nothing else is tolerated. Misdeeds or mistakes are inexcusable and are immediately followed by punishment with little heed to compassion and forgiveness.

Embedded within this message are other, more subtle messages. And within these are even subtler messages. Like Russian dolls, the messages go on and on until they become so subtle they are virtually impossible to discern. And yet, all that delicacy is surprisingly effective. The messages are evil; the methods of inculcation, barely perceptible; and the combination is so ruthless and efficient that without much trouble the entire infrastructure succeeds in embedding itself in my being without my having any idea that it is so.

As I look on both in awe and disgust, I see now how it was, how those at the top deployed many very powerful tools, not the least of which was religion, to control our society. Rationality dominates society at the expense of spirituality. It is revered like a God. What feeds the rational mind is knowledge—but only of a certain kind. For facts that bolster its foreordained conclusions, it has a ferocious appetite and its reservoirs seem limitless in capacity.

And who is at the top of this hierarchy? Who is carrying out all this control, enforcing these punishments on a day-to-day basis? *White Males*, always white males, and only white males. White males are the biggest of the dolls. They are the ones who hold all the power in society; they are the ones in control. The next smaller doll goes by the name of White Woman. But even that doll (only one tiny, doll-size down from that of the white male) represents weakness. Outside of motherhood, I am taught, women are basically irrelevant.

The dream fast forwards again and I see myself now as a young man, one of many. We have all been primed to achieve success in the material world, our one and only purpose. We emerge from our conditioning a tight-knit club of fellow gladiators, our thinking and behaviors governed by a myriad of rules. I, too, think I am a strong man, fully in control of his life. That is what defines me.

The brainwashing is now complete. And yet, even as I recognize myself as this confident, young warrior, I know it is not the complete truth. All the while a feeling of alienation has been slowly infiltrating my psyche. I watch it growing stronger with each passing year. I still follow the rules, but I am becoming increasingly angry, anti-social, and isolated.

As we want to do in dreams, I observe myself all the while becoming more and more agitated. How far removed I am from that free soul in the womb! My soul has been systematically hijacked, pushed farther and farther into the background, replaced by something I have learned to tolerate, but *it does not feel right*. In fact, it hurts. Like hell. Was that why I hit a breaking point when, at seventeen, fighting back feelings of utter helplessness and not knowing what else to do, I chose to run away? Then another realization hits—here I am thirty-seven years later, and I am still running.

I awoke with a start, bathed in a cold, clammy sweat. Feeling some-what dizzy from the intensity of the dream, I stabbed at the stewardess's call button and requested a cup of coffee. I sipped the hot, bitter liquid and tried to get a handle on my nerves. I wasn't just suspended in a jetliner over a vast ocean, I was at sea in every way, and I shook with frustration and rage.

Fully roused, I began to dissect the dream.

And then I saw. I had graduated summa cum laude from that system and entered adulthood believing that I was free, independent, and in total control, but I was not. The apartheid system is widely understood to be a political system, a form of social organization only. But nothing could be further from the truth; it is much more than that. Apartheid is a cancer; it spreads and metastasizes until the mind is subsumed into its order, until one sees *life itself* as black versus white. This is what had been imprinted on my young, still-forming mind. I had become not just the child of a racist regime but a product of something even more insidious; I had become the child of an *apartheid of the mind*.

Staring out the window at the deep blue sky all the way down to the falling horizon, I came to an even darker realization. I had been given a cell just like those on Robben Island, where South Africa incarcerated Nelson Mandela and its other political prisoners. The only difference was that my cell was *inside me*. I was still confined in that little cell. It was holding me constricted, and I didn't know how to break free. Perhaps that was why at certain times throughout my life I had inexplicably broken down and wept. Thankfully, it only happened when I was alone, but it embarrassed me, and I never understood it. Now, at last, perhaps I did. Perhaps I was finally beginning to see how all this had shaped me, how it had taught me to see the world. Yes, it had paved the way for me to attain a certain degree of material success, but at what cost? What it hadn't done was nurture me. It hadn't ever allowed me to be my true self—whoever that was.

And then I realized something else, even more profound. Despite all that relentless conditioning, there was *a part of me* that did not succumb. All those years, I had had no conscious awareness of it, but the pilot light of my spirit had still been lit, flickering in all that darkness. Even though there was every reason that it should have been extinguished, every reason that it should have given in and given up, it was still glowing, still glowing despite my early conditioning and the roaring cyclones, volcanic eruptions and earthquakes that so often constituted the daily phenomena of my inner being after Ofir's death. Through all, it kept casting light out to me. I just couldn't see it. Now, perhaps I could.

At last, I was standing face to face with the nuts and bolts that held my tacit infrastructure in place. For the first time in my life I was seeing myself with a clarity I had never imagined possible. As shocking as all the revelations were, if I wanted to take the next giant leap in my journey I had to address them head on. I sensed this was the only way to find Ofir.

Sitting back in my seat at 40,000 ft., racing through the razor-thin air at 450 knots, I wept. No, I howled. I silently keened for all my losses. And yet, while I mourned and paid respects to all those losses, another part of me welcomed the new me into the world.

I landed at LAX on March 31, 2011 with much to process.

❖

Who seeks shall find.

—Sophocles

18. The Ride

No matter where one might be driving in our valley during the fall, winter, or spring, there they were. Bicyclists were so numerous, that they just became a part of the landscape, their bright, multi-hued shirts infusing the scenery with splotches of audacious color. It was rare to see a cyclist laboring in the oppressive heat of summer; but when one did, their attire really popped against the neutral desert hues of brown, tan, and grey. I had never paid attention to them before. Now, though, I found myself noticing, watching intently. Something was stirring.

Since my return from South Africa, a lot was happening inside. I wasn't entirely sure what it was, but it felt like my tacit infrastructure was actually getting re-arranged, Big Time.

I'd come to think of myself as being a little like a caterpillar in a chrysalis. Sometimes it felt like my inner being was undergoing so much change so very rapidly that something new and different was about to burst forth; sometimes I even felt I could sense some microscopic tears in the chrysalis. Externally, however, I was still struggling with the grief. Even though I knew I had made significant progress on my journey, I could rarely feel at peace. Especially when I was alone—and I was alone a lot—my sadness and pain would take over, overwhelming me all over again. And whenever my emotions ran amok, they ran the show and whatever progress I was making on the inside came to a grinding halt. I needed something to take my mind off the grief, and history was telling me that strenuous physical exertion would help. Maybe I needed to try cycling.

The minute the thought occurred, I went into action. In the late spring of 2011, I purchased a bike. I was thinking that cycling would supplement my hiking; but after just a couple of rides, it became evident that it was going to become much more than that; this was a physical activity I could really bury myself in. Biking was way more physical, even "macho," in its nature than I'd ever thought. Once I experienced that, I knew I was onto something. Over time, I had begun to realize that physical pain was infinitely more bearable to me than the searing emotional pain that was my companion. In fact, if I pushed myself enough physically, I no longer felt the emotional pain. Biking offered that escape, so it quickly became my new obsession. I liked the hard, tarred surface; the maneuvering, the dodging and, frankly, the play with traffic. Sometimes I would feel metal graze my arm or leg. The element of danger attracted me; it made me feel alive in ways I could not otherwise.

My initial rides were not long at all, and before I could attempt longer distances, the summer heat was upon us. I waited it out and the minute the temperatures began to drop, I took back to the road. By December I had managed to work my rides up to about seventy miles. This was the month of Ofir's birthday, so I decided I would attempt my first century (100-mile) ride in his honor. On December 18, 2011, which would have been Ofir's 27th birthday, I set out.

It was a cloudy, cool day, perfect for cycling. I rode for hours thinking of and at times talking to Ofir. Things were going really well until, at mile eighty, I began to struggle. I pushed through. Then, with only five more miles to go, I hit another wall; the ride became intolerable. Then, just as I was about to drop, the clouds suddenly opened up and the sun appeared for the first time. I took this as a sign that Ofir was gazing down, encouraging me through those final miles. I know that sometimes we want something to be true so much that we fool ourselves, but I did not care. I just knew it was Ofir, and I had to tell him I knew. The following day, I wrote him a letter:

December 19, 2011

   Ofir hi,

*What a birthday we had yesterday! I decided to do a 100-mile bike
ride in your honor. You were with me all the way. Without you I would
never have made it. So many times, I wanted to quit, but you kept me
going. Going down Dillon Rd. towards HWY 62 was very tough. It was
cold, windy, and wet but you pushed me on. It was so special on mile
ninety-five when I felt like I had nothing left in my legs and suddenly the
sun came out for the first time all day and smiled at me. I felt like it was
YOU smiling and encouraging me on. Suddenly and miraculously the last
four miles were not tough anymore. Even though it is my goal to honor
you each and every day, I will try and do something special and maybe
even extreme in your honor every year on your birthday.*

   *I am still reading and writing. I write essays and poetry. I continue
to journey and walk the path. You are never far from me and I know it
is you who is guiding me.*

   *Over the past year I have been given back the gift of gratitude. I am
grateful for many things, especially for all the lessons you have bestowed
on me. I have so much more clarity now and understand that control
is an illusion; I have become accepting of the flux of the universe and
embrace all that is. Even though my ego mind tries to retain control
through the illusion that it grants me control, I now know better. Now,
my heart center leads, so my journey is authentic and with deep meaning.
I continue on with you in my heart and for that I am grateful. Miss you
so much, each and every day. You are in my essays, poetry and everywhere
I journey.*

   LOVE,
   Dad

Shortly thereafter, I became friends with a woman who was an avid
and experienced bike rider. She encouraged my enthusiasm for cycling

and one day told me that she had a video she wanted me to watch; it was about a bicycle race across America. That did not compute in my mind, so I blurted out that riding a bicycle across America was impossible. She assured me that nothing could be further from the truth. As evidence, she showed me not one, but two, documentaries. The first was about professional riders and the second about an amateur, a regular Joe, who had biked across America.

With that, the wheels of my mind began to spin. I started thinking that maybe I wanted to try a cross-country ride. It wasn't long before I decided to do it. The truth is, I didn't have a choice. The grief was still so overwhelming that my inner process had come to a standstill; I could feel it, stagnant. My only hope was to take to the road. I hoped that the physical beating of a 3000-mile bike ride would distract my emotions enough that whatever had been happening on the inside could pick up and continue.

Either that or it would kill me.

Over the next few days I made my preparations. I purchased items I needed: a tent, a sleeping bag, gloves, a cooking stove and warm riding wear. I organized my trip into seven maps, which I enlarged and divided into 107 pages, each one representing one leg. I attached a phone and map holder to the frame of the bike. I made sure I had adequate reflectors on my helmet and shoes and added two red, blinking hazard lights to the rear of the bike. Most importantly, I installed a set-up to hold a flag with Ofir's picture on it. I would not be doing this ride alone; I was going to do it with Ofir. I knew that it was only by his grace and wisdom that I could possibly make it to the East Coast. It was Ofir's job to guide and protect us. I figured I had the easier job, just peddle and not stop peddling until the ocean, hopefully, the Atlantic, appeared before us.

I knew nothing about bike maintenance and repair, so I went down to our local bike shop and paid one of the kids who worked there to show me how to patch inner tubes and make other general repairs. Lastly, I packed up my saddlebags. When everything was said and done, the bags weighed in at about sixty pounds.

Finally, I was all set and ready. On the night before liftoff, I lay in bed in a motel in San Diego with a thousand questions and self-judgments circulating through my head: *What in the world are you thinking? No way you should be doing this. You have minimal experience, having only been riding a little over a year. You have never even changed a flat tire! You are doing this totally unsupported—you are going to ride a bicycle 3,000 miles. . .for what?* I wondered if my grief had finally driven my sanity to the brink.

In the end, though, I figured my guides were behind this. I told myself, very unconvincingly, to trust them. In return, I was told that I would be 100% safe. With that, I let go.

Before drifting off to sleep, I looked one last time at my bike standing against the wall. What a sight it was! On the rear of the bike were three saddlebags; on top of them, the tent and sleeping bag, two red lights and the flag. On the center of the bike, attached to the frame, were three water bottles. And, finally, on the front attached to the handlebars, were my phone, light, and maps for the first day's ride. It was a very intimidating sight indeed. Once more, the head games took over. I was feeling so alone and wondering if I had finally bitten off more than I could chew. Eventually, exhaustion won over. I drifted off, but that night's sleep was anything but peaceful.

Early the next morning, we set out. The first three days of riding went well, and we covered 250 miles. On the fourth day, I hoped to make a 120-mile ride from Blythe, California to Wickenburg, Arizona. I was feeling strong but nervous because this was to be the longest day's ride I had ever attempted. I left Blythe at 6:00 a.m. with Ofir riding shotgun, and we rode into Wickenburg at 7:00 p.m. I was feeling physically tired, but mentally strong. The next day we made it to Apache Junction, 101 miles away.

The following day, while biking the leg that would take us from Apache Junction to Globe, Arizona, I saw what looked like a fairly steep

Bike in motel room in San Diego on the night before "The Ride"

climb coming up ahead, so I stopped at a little store conveniently located at the base to stock up on liquids. On my way back to the bike, a lady stopped me, pointed to the winding road in the distance and asked in all probability, rhetorically, "You're not climbing that on a bicycle, are you?" I very nonchalantly answered, "Yes." She frowned and did not say another word, but as she walked off her body language was screaming back at me, "You are nuts!"

I did not take her question seriously, thinking it stupid and uninformed. I had climbed many a steep grade up to that point and, as far as I was concerned, this was just one more. I did not know who the real uninformed, stupid person was until I actually began the climb.

The first hint of danger lay in the degree to which the road was both narrow and precipitous. I ignored this and kept climbing. It was soon thereafter that the full reality of the terrible conditions facing us became abundantly clear. There was no bike lane, no shoulder, and the stream of traffic, mostly large trucks, whizzed by, non-stop. The trucks were so close that each time one passed, I could taste their metal in my mouth as the cold steel shot by, nearly grazing my body. Now add to the mix that most of the weight was on the back of the bike. As a consequence, on a steep climb like this, the front wheel was barely making contact with the road. This made steering extremely unresponsive, close to impossible. I was soon convinced this would be my last day on Earth.

And yet, after what seemed like an eternity and having cheated death hundreds of times, we made it to our next destination. That night, I made a vow. Having survived a day that defied all the laws of physics, let alone common sense, I decided that I owed it to Ofir and my guide to finish the ride all the way to the Atlantic. Anything less would be completely unacceptable.

That night, I took out my maps and began to study them again. The route ahead was to take us through the rest of Arizona and into New Mexico, then through Texas, Louisiana, Mississippi, and Alabama, and finally across Florida to the Atlantic. Yes, I could do this. I did my nightly preparations, got into bed and in the morning set off again.

I got into a rhythm, a kind of routine. I would leave before sunup every morning and arrive at our destination around nightfall, sometimes as early as 4:00 p.m., sometimes as late as 9:00 p.m., but always within that window. For all intents and purposes, I was alone with Ofir and my guide. I made no effort to meet or talk to people, but some approached us; and the ones who did were very kind and helpful. The weather for the most part was good with only a few days of rain and cold, and the sunrises and sunsets were spectacular.

Each evening, as I prepped for the following day, it always surprised me how much time it took. The first order of business was to find food, which was time consuming depending upon how far I had to cycle to find a restaurant or convenience store. Food had become a priority only after I discovered how oblivious I actually was to food and nutrition on the day I fell off my bike and was forced to take a day off to rest my leg. That day was the first time I paid any attention to my physical condition. Standing naked in front of a full-length mirror, checking for bruises, I was shocked to see how much weight I had lost and how gaunt my face looked. Only then did my brain and stomach begin to communicate, and an overwhelming hunger kicked in. Suffice it to say that I consumed more food that day than a 1,000-pound gorilla, and I resolved to double my daily caloric intake. So that, too, became part of my routine.

Every second night after dinner I did laundry, charged all batteries, studied the maps, performed any necessary maintenance on the bike and unpacked and re-packed my saddlebags. Sometimes this ritual would take hours, but that didn't matter. It comforted me.

It seemed like I had just settled into that routine when the trip began to change. It started with the smallest of things. For some odd reason, I began paying attention to the names on the different street signs I encountered. I remember seeing one with my mother's name on it. Then, when I spotted a street named Argyle, I slammed on the breaks. I got off my bike

Lunchbreak on the road

and went over to inspect it more closely. Why, I'm not sure; but by the time I got back on my bike, the decision was made. My guide finally had a name, Argyle. Why Argyle? I don't know; ask Argyle.

Soon thereafter, I crossed the border into Texas. Something about riding through Texas reached me on another level. I couldn't put my finger on the change and it puzzled me.

My last two days in Texas were spent riding through the Sam Houston National Forest. It seemed to go on forever. I learned later that the forest was, in fact, immense, covering 160,000 acres and extending over three counties. Being the only human for miles around, save the occasional passing car, I began to feel not only surrounded by the forest, but absorbed by it. Soon, I got the eerie feeling that the animals in the forest were not merely observing me from behind the tree lines on either side of the road but were staring at me intently. They, for sure, were the guardians of the forest. No way was I messing with them. Then, at other times I would listen to the beautiful sounds of the forest. It seemed to be one giant symphony playing music while all the trees and shrubs danced along.

Listening to the pines, to the landscape and the animal life gave me a profound sense of its majestic power and beauty. I say "its" singular because the forest was one. I knew that each tree was not just an independent organism, that it was also interconnected with all the other organisms in that entire forest. *Everything* in that forest was connected, which gave the forest great power. This insight reinforced my previous sense that everything in the universe was connected; the forest was simply a small section of that larger hologram. Not only that, but the forest was profoundly *alive*. Not for the obvious reason that it was made up of organic matter, but because I saw and felt it as a being of sorts. I could feel its heartbeat vibrating; I could listen to its intelligent brain communicating with me; I could almost see the blood flowing through the various veins and arteries. Finally, I could see the intricate web that was its nervous system. I felt a part of my surroundings but with the clear understanding that it was I who was being graciously hosted by the flora and fauna; it was by no means the other way around. I would not have dared to break a live branch, cut a leaf or pick a flower for fear of causing the forest to feel pain or to bleed. Knowing how it was watching me, I was respectful in my thoughts and behaviors. Not for a second did I place a higher value on my life. I knew that the forest was as intelligent as I, if not more so. I was not more evolved than it; nor it, me. We were just components of a much greater whole, a whole that I was not able to describe but felt. This might sound nuts to some, but the truth is I had never felt anything so strongly. I can still feel it now.

Those two days in the forest alone left a profound impression on me. I had fallen through a rabbit hole and landed in a world that, though it looked familiar, was vastly different from anything that I had ever known. Another metaphor to describe what took place between the forest and me I take from the movie *Avatar*. In the same way that the Navi people would hook their own tails to their horse's tails, allowing their consciousness to merge into one, so it was with the forest and me. We had merged into one consciousness, one thought, one knowing, and we were able to do it by "wi-fi," not needing tails or any kind of hard wiring.

I reflected on what I had learned at the dialogue in New Mexico: Western culture is organized around the concept of time while indigenous cultures are based in place with a deep connection with the land. In Australia, the Aboriginals do a walkabout along ancient songlines remembering how their ancestors emerged from the Earth to form the landscape. Each verse of a song belongs to a certain area or place. Had I just heard the songline of the forest? Had it heard me back?

I soon crossed the border into Louisiana and entered yet another world, another subset of a greater whole. As the miles rolled by, I realized that I was feeling very different things from what I had experienced while riding through Texas. While in Texas, I could not help but feel a very strong, forceful energy emanating from the land. The feeling was palpable, even overpowering at times. The areas I was passing through in Louisiana, though, seemed to hold a very different energy. The energy there felt subtle, soft, welcoming, and beautiful.

It felt feminine.

Feminine? Where in the world had *that* come from? I tried to get my head around it. Where had the idea of land having energy come from? And even more bizarre, why was I sensing feminine energy and why did it feel so different, so much better? And why was I even thinking in terms of masculine and feminine energy?

Confused, I pushed on in my usual way, punishing my body. Then, an answer started to come. It was because I, too, possessed feminine energy. That's why I was able to recognize it—because it was within me, too. In perplexed disbelief, I pondered this idea. Could this possibly be true? The idea, as uncomfortable as it was, was strangely persistent, gradually embedding itself in my mind.

Pedaling furiously now, I continued to explore the unfamiliar thoughts that were now bubbling up, no, gushing up, as if I had just pried the lid off something. Was it possible that humans were born with both types of energy? If so, then I, too, was born with both. But if that was so, then what happened to my feminine energy? Masculine energy was all I had ever known how to express: be strong, dominating, rigid and power-ful to the point of being overwhelming. Was it possible that I had actually emerged from the womb with a certain amount of feminine energy, but something had happened that caused me to suppress it?

I was having flashbacks now of South Africa, of authority figures, of beatings and canings. I pushed those painful images down and forged on, taking the grandest of leaps: if the feminine/masculine energy concept was real, then was it somehow connected to my journey? Was it at all possible that, in order to find Ofir and the Ultimate Truth, I had to allow both these energies to work in my life? I felt I already knew the answer. This was *definitely* a possibility because over the past four years my hard-ened, aggressive, masculine, outer shell was being slowly and systematically sandblasted away, revealing something much, much softer within me. Something I could now only describe as *feminine*. This, too, was me—my inner feminine.

These thoughts were incredibly bizarre sounding to my rational mind; yet, they felt like truth. Somehow, through this journey and because of it, my inner feminine was clearly gaining strength, albeit very slowly. It was still not strong enough to stand up to the carbon fiber-encased titanium shell I had built up over my fifty-one years prior to Ofir's leaving; but feminine energy is patient, compassionate, nurturing and loving. It understood that it was pointless to attempt to overpower the masculine—it would never be able to beat it at its own game—so the feminine simply provoked the masculine into expending all of its energy. The genius of this actually brought a smile to my face. My inner feminine was just sitting back and waiting for my outer masculine to wear itself out by indulging in one physically exhausting endeavor after another. At this moment, that endeavor appeared to be cycling. My head saw this patience as a brilliant strategy, but it was nothing of the sort. It was pure Wisdom in action.

And where was this all heading? Was the masculine supposed to capitulate to the feminine? No, I thought, the goal must be for the energies to come into some kind of balance.

And then, my thoughts turned to Rachel. I realized that I had been hoping against all hope that somehow on this bike ride, I might be gifted with some insight about her. I very much wanted to overcome the huge rift that existed between Rachel and me. I wanted us to find a way to at least be able talk to each other without acrimony. I wanted desperately for her to understand. I wanted her to know that I did not walk out on her because of anything she did or, God forbid, because she was not enough for me. She had been my world, but my world had been shattered and I just did not know how to put it all back together again.

I wanted her to somehow acknowledge my pain as well her own; but so far, she could not. This never angered me, and I never resented her attitude towards me. Rachel, the mother of Ofir and my wife, did not have a bad bone in her body; and if anyone knew that, I did. If my world had been shattered, then hers had been obliterated. I not only understood that; I took full responsibility for it. I knew forgiveness was too much to hope for, but I longed for mercy.

At this thought, tears began to fill my eyes, and I had to pull over for a moment to gather myself. It wasn't that I didn't love Rachel. I always had, and I always would. But I was a different person now. I didn't know who I was at this point. I was so raw and unfinished, but I knew without a doubt that I could never again be the man I was. And, so, I could never again be Rachel's husband. I hoped she could one day find it in her heart to accept that, but I did not know if she could and that caused me so much pain it was almost suffocating.

With a heavy heart, I mounted the bike again and pushed off. The rest of the day's ride went by like a blur. That night, I pulled into a simple inn, ate a simple meal at a nearby restaurant, did my chores, and turned in early. All the while, I was cognizant of feeling the energy of Louisiana around me, like a soft embrace. I realized that Rachel couldn't forgive me until I forgave myself, and I was still miles or maybe years away from that. Those were my last thoughts before I finally fell into a deep sleep, cradled by the nurturing energy of my surroundings.

Louisiana was memorable for another reason. The next day, as the day before, I had been beaten up by fierce headwinds blowing on the order of twenty to forty miles per hour. On this day, I had been riding for about fifty miles when I began to feel I was running on empty. I still had another forty miles to go, and I honestly did not know if I was going to make it.

I came to a steep hill. It was in a very rural area, and I was climbing very slowly, just limping along. Halfway up, I passed a trailer house near the road. Outside, there were four African-American kids playing. I waved at them and they waved back, but I kept pumping. I was too exhausted to stop and chat, too committed to getting to my next destination. But, then, after I was well past the children, I experienced a very strange feeling. It was like I was being pushed to turn around and go back to visit with the kids. I resisted. I did NOT want to have to re-climb this hill. I kept

Me with three of the boys I was so fortunate to meet in Louisiana

pedaling, but it was futile. As if the bike possessed a will of its own, the steering wheel veered left and then left again, and I found myself heading back down the hill.

They saw me coming and greeted me as if this were nothing unusual. They were young teens, full of smiles. We laughed and joked and chatted about my ride and about nothing in particular. Despite the differences in our ages and race, I felt totally comfortable, as if our hanging out like this were the most natural thing in the world—and maybe it was. Finally, I knew I had to be off. They begged for a picture, so I gave in, and one took a picture of me with his three brothers. I hugged those four beautiful kids, got back on my bike and again approached that dreaded hill.

The most amazing thing happened. Not only did I climb that hill at double the speed, but I also felt totally refreshed at the end. How was that possible? I checked my bearings. Yes, this was the same hill and the headwind had not changed—then it hit me, bringing tears to my eyes. I had once read a book that talked about how we are able to give and take energy to and from each other. This is exactly what had happened. Those amazing spirits had given me some of their energy! It was what some might call a miracle, and I will never forget it. As I rode away I sent my gratitude and blessings to those boys.

And then I began to wonder: why did I go back down the hill? My guides wanted me to, that much I knew; but why did they want me to spend time with those boys? Was it because they knew I would get an energy boost when I really needed it or was there another reason? Was it somehow connected to South Africa? I think so. I felt so much love and joy from those boys, and I bathed in its glowing warmth. The racism I had experienced in my youth had saddled me with immense guilt by association. Through this beautiful encounter I was finally granted the peace I so desperately needed.

At last, we hit the Florida border. We crossed the Panhandle, and spent a night in Bonifay. Then, on the ride from Bonifay to Quincy, I had another odd experience, also involving energy. The day was overcast and very chilly;

and even though I was wearing every last piece of warm clothing I had in my possession, I was still cold. In fact, I was shivering, tired, and miserable. When I'd set out that morning, I knew I had a long, 115-mile ride ahead of me. Even with that foreknowledge, as the day wore on and the temperature dropped, my attitude deteriorated. Now, less than halfway to our destination, all kinds of emotions were running through me. Anger always seemed the first to surface. I was angry at myself, at the world and the entire universe, for that matter. I tried to use it as fuel and kept on pedaling.

Then, through the mist, I saw another biker appear from the opposite direction. As he approached, the first thing I noticed was that he was wearing shorts. When he cut across the road, it was obvious that he wanted to chat, so I pulled over and stopped. He greeted me in a very calm voice, but my response was so strange, it surprised even me. I snapped back with, "You are wearing shorts. What the hell?" It was as if I were actually angry at him for being lightly dressed while I, trussed up in full Antarctic sub-zero protection gear, was freezing cold.

Undeterred, he ignored my inappropriate remark and continued making small talk in his calm and friendly fashion. Ordinarily this would have irritated the hell out of me, but with each syllable that came out of his mouth, my anger began to recede. In fact, my attitude improved at what seemed like light speed. When we were done exchanging stories, I meekly returned to the issue that had sparked my badly chosen greeting and asked if the cold weather did not bother him. He explained that he was from Denmark and that he was accustomed to this kind of weather. I told him that I was from the desert and that these temperatures, coupled with the winds, were very difficult for me to cope with. He nodded his understanding; and after a few more minutes of chatting, we said our farewells and pedaled off in opposite directions.

I thought nothing more of it until, after riding for a little while, it hit me: I was no longer cold, no longer tired, and above all, no longer angry! I was, however, confused. The weather had not changed nor had any of the other riding conditions, so how was it possible that my world had so suddenly changed for the better? Only after some time did the meaning come to me. Apparently, the biker from Denmark had also graciously given me some of his positive energy to help me over the seventy-odd miles I still had left.

With tears in my eyes, I took this in. I'd been pursuing all these ideas, but did I really believe them? Maybe this was the proof I needed to finally accept the truth—*we really are all connected*. It's not just an intellectual idea. There really is some larger order, and things really did happen for a reason to teach us whatever it was we needed to learn.

Of course, my mind kept distracting me with questions: How did these exchanges of energy work? Was he now cold and miserable because of our exchange? Did he realize what had happened, as I had? But I knew those questions were all beside the point. I finished the day with much gratitude to him, hoping that our exchange of energies did not adversely affect his day and his ability to ride strong.

Our final day's ride of ninety-five miles was to take us from Gainesville to St. Augustine. The night before, I sat in my motel room reflecting on the journey thus far, and wrote the following:

> *Thirty-two nights ago, I sat in a motel room by the Pacific Ocean, unsure and confused. Tonight, I sit in a motel room one day away from the Atlantic with a lot more clarity. Tomorrow we finish. It has been a humbling and enlightening experience. Argyle, you never let us down—you never do.*
>
> *And, so, it is and so be it.*

A poem I wrote a few months ago.

ETERNAL WANDERER

I wander and I wonder
So much to ponder
So many whys and y's
So many what's and how's

I journey in awe
Alone from door to door

The doors are infinite
With the journey I sit

I journey to remember
From January through December
I want to go home
I journey alone

Yet, most of all, I seek him
And sometimes things seem so dim
Is he inside of me?
Is it this that I do not see?

My work is set
This I do get
I am deeply committed
And it is to him that I am eternally indebted

Is this his lesson for me
To simply be?
He is in my heart
It pierces me like a dart

I carry him within
Have I become him?
If this is true
Why do I miss him every minute anew?

Our final day was an exceptionally tough one due to adverse weather conditions. We fought a head wind all the way in as well as a light rain for the last third of the ride. Time and distance progressed as slowly as I had ever experienced. Even worse than the physical difficulties were the head games. Somehow knowing that I was in the final hundred miles of a 3,000-mile journey with the finish line so close, I was, from the moment I set out, like a child in the back seat of a car asking repeatedly, "Are we there yet?"

When I finally entered the town of St. Augustine, as absurd as this may sound, I could not find the ocean. Unbeknownst to me, the town does not sit on the ocean; it sits on the west side of the Matanzas River. Exasperated, crossing the Bridge of Lions, I continued to ride eastwards, where I was sure I would run into the Ocean; but I only came up on another area of water that was still not ocean front. Despite being exhausted, wet, and miserable, I refused to give up. Unable to go any farther in an easterly direction I rode south until finally I saw a sign that said, "To Beach." With a huge sigh of relief, I followed the signs until I finally arrived at the Atlantic Ocean. Not a soul was in sight except for a young couple leaving the beach. They were nice enough to take a few pictures of me standing with my bike on the sand and the Atlantic Ocean in the background. So, with little fanfare and somewhat anticlimactically, our 3,000-mile journey ended.

The trip had taken thirty-three days. The longest day's ride had been 131 miles and the shortest, the first day, was fifty. It was in New Mexico where we traversed the highest peak of the ride, Emory Pass, at 8,200 feet. We crossed the mightiest of rivers, the Mississippi, and many others. We had four flats and replaced one tire. I fell off the bike three times with one fall injuring me to the extent that I had to peddle half a day with one leg and take the following day off—our only day of rest. We had some peaceful, beautiful, and inspiring days and a few days of high stress, sometimes involving moments of sheer terror. We encountered a myriad of dangers, the biggest problems being traffic—particularly logging trucks with their branches hanging off the sides—and vicious wild dogs. All in all, it was a miracle that I did not die. But then again, I had help. I honestly felt that both Ofir and Argyle were watching out for me at all times. Although I sometimes had conscious doubts, deep within I trusted in them.

After touring Florida for a month, I returned home on December 25, having been on the road a little more than two months. Had I accomplished my mission? Had I kept my emotions in check long enough for the old me, that crusty caterpillar, to finally dissolve? I hoped so. More tears in the chrysalis were appearing; I could feel it.

Made it – The Atlantic Ocean

SURRENDER

Universe the story is yours
The illusion is mine
I do not control
Only participate

Your story hurts
It is not mine
Why?
What is the purpose?

You took half of me
What remains?
I function not
I exist

You are and have reason
Your goal is evolution
I am you
Why do I not understand?

The pain is raw
Reveal the purpose
I surrender in humility
Allow me dignity

—M.C.

19. White Flag

ALL THOSE DAYS I spent alone chasing the white line had been a time of deep reflection. I had used the time to practice Authentic Listening, and this had led to profound insights. I knew now that it all came down to energy. I certainly had run into that idea many times before on my journey; but only now because of my direct experience was I finally beginning to understand it. I was coming to see that in our essence we are not matter, but energy. To use the image of the ocean, we are all like individual waves in a huge Ocean of energy. We emerge from that Ocean, interact with all the other waves, return to and merge with that Ocean, reemerge again and on and on in one great, eternal cycle. That is how we are all connected. We are not aware of it, but our consciousness is not individual or our own. It all belongs to one infinite, unbounded whole. I do not have the language, but suffice it to say that energy, consciousness, or whatever one chooses to name it, is all one and the same. I felt it when I stopped to chat with those four kids in Louisiana and I felt it with the rider I met on that cold miserable day. I felt it in the Sam Houston National Forest, where I gained a deep understanding that animals, plant life and even things we consider inanimate are conscious, the only difference being in the level or depth or intensity of the consciousness—same Ocean, different waves—that's all. I brought back part of that forest with me and left part of myself there; *we exchanged energy*. Life is a never-ending exchange of energies. It continues, just in a way that is veiled from our perception.

In many ways, I felt the biggest lesson I received on my trip was the one that came while riding through Texas and Louisiana, when I was shown that energies in this physical realm manifest as either primarily feminine or masculine. These two forms of energy are complementary and recurring. Coming to understand that, coupled with the knowledge that all is connected and part of a greater whole, was the greatest insight by far.

More importantly, I felt that these insights were catapulting me straight towards Ofir and the Ultimate Truth. I returned feeling very encouraged, feeling that it was definitely within the realm of possibility that I would be able to embrace my son again. In fact, I was convinced that I was standing at the very edge of finding everything I had searched for. Ofir, the Nature of Reality, they were both right there, just on the other side of an invisible threshold and all I had to do was cross it. I felt carried in the wake of the bike ride. Just as I had made it to the shore of the Atlantic through sheer determination, I hoped to sustain the momentum of discovery through my reading and writing, which I resumed with renewed zeal.

But, then, after a few weeks, I hit some kind of imperceptible barrier. No matter how much I read, wrote or meditated, I was stuck. It was like, unchallenged, I had the football at the one-yard line, but my legs were frozen stiff. I just couldn't get it across the goal line. I responded with characteristic relentlessness. I beat at the barrier mercilessly. I beat and beat and beat until I had nothing left, but my blows just bounced off like a rubber ball off a brick wall. As hard as I tried, I simply could not get through.

I pulled back to reassess. I had come so close to finding Ofir, to discovering the Nature of Reality, that I could almost see, taste and feel it; but apparently there was a missing link—something beyond recognizing my guides and energy and the interconnectedness of everything and even beyond validating my inner feminine. Whatever I was missing was as elusive as the brilliant colors of a rainbow are to a blind person.

Instead of taking that one last final step over the finish line, the inconceivable happened—I began to go backwards. Everything felt "off." Reading no longer stoked me, so I invested in it less and less. Frustrated beyond words, I soon began to drift listless in a sea of days. After about a month of this, a wave of loneliness and depression swept over me like a tsunami. To my horror, I realized that my determination to find Ofir and to discover the Ultimate Truth—the very thing that had given me hope and kept me going all this time—was slipping inexorably away. Like water from a leaky basin, everything was draining out of me. I had always felt that I had inside me a bottomless reservoir of passion, energy and focus; this was what I drew upon to fuel my journey, to keep going in the face of all obstacles. But now, just when I seemed to be on the brink of finding Ofir, something had pulled the plug.

I fought this, of course. I tried everything I knew to try to re-awaken my enthusiasm, but nothing worked. By March, I had to admit the truth, the reservoir was bone dry. With that admission, a cloak of darkness began to settle down over me. I saw then that the hope that I would find Ofir had been a candle, only one tiny little flame, but it had been enough to light a way forward for me. It had kept the Beast at bay, and it had helped me stave off all the darkness that had been patiently waiting to devour me. For the past four years that candle had burnt strong and bright; but now, with one last flicker, it just went out.

One afternoon, shortly after realizing this, I sat stock still, trying to penetrate the darkness, trying to understand what was happening—and then I saw. Grief had finally prevailed. It had finally consumed all my energy. I knew then that I had reached the end of the road; my journey was over. It was time to surrender to a life of sadness, pain, and guilt. Head down, I raised the white flag.

I had failed; I had failed in protecting my son and I had failed in finding him. The only thing I needed now was someone to punish me.

In April of the previous year, I had had a brief, intimate encounter with a woman. Within days of our first meeting, I knew that a relationship with her could never be anything but dysfunctional. She was too lost and damaged and so was I. Nevertheless, I had entered into it. True to my intuition, it turned out to be so dysfunctional that she broke it off. Just last month, however, she had re-contacted me indicating that she wanted to renew the relationship. I knew immediately that I had found the perfect candidate to help me achieve what had to be done. I needed to be punished, and here was someone who would mete out that well-deserved punishment and at the same time give me all the "feel goods" that would enable me to endure it. I would allow her to punish me for my pathetic failure to protect my son and the subsequent pain my ex-wife would have to suffer for the rest of her life. There was no doubt in my mind that this was how my life needed to be for the rest of my days. Thus, it began.

During the entire time that I was in that relationship, my inner journey was at a complete standstill. I quit reading altogether, stopped attending conferences, and ceased investing any time in nurturing my inner being and its evolution. Only very occasionally did I engage in any writing and when I did, I wrote poetry, ironically, on the subject of love. I could only imagine true love through the medium of poetry because I certainly was not getting it in real life. I ceased writing about Ofir, my spiritual journey or any metaphysical topics as had been my norm.

As far as I was concerned, my journey to find Ofir and the Ultimate Truth had failed and with it the new life I had tried to create after Ofir's passing had also collapsed with one giant implosion. To some degree, I think I was relieved. In many ways, it was easier to live the way I was now— without goal or purpose, just letting the hours, days, weeks, and months pass by. I had been reduced to mere organic matter and I was slowly but surely rotting away. I not only accepted that, I embraced it. I fully immersed myself in the soul-destroying drama that had become my daily existence. I suspect that this woman whom I chose to be my punishment saw our life as a kind of Woody Allen screenplay, a bit neurotic but ultimately charming. I, on the other hand, felt like I was living in a Stephen King novel that had been adapted for the screen by Quentin Tarantino. Looking back at those "movies," they could easily have been called the *Kill Martin* saga. Perhaps that is why, when I learned of an opportunity to partake of the South American medicinal plant called "the vine of death," I accepted.

Meeting up with Mother Ayahuasca was a deeply personal experience, so I will only say the following: during the twelve-hour ceremony, I had no contact with Ofir nor did I come closer to understanding the Nature of Reality. However, my father and brother appeared with my dad dressed in a suit, of all things. I found the experience to be reminiscent of the time I spent with my Aunt Bella in South Africa, but the ceremony did not yield as much as I had hoped for and I left somewhat disappointed. Looking back at my state of being, however, it seems no surprise. It is likely that I didn't feel Ofir's presence because I was so mentally shuttered.

By October, I was feeling so worn down that I had to run again, so I flew back to Israel to visit my family. After a week there, I knew that even that escape was not enough. I needed to get even farther away, to lose myself. So, on a whim, I booked a ticket to Greece.

Early in the morning of October 15, 2013, I found myself flying from Tel Aviv to Athens seated on a plane belonging to some obscure airline. By the time we reached altitude, my brain was in overdrive, keeping pace with the turbine jet engines pushing the plane to its destination. If someone had been able to eavesdrop on the disjointed conversation raging between my ears, it might have been justifiable to wonder whether I was suffering from hypoxia or some other brain disorder related to oxygen deprivation. The cabin's air pressure, however, was functioning just fine.

The flight was very short and in no time the pilot greased a landing at Athens International Airport. We were still taxiing to a stop when I grabbed my carry-on containing what was to be all my worldly possessions for the next twelve days or so. With a sense of unfounded urgency, I pushed through the queue of disembarking passengers and made a beeline for the car rental agency. There, I found an employee who had trouble understanding English.

I knew the problem was not me, as I was well versed in both the Queen's and American English. I wanted to let loose a zinger like, "Apparently, English is Greek to you," but held back. It pleased me to note, however, that the old, aggressive and combative me had re-surfaced.

I was shown a car, but didn't like it. I did not like the next one either—
it was the size of a matchbox and seemed more toy than real car. I noticed,
however, that it was a diesel made by Opel, a model I was familiar with
going back to my youth. My Auntie Bella had driven an Opel, though
much bigger than the one I was looking at. Then, just as I was about to
walk away, I noticed the stick between and forward of the bucket seats,
and froze. Suddenly, I was hurtling through a wormhole not dissimilar
to the one Jodie Foster traveled through in the movie, *Contact*. It took me
back seven years, back to the time when Ofir and I had been together in
the showroom of our local car dealership checking out a low-end sports
car. True to his nature, Ofir had done his research. The car was well
within our agreed-upon budget; and he wanted it mostly because it was a
stick shift. At age sixteen, he had learned to drive a stick, which was highly
unusual for a young kid of his era. But of course, there was nothing usual
about Ofir. I remembered thinking to myself at the time, *A stick? It has to
be a control issue! I wonder who he might have picked that up from?*

Arriving back in Greece via the same wormhole (I think), I refocused,
turned to the attendant and without a wisp of hesitation told him I would
take it. I think I caught him off-guard because his nod was accompanied
by a look of surprise. He walked off to get the contract, obviously relieved
that he was about to get rid of a car that nobody wanted. If only he knew . . .

I quickly handled the paperwork, got in, stabbed the key into the
ignition and started the car. It had been a long time since I had driven a
stick. I eased off the clutch and simultaneously pushed on the gas. The
car lurched forward, hiccupped a few times and stalled. I glanced into the
rearview mirror and saw the attendant smiling from ear to ear. I started
the engine once more, getting it right the second time, and took off, issu-
ing a loud "screw you" to the smirking fool behind me. I definitely liked
the way I was thinking and behaving—some of my old grit was back. I
thought it was a good start.

My destination that first night was Diakopto about a four-hour
drive west of the Athens airport. Along the way, I decided to stop to

look for a SIM card for my phone. Korinthos seemed a good bet, so I pulled into the town center and began looking for a parking space. Nothing. I drove around in circles for a while wondering what the secret was. Then, after a couple of rounds, I began to notice all the cars parked on the sidewalk. I said it out loud, "Oh well, as in Rome . . ." I found a spot on the sidewalk for my matchbox and headed off to locate an electronics store. As I walked, it occurred to me that I had talked to myself a lot over the past six years. For the most part, I had not wanted company; on the other hand, I don't think company particularly wanted me, either.

An hour later, I returned to the car, relieved to find that it had not been towed, and drove off, functioning phone in hand. As I got back on the freeway, I realized that I was getting a good handle on up shifting and down shifting, using the brakes very little. Ofir immediately came to mind. I bet he did it better than me.

I reached the hostel, dumped my stuff in the room and decided to go on a hike up the Vouraikos Gorge. I finished the hike as the sun was setting, ate dinner and went to sleep.

The next morning, I set off early, heading north into the Pindus Mountains toward a town called Karpenesi perched 3,300 feet above sea level. To get there, I crossed the Rio-Antirio Bridge. It stretches over the Gulf of Corinth, a deep inlet of the Ionian Sea, which separates the peninsula of Peloponnese from western mainland Greece. The bridge itself was strikingly beautiful with its intricate web of cables, so complex in form that it left me wondering whether the design was primarily structural or aesthetic.

The day was cool and overcast by a layer of black, threatening clouds. As the car began to climb, I was struck by the fact that I had chosen to explore the rugged mountains rather than collapse on the tranquil, relaxing beaches of the Greek Islands. The fact that I opted for adventure over comfort or relaxation was another glimmer of the old me; and, again, I took some solace in that.

I continued on via the Pindus Mountains roads. As I was soon to discover, these roads were treacherous in every way possible. They were exceedingly narrow, one and a half lanes at best, even though traffic went in both directions. They were also badly paved and in places strewn with rocks, some the size of boulders, that had fallen from above. To top it off, the roads were devoid of any barriers that might prevent a hapless car and driver from pitching straight downwards into the jaws of the valley below. As if all this were not enough, one had to constantly negotiate hairpin turns that were both extremely tight and blind. Driving under those conditions got my juices flowing. I was aware of a potent concoction coursing through my veins that was part fear and part excitement mixed with, strangely, a powerful feeling of being alive that I had not felt in a long time. How I loved those moments when adrenaline would flood my brain, leaving no room for thought or grief.

I drove like a man possessed with music blaring and the windows wide open to suck out any remnants of caution that might still be lingering. As I kept pushing the accelerator—and myself—harder and harder, it became obvious, even to me, that I was tempting fate. If I kept this up, it could lead to only one outcome—a single-car accident resulting in certain death.

Then it hit me. Everything was so eerily similar: driving a stick shift, speeding, negotiating dangerous turns. It was hard to ignore the fact that I was doing my best to duplicate everything that had happened the night of Ofir's accident. The only difference was that I was in the mountains of Greece while he had been on Torrey Pines Road in La Jolla, California. It occurred to me that I must have created all this in a desperate effort to meld with him, to know what he was thinking and feeling in those last moments. Was I trying to bring him back to life by becoming him in my mind?

I had always been concerned about Ofir's passion for life, the passion he had inherited from me. Would he learn how to handle it, to temper it, or would he push himself too far? I'm sure it was because I was in Greece, but a strange thought came to me. Had we been like the mythical Icarus and Daedelus? Did he, like Icarus, think he had to surpass his father? Did

DRIVING MOUNTAINS IN GREECE

he believe he was invincible? Did he, too, fly too close to the sun? Is that what happened that night on that dark, luge-like tract in La Jolla? Like Daedelus, I had tried to advise, to warn, but I don't know if he heard me. Could I have done more?

If I were to shine a laser beam on my very lowest point, that moment was it. Everything seemed to go blank and all I remember is this one last thought—if I am not able to find Ofir, then so be it; I will join him.

But instead of crashing, the car simply trekked on, taking me with it.

When I finally came out of that trance-like state and took stock, I was surprised to feel that my face was soaked, and water was dripping down onto my tee shirt. My first thought was that it had to be raining; but as I looked out the open window, I was startled to see that, although it was dark and cloudy overhead, it most definitely was not raining. At that same moment, my tongue happened to intercept a droplet falling off the tip of my nose and, to my surprise, it tasted salty. Only then did I understand; I had been crying profusely the whole time.

Of the twelve days I spent in Greece, a full six were spent driving those mountains like the madman I had become. Gradually, as the days ebbed away, I found myself calming. Being in Greece was like going back centuries in time. The roads, structures and even the people all seemed to exist in another age, which made certain practical things like navigating almost impossible. Road signs were either non-existent or old and unstable with arrows pointing in whatever direction the wind was currently blowing. Not to mention the fact that the signs were in Greek, which was, yes, Greek to me. I decided that I understood why they named their language "Greek." It was because no one could read or understand it, kinda like quantum physics. Well, at least I could joke.

Given these circumstances, navigation had to be accomplished through a combination of ignorant guesswork and blind rerouting after making what were, presumably, wrong turns. When I was lost, which was all the time, I had only one resort, human interaction. However, if I somehow managed to track down another human roaming the area, communicating was a real challenge. I didn't speak a word of Greek, which by definition made me a bona fide barbarian, and no one in the countryside spoke English. So, to a person, the strangers I accosted would revert to giving directions with their hands. After they had waved and flailed their hands about in virtually every direction for what seemed like hours, I would politely thank them and drive away without even the remotest idea of what they had been attempting to tell me. Often, I would drive off in the exact opposite direction from where I needed to go. Looking in my rear-view mirror, I would see the hands going up again, gesturing wildly. Those were the only times that I fully understood what they were telling me, which I'm sure was, "Moron, I have just spent an hour kindly explaining to you clearly where to go, and you immediately drive off in the wrong direction. Oh well, what does one expect from a barbarian?" To this day, I bet they are still telling stories to their grandkids about the "The American Moron of the Mountains."

After visiting Karpenesi, Zagori, Vikos Canyon, Monodendri, Ioannina, and Klambaka, I found my way to Meteora. I had heard that it was an extraordinary place, and it did not disappoint. First, there is the mountain itself, which rises up to touch the sky. Then, looking up, one can discern six monasteries perched upon it. At first glance, they seem a part of the mountain, carved out of it, causing one to wonder if the monasteries were not appendages of the grand mountain. Did the mountains give birth to the monasteries? Or had they, perhaps, fallen out of the womb of heaven and landed on the mountain? Whatever the answer, it was an awe-inspiring sight for sure.

I felt called to climb up to one of the monasteries, so I found a place to park and looked for a trail. As I began the hike up, it soon became evident that I was the only one on the trail. Apparently, there was a road to the top and most people chose to drive. The hike did not take long, but it was very steep in places; so, when I finally reached the top, I was feeling exhausted but also exhilarated from the flood of endorphins. As I made my way towards the monastery, anticipation rose. For the first time in

Monasteries "growing" out of the mountains in Meteora

More monasteries "growing" out of the mountains in Meteora

ages, I was feeling open to engaging with something spiritual. However, just as I reached the entrance, a young monk in a long robe rushed up. Taking me by the arm, he promptly ushered me outside, informing me that I could not enter wearing shorts. He said this in perfect English.

For a moment, I stood there, incredulous, staring open-mouthed at his receding back. How could this be? After investing so much effort to reach that holy place on a mountaintop, I had been firmly ejected, rejected as unworthy. I took it as a sign. Now it was confirmed; the realm of the spirit was closed to me.

A depression the likes of which I had never before experienced moved into my soul like a suffocating cloud. Through the fog I saw the flash of the Beast's eyes. I was just about to beckon him when I felt a bitter bile rise in my throat—the old familiar taste of anger. A flash of fire sent that dark mist packing. Well, if the spirit world did not want me, then I did not want it, either. I turned my back to the monastery and proceeded to hike back down. As I descended, my emotions began to settle into an old, familiar groove. While at first I felt humiliated and disappointed, those feelings were now replaced by a sense of satisfaction. What had just occurred reinforced the reason I had come to Greece in the first place: to stop this insane effort to change and grow and to reconnect to my rational roots. Greece, the birthplace of rational thought, seemed the perfect choice to re-entrench myself in my old way of being.

It was with this mindset that I returned home to the United States and resumed my life as before, giving myself over to this woman, to her drama, to her chaos—and to my punishment.

The months went by, drifting one into the other: same woman, same dynamic, same me, my search but a vague and distant memory. Then, in July of the following year, something inexplicable happened. One morning, I opened my sleepy eyes and, barely awake, walked over to where she was sitting. I looked at her and without provocation made the following statement, "You repulse me." Then, just like that, I turned around, got dressed, packed up my stuff and drove away.

Finally, finally, finally, I was done, and nobody was more shocked than I was. My thoughts were racing, this question pounding over and over in my ears: *What the hell have you done?* I was scared to death. I had just thrown away my crutch, the drama that had kept me from feeling my grief. What on earth was I going to do?

Physical pain dictated the next step. A few months earlier, a lifetime of back problems had reached the point where the pain was intolerable, partially thanks to a year and a half of deep emotional stress that characterized the relationship I had just ended. Hardly able to walk, I was told that my only option was surgery. I swear that the thought of going under general anesthesia was so attractive that it became my primary motivation for deciding to go through with it. Finally, here was an opportunity to sleep without continuous waking, twitching, and nightmares! I just wanted some relief from feeling. But of course, relativity being what it is, the time I spent in a state of "not feeling" seemed like a second. Funny how escape never seems to yield what one hopes for.

After the surgery, I spent ten days lying in bed recuperating and also berating myself for all my failures, not the least of which was losing Ofir. One night, not able to sleep, I decided to text Rachel. Despite knowing that she would never reply, I typed in my standard mantra, the single line I had been texting her for years, "I am so sorry." This time, however, to my utter amazement, I received a reply. It came in the form of a question: "Why do you keep texting me that you are sorry? Sorry for what?" I stared at the screen. If nothing else, this exchange was a testament to how far apart we were in our understanding of each other. Before Ofir, we had been a devoted couple, virtually inseparable, but Ofir's leaving had been like an atomic blast that split us into a million parts, the likes of which physics had yet to identify.

I wanted to answer her question, to make her understand, but knew it was futile. I wasn't even sure I understood myself. In fact, I was desperate to understand, so I tried to write it out. I began writing furiously, putting all my feelings to paper. What came out was an essay I entitled: "What

It Means to Be a Mother." I wrote it from the perspective of a father, a husband, and a man whose child had left. The premise was that a mother is second only to God. Believing this with all my heart and knowing that Rachel was an amazing mother, I could not fathom why God would allow her to suffer such an injustice. I could somehow understand God doing something like this to a man, but to a mother? It made no sense and it made me angry. And I felt 100% responsible. As a man, it was my charter to defend and protect God's second-in-command, and I had failed in my duty. How does one ever make peace with that? Unfortunately, I never finished the essay and never sent it to her. I could not convince myself that it would yield any results.

After some time, it became evident that the surgery had not been successful. The pain persisted; in fact, the pain was sometimes excruciating. I began to wonder if I was doomed to a life of pain on every level. In addition, being alone again was extremely difficult. With all of this to contend with, I decided to see my therapist, whom I had not seen in several years.

Perhaps some growth had actually occurred because I found I was able to get much more out of therapy this time, and I was appreciating my therapist much more as well. She is an incredible spirit and I am forever grateful to her. One day, I recounted to her what had happened in Meteroa and was adamant in telling her that I was done with my search and with spirituality and that I had returned to my original identity—a rational man. I had barely finished what must have seemed like a bit of a tirade when she suggested I read a book called *I Am the Word: A Guide to the Consciousness of Man's Self in a Transitioning Time* by Paul Selig. The book is a channeled text given to Selig by entities who are guides or ascended masters. In brief, the book is about setting intentions. The message is that one should set an intention and then trust in it. In time, whatever one has intended will come to fruition. The book stresses that we are not to expect things to happen immediately.

Upon reading this, I was filled with ambivalence; this method seemed way too magical and ungrounded for the new old rational me. But I was also desperate, so I reluctantly wrote down some intentions based on what I had come to understand about myself. I had no expectations of results, so I put away what I had hurriedly written down and promptly forgot all about it.

At this point, I was also facing a decision. I still needed to recover from the surgery, but staying in the Coachella Valley was no longer an option. There was simply too much painful history there. Sadly, the place we had called home for thirty-five years, the place where we had built a great life and raised a family, the place I had grown to love, no longer felt like home.

Feeling both homeless and directionless, I made a quick decision. I chose to go and spend the next month in a small town just north of San Diego. It seemed like a good fit since some close family friends lived there. It was also the home of the Yogananda Self-Realization Fellowship, so I figured it had some good spiritual energy (as if I really cared, I told myself). And it was by the beach. I rented a place online, threw some things in the car, and departed on August 16, 2014.

My departure from the Coachella Valley that day with a few belongings tossed haphazardly into the back of my SUV seemed like a defining moment. I had hit rock bottom. I was utterly and completely exhausted. I drove toward the coast in a state I can only describe as fading in and out. It was as if I were being put under anesthesia, only to be immediately revived, over and over again. Actually, the idea of being put to sleep for a very long time had great appeal, so why was I being repeatedly awakened? And then, I heard something. At first, it was very faint, like the sound of a bird's wing off in the distance. I hearkened; but when I tried to listen, whatever it was couldn't be heard over the raging commotion in my head. I shook it off, sure I was imagining things; but then I heard it again, as weak as a whisper. *What was that?*

Was it life?

Confused, I turned to my rational mind for help. Mentally, I rifled through my past readings about physics looking for information, for insight. My consciousness lighted on a specific page, and I scanned down the text with my mind's eye. It was a passage about a concept in physics called "the conservation of energy." It basically said, among other things, that energy/matter can change form, but it cannot be destroyed. *What did that have to do with me?*

It took the entire drive but, by the time I arrived, I began to see. By the reasoning of physics, even if my journey had come to a screeching halt, all the energy that had been driving me was not gone, as I had thought. No, it had just been co-opted; it had been poured into sustaining the dysfunctional life I had chosen. But maybe all of that energy had not yet been siphoned off. Maybe some of that energy was still inside me. Maybe, just maybe, if I could find it, I could fight my way back.

I was shocked that I was even considering this idea. In my eyes, the fight was over; it had been over for nearly two years. But as I pulled into the driveway of my latest escape, I decided to keep an open mind. Why not? I had nothing more to lose.

LIFE RENEWED

The tundra of my heart
Self-banishment its destiny
Eternally cold, sad, alone
Uninhabited- forlorn its surroundings

But wait! Who goes there?
I feel a presence
I hear a voice
I feel a touch

Life has entered my heart's landscape
The sun reignited, warm and nurturing
My being bursting in color
Peace raining down in a gentle drizzle

Now, The heavens above a deep blue
The earth below a dark, peaty brown
Flowers are blooming
Nature has returned in all her splendor.

Life feeds me once more, and I it
Unbounded love the source
My senses bursting - life wide open
Finally, you have come for me

—M.C.

20. Epiphany

I'D RENTED THE HOUSE IN ENCINITAS, sight unseen. I pulled into the driveway, shut the engine off, and stared at it. It seemed to stare back. What had I done?

I had chosen this particular house because of its location only a short walk from the beach. After all the chaos of the past year, I felt called to spend time by the ocean. Why, exactly, I was not sure. Up until this moment, the ocean had never been that important to me.

With some trepidation, I got out, went up to the door, unlocked it and took stock. Besides being a thousand years old and needing a lot and I mean a *lot* of work, it was fine. Or was it? I was feeling agitated, in need of distraction; however, looking around, I knew this was *not* the kind of place one would want to bring a woman to. Yes, of all the issues rattling around in that mush brain of mine, for a moment, that was my biggest concern. But the truth was, I really did not care about that or much of anything. Heaving a deep sigh, I went back to the SUV, retrieved my few belongings and carted them inside. If this was to be my life now, I accepted it completely.

Very quickly, I settled into a routine. Despite the constant pain in my back and foot, I began each day at sunup with a three-mile hike along the shore, which I then repeated at sundown. In the evenings, I fell back into the same pattern that had held me in its grip for the last six years. I went out, hoping to meet someone. I told myself that it was different this time, that I was finally ready for a "real" relationship. That's what I told myself, but it wasn't true.

So, at night, old habits held sway; but in the daytime, things felt different. For the first time in years, I was not engulfed in any drama or chaos—my own or anyone else's. At first, the very idea of being alone had been terrifying, but I found myself actually starting to enjoy it a little. In between my walks on the beach, I began to read again, both books and some of my own writings that had accumulated over the years. I found a good spot—a comfortable chair by a window that looked out over the beach—and read, vaguely wondering why I had developed a renewed interest in reading my own work.

All along my journey, reading and writing had been very important to me. Not only had they helped me in my search for Ofir and the Ultimate Nature of Reality, but reading had also become a kind of meditation. Over the past two years, however, it had stopped working, and I had become so discouraged that I stopped reading altogether. Now, though, change was definitely in the air.

The first three days passed with me walking and reading and thinking. Then on about the fourth day, while sitting by the window reading, I felt a strange uneasiness. I could not identify its source, so I dismissed it. But as the morning wore on, it grew too strong to ignore. I put down my book, sat quietly, and allowed my mind to wander and wonder. After giving it my full attention, I realized the source of the uneasiness—the raging voices in my mind had gone quiet. It had been so long since I'd had a quiet mind, it felt like a foreign territory.

The more I read, the calmer my mind became. And the calmer I became, the more intense and focused the reading became. Each was feeding the other. I wondered if the constant flow of fresh, crisp ocean air through the window where I was sitting was functioning as a powerful detoxifying agent cleansing my soul.

A few days after that, Tal came down to visit with his new girlfriend. Watching them interact as innocent young lovers do, I felt shivers running up and down my spine. In them, I saw Rachel and me thirty years prior and instantly knew how good she was for Tal. When the shivers subsided, a forgotten feeling washed over me. I think it went by the name of "happiness." Once again, Tal taught me a lesson, one for which I am eternally grateful: that apparently feelings of happiness and even joy were still possible, even for souls as lost as Rachel and me.

When they left, any desire to go out at night went with them. I continued on with my reading and my walks on the beach, both of which helped me to reflect and take account of myself. Something was definitely happening. I noticed that for the first time in a long time I was able to get some distance from my sharp, harsh emotions. I was also beginning to see things on multiple levels. Somehow, I got the insight that I had chosen to live a life of chaos and that all that drama in various forms was just a way of preventing me from feeling things, especially grief, the Beast I feared would devour me.

Snakebit as I was from all the years of up and down, hope followed by hopelessness, I slowly, hesitantly, began to open up and allow in the feelings I had so long pushed away. As I did so, a very curious thing happened. The Beast was still there, but somehow, it didn't seem as vicious and I wasn't quite as afraid.

Then other things began to happen. Typically, my walk to the beach took about ten minutes; I was always in a hurry, anxious to get to my destination. But one morning, everything changed. It started with the flowers in people's yards. I'd walked by them every day, not paying attention. But on that day, it was impossible; their riotous colors could not be ignored. As I beheld them, they radiated a stunning beauty such as I had never seen before, and I was mesmerized. All the trees and shrubs looked different, too. They seemed to be beckoning me closer, enticing me to stop to inspect their meristems, like proud parents parading their newborns. As I leaned in to examine them, I witnessed life itself exploding forth from those tiny, young leaves. Even the bugs on the plants seemed to be smiling at me, inviting me to watch them feed.

And that wasn't the only thing. With every step, I felt the earth beneath my feet sighing in joy as it, too, greeted me. I can't even remember walking; it seemed more like gliding. My walk, once a mere necessity or obligation, had transformed into an *experience*. Now, instead of ten minutes, it took . . . how long? Who knows?

I luxuriated in the deliciousness of it all. Like a kid let loose in a candy store or a starving man, I feasted on Nature's beauty until I was nearly delirious. The beach, too, seemed to come alive in a whole new way. I sensed from it an infinite patience, which was soothing to my active temperament. It did not matter to the ocean what time I arrived; it kindly hosted me and in return asked only that I acknowledge it.

This enchantment continued for days. All the while, I was highly alert, intensely aware of my surroundings, but I also felt calmer. The constant chatter in my head was dissipating and a sense of peace and love began to pervade my being. Yet, these alien feelings were all quite unsettling, and I felt a tinge of fear as if a giant wave were looming, threatening to sweep me away. I began to recoil at the thought of being swallowed up and lost in it.

The scope of the changes taking place and the speed at which they were happening seemed to feed off each other to such an extent that it was becoming impossible to process all alone. I needed to talk to someone, so I decided to call my therapist. I was hesitant to tell her I was afraid, so instead I divulged to her how guilty and confused I was feeling about being at the beach and being so non-productive. She said something in response, and we moved on to another topic. Then, many topics later, I suddenly cut her off and blurted out the following, "It's okay to be non-productive on the outside. It's on the *inside* that I need to be productive."

The rest of the conversation is a blur. After I hung up, I stood transfixed. What had I just said? *It's okay to be non-productive on the outside. It's on the inside that I need to be productive.* It took me a moment to grasp the significance of my own insight; but when I did, it came with the force of two immense spikes being driven through my feet nailing me into the ground. I wonder even now how it is that I do not bear stigmata. In the moment, I realized something. *I was on the inside.* This is very difficult to articulate. I don't know how else to say it, other than *I was on the inside of me* for the first time in my life. For the very first time, I was not in my head but in another place entirely.

That insight cut a mile-wide hole in a seemingly impenetrable membrane, and I suddenly found myself not only inside myself but inside the very Womb of Reality! In that moment, I came face-to-face with my true self, that pure, untainted spirit that had been floating and rolling around its mother's womb fifty-seven years earlier.

At first, it was very disorientating to find myself in such a numinous space, but then things began to come into focus, illuminated with a lucidity I'd never before experienced. I was no longer afraid, but I was deeply curious. Had I really stumbled upon the Ultimate Nature of Reality?

No sooner had I thought that, than another insight came. I realized that I had spent my entire lifetime thinking that the most important things in life—the only things that really counted—were the things I accomplished in the external world. Up until then, my whole existence had been about *doing*, about being productive, as measured by such things as success in business.

For sure, this belief could be traced back to my extremely disciplined upbringing in South Africa and to the example set by my father. And what had my young, impressionable mind made of that? It had come to believe that only matter mattered, that non-matter "non-mattered," that it was just make-believe fantasy, even that the spiritual was spurious.

This led to another realization: I had dismissed and neglected my inner life, even on the rare occasions that its existence registered in my consciousness, because I'd never felt it was very important. That's why I wanted to leave the room when Woman Stands Shining first spoke about the buffalo. This, too, was explicable. South Africa was a closed culture; there was a resistance to taking in anything from the outside world—most especially when it had to do with looking inward. We were so preoccupied with following rules and laws and with avoiding punishment that we had very little time or energy left for any kind of inner life. My realization of that neglect hit me—no, it slammed into me—and jolted me awake.

I was well aware that many spiritual teachings speak about our having to go inside to find what is true and authentic. This point has been made

over and over again throughout human history. Jesus says it clearly in the
Gospel of Thomas. The words "Know Thyself" are inscribed on the *pronaos*
of the temple of Apollo at Delphi. It is the cornerstone of meditation and
yoga, and many sages throughout history have preached it in one form or
another. Yet, I had ignored that wisdom. Even worse, I had looked for things
outside of myself to take away my sadness and pain. Now, though, I knew
with undeniable certainty that it was what was *inside* that mattered most.

This came to me as a sudden, deep, inner gnosis, powerful and absolute; I felt it in my heart, my soul and my entire being. In fact, it was as
if the statement itself held some ancient secret code, some spell recorded
in the Original Laws, because from that moment onward my inner and
outer were now one. It was no longer the inner *versus* the outer. It was the
inner *and* the outer, synchronized, like a single heartbeat.

After that, things began moving very fast. I was reading all day and
vegging out at night, and, all the while, I was being visited by a series of
profound epiphanies.

In essence, I came to understand that there exists two me's: one, my
ego self and the other, my higher Self. Again, this may seem obvious to
many, but experiencing life through my ego self was all I had ever known.
Over the previous fifty-seven years, I had perfected it. Yes, I had always
had the benefit of strong intuition, a trait that others have called impetuousness; but I had never understood that what I thought of as intuition
was actually my Self. Now, at last, I did. This is not something that I can
explain in rational, everyday terms. The best I can say it is that it happened in a flash of awareness. One second my awareness of my Self wasn't
there, and the next it was.

And with that, I knew that *I had found Argyle*. He had changed from
being a feeling to a full, head-on encounter. I came as close to shaking his
hand as I ever could. Argyle was my Self. Why had I created a persona
named Argyle? Well, that was Self's way of making things easier for itself.

And then my mind took me back to my ride through Louisiana where
I had posed the following question: If the concept of feminine/masculine

energy was real, then was it somehow connected to my journey? Was it at all possible that in order to find Ofir and the Ultimate Truth, these energies needed to come back into balance within me? As I was considering these questions, I heard these words: *What could be more nurturing than sitting in the womb of the Divine Feminine?* And so, the forest fire that had raged within me for the past seven years had finally burnt itself out, and I was finally ready to be nurtured back to life by the Divine Feminine. And with that, another duality—the separation of the Masculine and Feminine—fell.

I had never felt so complete in my life. All of my parts—including those that had been so brutally and systematically beaten out of me as a boy—were all finally reunited. The spirit being who had had such awareness in the womb had returned. This was not unlike an earthquake in my little world; and so, indeed, just as with an earthquake, the aftershocks came, one after the other in the form of even more epiphanies, realizations, and insights.

The first hit me like a Gamma ray burst, with the blinding intensity of 1,000 supernovae: ***Ofir was never lost; you were.*** This revelation may have been short in content, but it was shocking to me and nauseating in its power. My mind reeled, trying to take it in, when another revelation hit: ***Ofir is not gone.***

I had gone searching for Ofir because I thought he was lost to me, but at that moment I came to see that he was never gone and will never be gone because he lives in my heart and talks to me from my heart. Wait! Where had I heard those words before? Then it hit me, the strangest thing of all. I scrambled through my writings to confirm it; and there it was, born out by my own words, over and over and over again. All the while, I had thought I was writing letters to *him*, but it was actually the reverse; *he* had been reaching out to me through *my* writing. I was actually writing *his* words, words sent to me by him! Again, I flashed back to New Mexico, three years earlier and thought about how spirit communicated through us. It was true! In rereading my letters to Ofir I witnessed it first hand:

- *From my very first letter to him, I had called him my "shining or guiding light." (I didn't know it then, but from the get-go he was telling me that he was guiding me.)*

- *"We were so alike," I wrote, "only you were a 1,000 times better." (My higher Self knew that we had come from the same Oversoul, but he was more advanced in his journey.)*

- *"You definitely are a very advanced soul." (This was Ofir saying, "So listen to me, dammit! I know what I am talking about, you stubborn mule!")*

- *"You are and always will be with us." ("Stop searching, you idiot, I am right here. I always was and always will be.")*

- *"You worked so hard and gave up so much so that you would be able to live out your dreams." ("Stop the craziness and wake up! I gave up so much to set you straight. Pay attention.")*

- *"I AM NOT HELPLESS AND OUR RELATIONSHIP STILL EXISTS AND I CAN BE THERE FOR YOU." (What in the world could be clearer than this?)*

- *"LOVE YOU and please know you are not alone, or should I say I am not alone??????????? (WOW!!!)*

Immediately thereafter, the next aftershock struck. I heard the words, **Not only was Ofir not lost, it was he who sent you on this journey.**

I scrambled to process this. Then I saw. Yes, we had come from the same Oversoul, and we are connected in ways beyond human understanding. So, when he saw how lost I was—how like a feral spirit I'd become—he sent me on a journey to find myself, to remember who I truly was. And even when I was not listening, he kept on guiding me down the path. No matter what, he was not giving up until I saw the light. He guided me in much the same way that we teach a dog a trick—repeating the teachings patiently, over and over.

Over the next weeks, insights continued to come. He was teaching me, still.

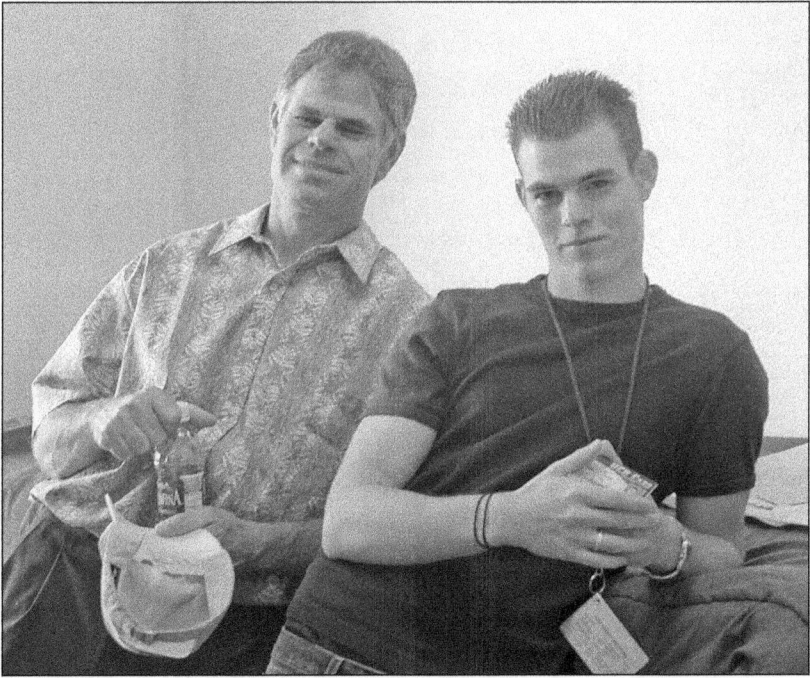

Ofir and I, together always

YOU – ME

My heart is my home
Your spirit its tenant
My heart is strong
Your spirit its sustenance

My heart is my guide
Your spirit its compass
My heart is wisdom
Your spirit its guru

My heart weeps
Your spirit its tears
My heart radiates with life
Your spirit its sun

I carry you in and with me
That is all I have
I don't have your physical being
I am you

—M.C.

21. The Alchemy of Grief

THAT MONTH AT THE BEACH was the turning point in my journey to heal my grief and to find Ofir. I know this beyond a doubt. I know because when I left I felt like the proverbial monk who goes into a cave and emerges years later an enlightened being. I am by no means saying that I had become an enlightened being, but I am saying that I had so many profound, enlightening moments that I emerged from that month a totally different man. Yet, there is no spiking of the football; I had only scored a touchdown. The game was not over. It is never over, or is it?

As I have said, these insights come from a place of no language, so they are almost impossible to articulate. Still, I will do my best to share my understanding of what I received:

- *The life-long illusion that I had held so firmly—that I controlled everything— was simply just that, an illusion. If I could not control what was most dear to me and loved so much, then I controlled nothing. We are all on a journey charted by our souls. We think we chart it and we cling stubbornly to the conviction that we are in charge, but it is the Universe who writes the story. We can resist what the Universe writes for us, of course. We have free will. But I prefer now to listen to Life and to follow where She beckons, for I know She leads me ever deeper into the core of my own heart and oneness with the Whole.*

- *I recognize now that we do, in fact, possess both Feminine and Masculine energies. These are both necessary and both serve a purpose. I still own a strong, kick-ass, aggressive male side; but now it is my*

Feminine side that guides the Masculine. I know, I know. To some men this sounds weak, maybe even repulsive or horrifying to hear; so, let me say it in another way that makes this whole idea easier to digest: wisdom guides knowledge. This is as powerful as it gets, and it works! Understanding and embracing this concept gave me my life back, and it is what allows me to move forward in engaging my deep grief with a wisdom that I did not have when I needed it most. For the first time in my life I feel complete as a human being, though I undoubtedly still have much work to do in maintaining and strengthening this divine balance.

· *I understand now that my inability to engage my Feminine side, coupled with my overreliance on my aggressive Male side ("I am fully responsible for everything that happens on my watch") was the cause of my conducting a chaotic war on the outside, when everything I needed was right here, inside of me. That need to solve and fix at all costs came at an extremely high price, not the least of which was the loss of Rachel's and my marriage. This does not change the fact that my love for Rachel is absolute and pure. What we had for all those years together, no one can take from us. It is recorded in the storybook of the Universe for eternity. I have the saying, "If you loved someone once and you ever stopped loving them, then you were never in love in the first place." I will love, honor and respect Rachel forever. I finally made peace with myself over our separation and have given myself permission to move on, find happiness and live a full life.*

· *The reasons for entering into and remaining in such a dysfunctional two-year relationship with another troubled soul also became clear. It was all about self-loathing and self-punishment and everything that accompanies that. It is now clear to me that the statement "you repulse me" was, in fact, aimed at myself. She had her own pain and demons, as did I. Sadly we chose to engage with each other through these. We were reflections of each other. We seldom got to explore, cultivate and experience each other's beautiful sides, even though we both knew they were there. By the time I left the beach, I was able to let her go and set myself free.*

• *I no longer take responsibility for Ofir's death. I no longer need to punish myself. After seven years of self-flagellation, I came to understand and accept that I was devoid of guilt. All was forgiven . . . no, there was nothing to forgive.*

After everything that had happened, I searched frantically and finally found the intentions that, at my therapist's recommendation, I had skeptically and hurriedly jotted down and put away weeks earlier, erasing them from my memory. Pulling them out, I saw in my own words a wisdom that went far beyond what my rational mind would have produced:

I understand, acknowledge and accept that I am part of, a son of, and a fractal of God, Creator and Universe. All vibrate in the frequency of love. So do I. I am as worthy of that vibrational love as any other form of consciousness. I accept creator's love unconditionally and, therefore, I accept love of the self. I will be content and at peace. I will no longer punish self, only be kind, non-judgmental, forgiving, and loving as my frequency transmits and receives love.

After setting the paper down, I sat motionless for a long time, tears streaming down my face. At the time I had written this, I was in the very depths of despair. It was clear to me now that it had to have been Self who had been the author of those sublime words because I had been too broken to have been able to string together even a single cogent sentence.

At last, I knew with certainty that this life was not only about the material/physical. There is a much larger, more profound dimension to everyone's life journey—including my own.

I set out on this journey, this journey of grief, to look for Ofir—or so I thought. But it was actually the opposite. It was Ofir who sent me on this journey, and it was Ofir who guided me and who ultimately introduced me to my real Self, my true Nature. I sought my son and found my Self, which in many ways is the same as finding Ofir. It is that simple—and that profound.

I believe, now, that my soul needed to go on this journey. It was necessary that I go through a deep process of grief—of loss—in order to find myself.

The calculus of this is beyond my ken. I cannot understand it; I only know that it is true. Like caterpillars, I believe that we humans also possess imaginal cells and that these cells represent our higher Selves. They direct our journeys if only we will let them, if only we will give up the illusion of control and Listen, if only we have the courage to endure the fires of hell that dissolve us so that we may ultimately reemerge as something else, something better, much better.

My journey was foreordained, written into my DNA, but it needed the strongest of catalysts to penetrate all my defenses and set it in motion. Up until then, I had been cruising through life, my dial set to "stupid happy." I believed I was in control. That was the be-all and end-all of life. I had forgotten, if I ever knew, the need to grow, to evolve. Then one day, my world was turned upside down. One moment, I was driving in my sexy convertible, music blaring and the air racing through my hair, fanning my obliviously smiling face; and the next, I was suddenly and violently wrenched from that vehicle and flung into a dark, scary container.

Nature in her wisdom knew what a crusty, old caterpillar I had become. She knew that only a very strong alchemical magic could get the job done. That agent was grief. Knowing this was the only way, Nature filled her syringe with grief and injected it into the chrysalis to bursting point. And the process of dissolution began.

I was in shock, afraid and disorientated. Yet, all the while, Nature was quietly, methodically and efficiently running its course. A lifetime of beliefs, behaviors, attitudes—in short, everything that I had become— was being systematically dismantled and dissolved so that it might be replaced by something beautiful and sublime. The progression was excruciatingly slow. It took almost eight years—eight, long, exhausting years—mostly because I resisted every step of the way. Since I had completely forgotten the natural stages of a life cycle, I had also forgotten the purpose of being in a chrysalis. That old crusty caterpillar did not care about process, butterflies, or anything else. It just wanted its old life back. So, for all those years, I fought the transformation; for all those years, I was angry and defiant.

I see now that during those years of chaos as I was flailing and sloshing around in the ugly, gooey muck of the chrysalis—and even before—my imaginal discs, my higher Self, had been surreptitiously and methodically prepping me, giving me instructions for my emergence into a new life form. I was a highly rebellious student, but Self had infinite patience. Self would keep on prepping me until I was ready. Then, one day, I finally stumbled upon the key, the one I had been incapable of identifying when I returned from my cross-county bike ride, when I had come so close before giving up completely. It boiled down to one simple word, okay, maybe two: *full surrender.* At last I saw that I did not have to *do* anything; that I just had to allow the process to unfold. When I finally surrendered, the energies came into balance; and, as soon as that happened, I was visited by another sudden flash of awareness. I became aware that Self did exist alongside self and that I needed to balance both. In other words: I needed to be present to the spiritual as well as the physical/material. And with that, I was propelled out of the chrysalis just as suddenly as I had been thrust into it. Finally, improbably and seemingly impossibly, a butterfly emerged.

For seven years, I was weighed down by fathomless, inconsolable grief. Now that weight has finally lifted, and I feel the breath of life filling my lungs, nourishing my humbled body and lifting my fledgling spirit. I have been transplanted back into the rich, organic soil of Life. For years, I thought that Life had abandoned me. But on the contrary, Life was embracing me every step of the way. It was I who, in the dark night of my soul, had abandoned Life. But with my surrender, Life came and got me. It loved and nurtured me back. And as I continue the work of resolving and integrating all those dualities, I know that this was no less than a blessed occurrence. It brings tears to my eyes every time I think about it.

My journey over those years was not an easy one, but it was an exceptionally rich and beautiful one. I do not mean beautiful as in pretty because many times it was not; often it was downright ugly, graceless, and clumsy. I mean beautiful in the sense that it was living life at its richest, at its highest level of authenticity and intensity. My journey was full of Life and love because it involved death and grief. Ultimately, I found that grief did not damage or destroy my Life; it enhanced it.

I finally understand that grief was never a vicious Beast. That was just something I created in my mind because I did not know how to grieve; my culture had never taught me. I was told to "be strong," "move on" and "prevail." And, so, I tried to grieve alone. When that failed, I tried to run away from grief. I tried to cope through my intellect. Nothing worked.

I know now that grief is not a monster; it is but the other face of love. Just as life and death are complementary to each other, so are love and grief—different sides of the same coin. One does not exist without the other. In the same way that we honor others with our love while they are in our lives, so we honor them with our grief when they are no longer in the physical realm. That is how it should be.

Grief is but love's calling card; it is meant to signal others to gather around those who grieve and to transfuse their stricken hearts with love. Drugs, therapy, and books cannot mend a grieving heart. It takes a village of loving hearts. Traditional cultures know this. Their communities grieve together as one, and this is how it should be for us too.

Lastly, I know that grief does not belong in the head; it belongs in the heart. Only when I finally opened my heart did I at last find peace. By the time I left the beach, the Beast was no longer my mortal enemy, but my teacher and friend.

I have come to accept that everything that transpired over the past seven years had to happen. Learning to grieve and to accept the passing of my beloved son was a necessary process, and I had to endure it all. There was no skipping of steps, no escaping or hiding. I had only two choices: endure the process or die. I chose to endure. I chose life. I am even able to feel grateful for the journey, which takes me back to that chance encounter with the director of SEED at the dialogue. I now understand and appreciate what Father Leon Secataro taught—we all need to be "thankful to the ancestors for everything that has happened to bring us to this moment in time."

The trajectory of my soul's journey—its true meaning and purpose—was revealed to me by my son. I call him my "son," but I am not sure I have that right. Sometimes I feel like I am anthropomorphizing our relationship, trying to make human something that is actually pure spirit. In the big picture, what we call each other is unimportant.

If one were to peel away all the layers of that onion that is me, one would still find at the core a deep well of sadness. The death of my son will always be a great source of sorrow, and I will carry that to my grave. But I hold that sadness differently now. Now I understand that my sadness is only an emotion; it is not who I am. I now embrace the sadness as part of me but do not allow it to rule my life, nor do I try to suppress or hide from it through negative behaviors or extreme physical endeavors. I understand now that emotions are like ocean waves. They are surface phenomena and they pass, but all the while the ocean depths remain undisturbed. This is another lesson for which I am grateful. Regardless of whatever emotion I may be feeling—happiness, sadness, anger—I am, in my depths, content and at peace. So, I simply wait and trust in Self to lead me on . . .

It feels like a resurrection.

Re-embracing Life

Epilogue

M Y EIGHT-YEAR JOURNEY WAS OVER. I had found Ofir, made peace with the Beast and come to understand something of the Nature of Reality. It was time to find a new direction, somewhere else to focus my energies. Yet, for some reason my mind was still not settled. How strange. What was missing? What else could there possibly be?

And then it hit me. I still had one piece of unfinished business. I owed a little boy an answer to that question he had posed to me not so long ago.

Determined not to let him down, I quickly wrapped up a gift, got into my SUV, and drove straight to his home. As always, we were happy to see each other. We chatted about friends, school, sports, and his life in general. The proverbial question he had not so subtly asked me one lazy, quiet day never came up. In fact, it had never come up since.

After spending a couple of hours with him playing the games that kids love to play, I told him I needed to get going. Protesting, he followed me to the front door. When I reached the patio, I stopped, turned around and knelt down so that we were face to face. I could see that he understood from my body language and facial expression that the mood was changing. The age difference melted into sublime silence. Calmly and patiently, I waited for us to dissolve into that stillness, all the while looking him deep in the eyes. Only when I felt sure that we were connecting on a higher level did I engage him about the true purpose of my visit.

"Do you remember a while back you asked me a question, one I was unable to answer?"

As if afraid to talk, he shook his head from side to side.

I responded by slowly pulling my phone out of my pocket and displaying the picture of Ofir a few inches from his eyes. I asked again, "Now, do you remember?"

Still staring intently into his eyes and beyond, I felt the contact; we were Authentically Listening in Rumi's field. The energy of the field that enveloped us was almost too much to bear. He stood in total silence, his eyes fixed on my phone. After maybe ten seconds, still mute, his head began to move up and down slowly. Then he broke the silence. "I asked you why are you are still alive if Ofir is dead."

"Yes, you did," I immediately responded.

Then, I, too, paused for a short time, looking back at him with an intensity that matched his when he had stared at the phone. Then I stood up, reached out and handed him the gift I had brought with me. "Well, here is your answer."

Without saying another word, I turned around and walked to the street.

As I drove away, still feeling the profundity of the exchange, those familiar shivers ran up and down my spine. I smiled and cried all at the same time. Although he was still too young to read my book, he was not too young to read the note I had hand-written to him on the inside.

I felt whole again. The journey was over. It was time to move on.

And to Ofir, I wrote again, this time with a spiritual maturity taught to me by him.

Dear Ofir,

I now understand that life took everything away in order to give me something precious beyond words: the opportunity to rebuild myself, layer by layer. Because I was willing to undergo that systematic destruction under the guise of searching for you, I was given the freedom to re-layer unconditionally. I have been doing that and it is an ongoing process. The beauty of this process is that not only can I add layers, but I can discard unwanted ones as well. *This gift of rebuilding and regeneration comes with a sacred responsibility, for what emerges will be of my own doing.*

My freedom came at an unbearable price. The terms were non-negotiable and the contract did not even require my signature. I had no choice, and I will always be sad that you are not here now with us in the physical realm. I grieve your loss deeply and miss you terribly, but I have accepted the agreement. In having done that, I will give it all my energy and attention. I just hope that this new me is able to honor and fulfill this agreement with dignity.

I now know that you were never lost or gone. You were always and are now right here inside me. Your home is my heart and you make it strong and proud. You live on in spirit and energy. I know; I carry it.

Ofir, it is because of you, through you and in conjunction with you, that I live out the rest of my life and do my work. It is because of you that I am able to receive these understandings with grace not anger, with an evolved not debilitating sadness; with presence, not aloofness and, finally, with love, not fear. Because you are very evolved, while I am still learning, I eagerly await what is to be revealed to me next.

I often ask myself the question: would the world be any different if Jesus, Buddha, Gandhi and all the other great Avatars had not come into existence? I still do not have an answer; but in the Gospel of Thomas, Jesus clearly states what I now know, thanks to you and Self. Jesus said, "If those who lead you say to you, 'See, the kingdom is in the sky,' then the birds of the sky will precede you. If they say to you, 'It is in the sea,' then the fish will precede you. Rather, the kingdom is inside of you, and it is outside of you. When you come to know yourselves, then you will become known and you will realize that it is you who are the sons of the living father. But if you will not know yourselves, you dwell in poverty and it is you who are that poverty."

Ofir, you took me out of poverty and gave me the gift of knowing my Self and becoming known. You were not found, for you were never lost. The irony is that it was I who was lost and I who was found.

In the Lakota language, there is no word for "goodbye," because life is forever. Instead the Lakota people say, as I say to you now: "Toksa akhe" (I will see you again). With a heart full of gratitude for all you have done for me, shown me and taught me, I release you now. I am well and I am strong. I am at peace in my sadness and will continue to feed life in the most positive way I know. I do it in your honor; and in my grief I celebrate, honor, and praise you.

Journey well, my son. I say this knowing that where you are now there are no "sons" and "fathers," only spirit beings. I do not know or understand where, when, or how we shall meet again, but until then, may you continue to walk your beauty path, as I will, and may those paths intersect again soon, yes, soon.

Oh, I almost forgot. Regarding the Ultimate Truth and the Nature of Reality—yes, I do know the answer. It is a simple one—we are not meant to know. We are meant to seek, to experience and to do our work. And through those endeavors, we are meant to evolve. We are each a fractal of the Universe and so in conjunction with the Whole of which we are a part, we are all on a journey to that Omega Point, at which time we will all go home. We are God's dream and we dream back the dream.

Love,
Dad

Author's Note

To be and stay alive is easy. To live life takes courage.
—M.C.

MINE IS NOT THE ONLY JOURNEY. If you see someone going through a journey such as mine, please be patient. Please be part of their village. And if it is you who is on such a journey, please know that you will one day emerge into the light. Let me be clear, sadness still pervades my being, but it does not cripple my life. It feeds and nourishes my life, albeit a very, very different kind of life than I had known prior. Please know, too, that this is not just my story. It is *our* story, God's story. I eagerly await the opportunity to listen to your stories for they, too, are our stories, God's stories.

I would like to leave you with the old Navajo saying, "Sa'ah Naaghai Bik'eh Hozhoon." May you continue to walk your beauty path. Journey well, my friends, into the light and beyond. I will see you there.

For further inspiration and additional references, please visit: www.fierceillumination.com

I am looking forward to hearing of your own Hero's journey, but if it has not yet begun, then hopefully this site and community will serve as a catalyst to embark on your own Hero's journey to find your true Self.
-Martin

www.ingramcontent.com/pod-product-compliance
Lightning Source LLC
Chambersburg PA
CBHW071315090426
42738CB00012B/2703